Artful Moments

Artful Moments

Building Meaningful Museum Experiences for People Living with Dementia

**Laurie Kilgour-Walsh,
Janis Humphrey,
Maureen Montemuro,
Kathy Moros, and Shannon Stanners**

ROWMAN & LITTLEFIELD

Lanham • Boulder • New York • London

Published by Rowman & Littlefield
An imprint of The Rowman & Littlefield Publishing Group, Inc.
4501 Forbes Boulevard, Suite 200, Lanham, Maryland 20706
www.rowman.com

86-90 Paul Street, London EC2A 4NE

British Library Cataloguing in Publication Information Available

Library of Congress Cataloging-in-Publication Data

Names: Kilgour-Walsh, Laurie, author.
Title: Artful moments : building meaningful museum experiences for people living with dementia / Laurie Kilgour-Walsh [and four others].
Other titles: Building meaningful museum experiences for people living with dementia
Description: Lanham : Rowman & Littlefield, [2025] | Includes bibliographical references and index. | Summary: "This book is an introduction and how-to guide for museum-based program development and implementation for people living with dementia. Exploring the potential that such programs have to improve the quality of life--the wellbeing, of participants, the book guides readers through an exploration of their museum's environment, approach, and activities, all firmly seated in knowledge of dementia and a person-centered focus"-- Provided by publisher.
Identifiers: LCCN 2024040304 | ISBN 9781538195413 (cloth) | ISBN 9781538195420 (paperback) | ISBN 9781538195437 (electronic)
Subjects: LCSH: Museums and people with disabilities. | Dementia--Patients--Services for. | Museums--Activity programs. | Museums--Psychological aspects. | Well-being--Age factors.
Classification: LCC AM160 .K55 2025 | DDC 069/.17--dc23/eng/20241009
LC record available at https://lccn.loc.gov/2024040304

Contents

Part V. Activity

Part VI. Engagement and Well-Being

Acknowledgments

There are so many people involved in a project of this scale, and over the years we have connected with people whose contributions and support have left their mark. Together, we offer our acknowledgment and sincere thanks.

To our friends and colleagues in healthcare, especially Esther Coker and Carmen Murray who provided their knowledge and support in our research for this book.

To the team at the AGH, including the many *Artful Moments* Artist-Educators and volunteers, including Tyler VanHolst, Aggie Zeglen, and Sonia Rogers, whose dedication and creativity continues to build our success.

And our friends Mat Kennedy, Hugo Gatsby and Veronica Dyer for their experience and enthusiasm as we began to work on a digital project to share our work with other museums—that development led us here.

To our program participants and their family and friends, who have shared so much with us over the years. Being able to share the art that we love with you continues to be a joy.

And to our families who have believed in us, cheered us on, and supported us through a huge endeavor and an emotional year.

This work is for you.

Foreword

By Shelley Falconer
President and CEO, Art Gallery of Hamilton

Museums have long held a core function of education and learning. Collectively, we have served student and adult visitors alike in a range of learning activities, sharing knowledge, skills, and stories specific to the collections and exhibitions that our museums hold. Increasingly, the area of health and well-being has expanded into our cultural spaces with museums as partners in the support and delivery of both healthcare interventions and practices, from prescribed healthcare visits to object handling, volunteering, and art-making to performing arts and music.

Freeman Tilden, in his seminal 1957 work, *Interpreting our Heritage*, encouraged capitalizing on curiosity—on the interests and personal connections of the audience to the objects under scrutiny in any interpretive work, and advocated provocation, rather than simply instruction as the chief aim of museum work. The term "person-centered" was not used until much more recently, but even in this early work, as museum educators and facilitators we see the ideals of following where our participants take us as a core strength of what Tilden would have called effective interpretation, and what has become one of the core beliefs in the methodology used by AGH Educators in our program, *Artful Moments*.

Moving forward to the early 2000s, we saw a shift in our ideals about who our visitors and participants might be, and in the role we as museums could play in their lives. No longer were we simply teaching about art, history, nature, or myriad other specialty collections, we began to consider the ways that those objects might impact visitors beyond just subject-specific interests, thinking more about the social role that could emerge. Museums began to think more about accessibility and inclusion, and new kinds of programs emerged, including programs designed to support people living with dementia.

In the early 2000s, the Museum of Modern Art (MoMA) was an early leader with their program, *Meet Me at MoMA* in 2006. Shortly after, other programs emerged at museums including the Walter Art Centre in Minneapolis, the Philadelphia Museum of Art, the Guggenheim and Metropolitan Museum of Art in New York, as well as important programs at the British Museum, and other institutions in the UK and Australia. By the mid-2010s programs were offered worldwide, including the Tate in London, The Louvre, the Van Gogh Museum, and numerous others. The Art Gallery of Hamilton's *Artful Moments* launched in 2011 and has grown into one of our key programs enabling us to reach a more diverse population and deepen our relationship with the community.

In North America and internationally, overburdened medical and social care systems indicate clear needs for health and wellness programs, and each year we see the list of museums offering programs for people living with dementia grow as many museums consider what role they may play to address our community health needs. We connect with our colleagues regionally, nationally, and with a growing international network. We share and learn from each other, and the innovations and impact worldwide are exciting. Even so, with an aging population, we see continuing growth in the number of people diagnosed with dementia each year. The WHO recognizes dementia as a public health priority with more than 55 million people living with dementia worldwide in 2024, and that number will increase each year.

Today, museums of every kind have embraced strategies and program development to support people living with dementia, and their family, friends, and care partners. But there are simply not enough programs to keep up with the need, and barriers persist including funding, required staff, and skills. With advances in neuro-aesthetics and professional evaluations demonstrating significant outcomes in caregiver/care recipient interaction, increased socialization and personal validation for this traditionally marginalized and growing segment of the population, programming to support people living with dementia can contribute meaningfully to our community health and social needs.

Having spent more than a decade evolving this practice, we have seen the impact and have learned from our work and our colleagues in the field. *Artful Moments: Building Museum Experiences for People Living with Dementia* is our contribution, sharing our experiences in the hopes of supporting others in embarking on similar work. We hope that this work resonates with you, and leads to new opportunities and connections across the museum field.

Laurie Kilgour-Walsh is a longtime professional museum educator, and we are deeply grateful to her for sharing her practice and methodologies with us. Together with her team, Janis Humphrey, Maureen Montemuro, Kathy Moros, Shannon Stanners, and the talented artists who lead our programs, Laurie's research, passion and leadership in the development of *Artful Moments* remind us of the life-affirming power of art and museums (or the aesthetic experience) to contribute to our collective health and well-being.

Part I

Museums and Dementia

Starting with a Museum

A Reflection by Laurie Kilgour-Walsh

Museums are places with charged histories, collections, and visitor experiences. They are also places filled with the potential for transformative encounters that can be both personally and collectively significant. As we move ahead with new perspectives on how museums may serve our communities, we must activate our strengths and opportunities to be places of connection, inclusion, and empowerment.

Acknowledging that I wear my professional bias very clearly, I have often reflected on a colleague's comment once, that we are a gallery that is *almost* the perfect size. Large enough that we have a significant collection and slate of activities to do some really exciting projects, but not so large that we become siloed into a singular focus. Though, who doesn't wish for just a bit more space, or staff, or budget?

The story of how *Artful Moments* began is described later in this chapter, but it occurs to me that this project might not have evolved the way it has in another place. My work at the time comprised many different audiences and activities—in the beginning, *Artful Moments* was just one project that I quietly worked on among many others. It had the potential to be a one-time partnership with time-limited funding. But, it *really* worked. We connected, deeply, with our partners (some of whom are co-authors of this book), with the participants, and with the art. I loved it and I wanted more. I was very fortunate to have the freedom to keep working at it as I wished—finding project grants and partnerships along the way, and letting the ideas and learning bubble away quietly amid all my other work. Slowly, almost without realizing it, this small project became something big. I had opportunities to talk about it with colleagues and peers and later to consider how to support other organizations in similar work. I built a website, wrote a chapter for a museum publication, and spoke at an international conference. And now, *Artful Moments* is a book—this book.

My path to this point was winding but led by encounters with the right people, the right experiences, and the right museum. My hope is to guide you with a more direct route to the program you want to create and to the experiences that I know you will have.

Artful Moments is about museums and people. It is talking and making, sharing and learning together. It is meaningful, powerful, and necessary.

1

What Is Artful Moments?

Artful Moments, a program by the Art Gallery of Hamilton, combines a deep knowledge of participants and supportive strategies to deliver meaningful, individualized, and engaging activities to people living with dementia. We use our collections and exhibitions to provide opportunities for creativity, self-expression, and social connection through conversation and experiential activations. By blending specialized dementia-care strategies with conversations and hands-on activities, *Artful Moments* fosters "in the moment" engagement and enjoyment for participants. The program also promotes social connection and shared experiences with family, friends, and peers.

SHARED EXPERIENCES, SHARED LEARNING

We believe museums offer a unique point of connection for people through the objects and stories held within their collections. Whether through a work of art that captures an artist's vision, an historical object that holds memories of the past, or a living specimen that reveals the wonder of the natural world, these objects inspire, capture the imagination, and offer points of connection with the people viewing them.

The programs we present are built on an understanding of our strengths—our collections and exhibitions, our approach to programming, and our audiences. This is combined with knowledge of and experience with people living with dementia as well as the strategies that we use to facilitate engagement and social connection.

Over the years, we have learned a great deal through our program and we are eager to share our experiences to help other museums create programs of their own. By building on the knowledge of dementia and best practices for successful engagement in their core programs, museums can become accessible, relevant, and empowering for people living with dementia.

In a national study conducted by the Art Gallery of Hamilton, we asked museum staff about their institution's readiness to deliver programs for people living with dementia. Most respondents were from small to medium-sized institutions, about half were from history museums, and nearly one-quarter were from art galleries. When asked about working with people living with dementia in general, most respondents felt that their community would benefit from this type of activity, though most had not been able to offer such programs. They embraced the idea of offering programs for people living with dementia, but many were uncertain how to get started. One of the biggest barriers cited was access to information about dementia and strategies for program design and delivery. Nearly half cited a lack of institutional capacity as a major concern, and many felt that accessibility was a barrier. Despite the challenges, over 80 percent of respondents shared that they would like to pursue a program for people living with dementia. While we cannot address issues of funding or staffing directly, we can show you how a program can be crafted to suit a range of museums from small community museums to larger institutions.

Each gallery, museum, historic site, or other cultural institution will come to this work with its own strengths and approaches to programming. We hope that by learning about our experiences, you will learn to adapt the work that you are already doing to suit the particular abilities and needs of this new audience. Much of this work is about adaptation, not invention.

This book brings together the experience and knowledge gathered over the past decade, to help other museums enrich their own programs using what we have learned. By sharing this work, we hope that more people will experience the joy and connection that come from shared experiences with museums.

The Roots of Artful Moments

We began our program with an idea and the vision of a better way to care for people living with dementia. From a simple experience of people enjoying art in unexpected circumstances, this spark planted the seed for what would become *Artful Moments*.

In 2009, a new wing was built at one of Hamilton's community hospitals with a specialty unit for people living with dementia. Most patients were in the later stages of dementia often with other complications. We were initially asked to coordinate artwork to hang in this new setting. What developed was a collaboration that allowed patients themselves to choose what would hang on the walls.

A team from the Gallery planned several visits to the hospital unit, each time bringing a selection of artworks by regional artists to be presented to a focus group of patients. The works ranged from representational to abstract with a variety of subjects, styles, and media. The Gallery team spent about an hour with a small group of people who resided there, along with several staff members, asking them what they thought of the work and telling them more about what they were seeing. The facilitators asked simple questions about what colors or subjects they saw, how they felt looking at the art, and whether they would like to see it in their home. The visits ran like a small focus group with each person being invited to answer questions with the help of the hospital staff.

In one session, we had an interaction with a particularly memorable woman. She spent most of the session sitting quietly, leaning forward in her chair. We thought that she might have fallen asleep and so did not engage her as much as others. Then we brought out a painting of a pond and asked her a question. It took a few moments, but then she lifted her head and said, "I see my summer fowl dipping their wings in the water." It was at that moment we realized we had made a true connection and that we needed to find a way to do more.

These focus groups were inspiring. The hospital staff saw engagement in the people they cared for each day that they had not seen before. And the Gallery team saw people making very personal connections with art using many different types of communication. They interacted differently than we were used to but they shared their thoughts in their own way. We realized that this kind of experience offered the potential for both engaging activities and enhanced relationships for people living with dementia far beyond just simply decorating the space where they resided. And importantly, the individual's participation was not dependent on their prior enjoyment of or experience with art or a predetermined level of ability.

During this simple act of looking and responding, we saw a temporary shift away from a focus on dementia to the sharing of experiences. Memories were sparked, opinions (sometimes strong ones) were shared, and we saw social engagement. Participants were living "in the moment," free of dementia. We knew then that there was a role for the Gallery to play in enhancing the well-being of people living with dementia in our community.

The program that emerged from this experience brought together expertise in museum education with the health care team sharing their knowledge of the impacts of dementia and proven strategies for engagement. From the start, the program combined theme-based "tours" in the hospital using their new art collection and complementary reproductions of art paired with hands-on activities, as well as in-person visits to the Gallery. The off-site excursions were initially thought to be too difficult to manage for patients in the later stages of dementia, but they were overwhelmingly successful with careful adaptations made to the environment and activities.

Evaluation focused on demonstrating engagement in our participants, measured by several clinical tools. While our primary research focused on engagement in the person with dementia, anecdotally we observed much more. Experiences were shared instead of directed, reminiscences were sparked, and participants experienced validation, success, and engagement. We loved the interaction we saw between family members, participants, and staff.

Since then we have expanded to work with people living in their own homes or a retirement community, often in earlier stages of dementia. The program combines looking and talking about selections from the Gallery''s exhibitions with hands-on activities over several weekly sessions. We evaluated the program for engagement and social connection and observed participants rekindling a love of art from earlier in their lives or discovering it for the first time. We use art as a tool to inspire conversation, sharing, and well-being. When the pandemic hit Canada in March of 2020 we closed our doors and turned to virtual programs, finding new ways of connecting with participants remotely.

The stigma or fear associated with a diagnosis or visible disability can shrink a person's social connections. A growing body of research shows that loneliness and social isolation have a serious impact on all aspects of health and well-being, equivalent to other serious risk factors. Social isolation and loneliness are increasingly being recognized as a priority public health problem and policy issue across all age groups, and we know that seniors and people with disabilities or other conditions including dementia are particularly at risk.[1] Our research demonstrated that *Artful Moments* was a viable solution for this challenge.

THE *MODEL FOR SUCCESSFUL ENGAGEMENT*

Program methodology is guided by the *Model for Successful Engagement (figure 1.1)*, created by the Art Gallery of Hamilton, based on our practice and evaluation of past programs. Inherent in the model is the idea that all components of the model are essential and interconnected to fully achieve our program goals. We also believe that when properly employed, the Model is broadly applicable to any museum or cultural experience and beyond.

- The **Museum** is the foundation of the Model, encompassing its collections, spaces, and staff. *Artful Moments* is a program built from within each museum using its assets and creative potential to create a unique, meaningful, and specific program. We touch on some of the ideas about the potential of museums, but the core of this component rests with you.
- The **Participant** is the person living with dementia and is the central focus, informing everything else. In a person-centered program, the understanding of the person living with dementia and their particular circumstances is the heart of the program. Everything else is built from this knowledge and refers back to it.

Three pillars form the structure of a program: **Environment**, **Approach**, and **Activity**. They are interconnected, with each one influencing the others. Most likely you will find that your development process will move in and out of each area several times before you have finished. We have chosen to use this order in our work starting from the *environment*, where we often have the least flexibility. Creative solutions are required that will in turn affect our activities later. Similarly, thinking about *approach*—how we connect with participants can affect our later work in planning *activities*.

- **Environment** comprises the physical and social space. A well-considered environment must apply the knowledge of the participants to support engagement.

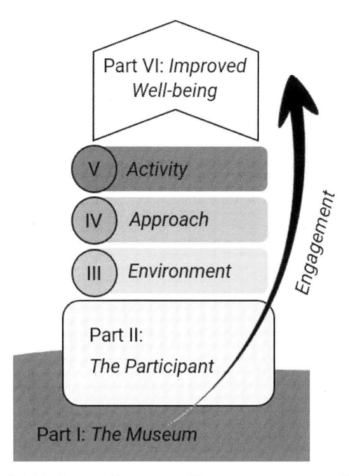

Figure 1.1   The Model for Successful Engagement. Effective programs must consider the museum experience as a whole. The model guides this planning, starting with the museum, centered on the participant, and moving through the pillars of engagement to arrive at the outcome, improved well-being. *Source:* Art Gallery of Hamilton.

- ***Approach*** is about communication, facilitation, and attitudes. To achieve engagement, the approach is individualized to suit the needs and abilities of the participant.
- ***Activity*** comprises the content of conversations and hands-on activities. Well-planned activities incorporate knowledge of the participant so you can support and respond effectively.

These pillars support the key process of the program, **Engagement**. We work to capture the interest and attention of participants through experiences that support their abilities, fostering connections, and encouraging participation in whatever form that takes for each individual. A certain degree of engagement may exist simply in the choice to participate in a museum experience, but as each layer of the methodology is added, that engagement grows by the focus and support that each provides.

The process of engagement leads to the outcome, of improved **Well-being**. Well-being can encompass balance in many areas, including positive feelings, self-esteem, social connection, and more.

STRENGTHS OF THIS PROGRAM

We have been thrilled to see engagement blossoming in participants who may never have visited a museum. We have been touched by the rekindling of a relationship that may have slipped into one that is so focused on providing care that shared moments of enjoyment have been lost. We have heard from participants and their families and friends about the positive impact that joining the program has offered them. *Artful Moments* is successful because:

- It provides responsive, meaningful, individualized engagement focused on strengths and abilities.
- It upholds rigorous and creative use of museum collections and exhibitions to provide rich, interesting content.
- It prioritizes enjoying the experience "in the moment" and social connection at every stage of dementia or level of ability.
- It is built on knowledge of dementia and best practices to achieve success.
- It is supported by research, experience, and learning.

We have been connecting with people living with dementia for many years. We have tried different things and learned a lot. It may seem that creating a new program for a new audience is a lot of work, especially if you are a smaller organization—and the truth is, it is. But, there are many ways forward and many ways to succeed.

Sharing Expertise

You don't have to do it alone.
One of the most important factors in our success is the reliance on sharing expertise and the transfer of knowledge. This program was born in partnership between a museum with lots of expertise in our field and partners with expertise in dementia care. We use a mutually supportive approach ensuring positive experiences for everyone involved. This approach encourages ongoing reflection, coaching, and responsive improvement. Sharing the success and the responsibility can only benefit the audience and the community.

In addition to healthcare expertise, most communities have many support organizations available. Look to the service organizations, the care facilities, and the support workers around you. The field of museum education is a community on an international scale. Look to your colleagues your peers, and to institutions across the country and the world. There are amazing programs happening and inspiration and support are often just a phone call or email away.

Adaptation Not Invention

Start with what you already do.
As museum professionals, you are already designing and facilitating great programs and activities about your exhibitions and collections for a variety of audiences. You have the content knowledge. You have the presentation skills. Our approach emphasizes adaptation over reinvention of museum activities and resources, making program design achievable for museums of any size. By carefully adapting what you already do you will be able to accommodate the strengths and needs of your audience.

Reaching Museums and Beyond

Artful Moments began with an art collection and activities in painting and collage. We continue to use art as our subject matter and have mined the AGH Collection and exhibitions for gems that incite deeply personal and engaging conversations and that inspire creative expression through a variety of art-making activities in our work with people with dementia and more broadly. We adapt the way we set up and facilitate to suit each audience based on what we know about them and the ways they interact with us. If you come to this book from an art museum you will likely already find resonance with our work. But our programming for people living with dementia does not end there.

This methodology will work in any museum setting with nearly any collection. We are convinced that it will work even more broadly for a range of social experiences from symphonies, to theatre performances, and even dining experiences. This work is about adapting what we already do rather than creating programs and activities from scratch. It is important to understand this concept, particularly if you are a different type of museum or cultural organization. This book is not about how to lead art programs, but rather how to lead interactive programs with many kinds of content based on many types of museums, collections, and exhibitions. By looking holistically at your museum, including every aspect of the experience, you will discover ways to connect and support your audience of people living with dementia in ways that promote strengths and social connection. Participants will come to the museum "as they are," with varying levels of experience, abilities, and knowledge of your contents and they will thrive.

Take what you learn and apply it to your own setting.

The program's philosophy, design, and facilitation techniques combined with your newfound knowledge of dementia will be applicable through all stages of a person's dementia journey. Learning how to observe and adapt to changing levels of ability is a core concept of this project.

Conversational and hands-on experiential activities can spring from any starting point—an artwork, a parlor chair, the cockpit of a WWII fighter, a radio or typewriter from years ago, an otter, a shark, or a passage of music. The options are endless. If you know your collections, exhibitions, and activities well, your program will bloom by applying what you learn from this book. While we cannot address every subject or type of museum we choose the word "museum" as a broadly relevant term for a place that holds a collection of physical or sensory assets. We encourage you to apply the term as freely as you wish so that you can connect with your own work.

Your work throughout this publication is to consider how our experiences can translate to reflect what you do in your museum. In your current programs, what do you talk about with visitors? What interactive activities do you offer? Then ask yourself how you can adapt to suit the audience. We have worked with museums in historical homes furnished to reflect the period of the original family who lived there. We talked about holiday traditions, reminisced about childhood hobbies, and made holiday decorations in the style of that time. We planned programs in a historical garden, smelling the fragrant herbs growing there, and making a small container garden. We worked with musicians from a large orchestra to think about ways to adapt music appreciation to suit the interests and abilities of participants. In each case the subject matter was different but the methods were similar. And the program that resulted was unique, engaging, and meaningful for the participants.

We cannot provide a prescriptive set of lesson plans that you can transplant into your work. We will show you how to build the essential knowledge of your participants, your museum, and the pillars of engagement to achieve a positive experience for your participants. We invite and encourage you to build on our ideas and accomplishments and apply what we have learned. Thank you for allowing us to help get you started.

NOTE

1. *Social Isolation and Loneliness Among Older People: Advocacy Brief* (Geneva: World Health Organization, 2021), 2.

2

Exploring Impact

"Dementia" is a general term for loss of memory, communication skills, problem-solving, and other thinking abilities that become severe enough to interfere with daily life. Rather than a disease itself, dementia describes a set of symptoms that may be caused by different illnesses. Alzheimer's disease is the most common and familiar form of dementia. Other types include vascular dementia, Lewy Body dementia, frontotemporal dementia, and mixed dementia (more than one type of dementia occurring simultaneously). There are over one-hundred other less common causes or types of dementia.

Dementia affects everyone differently. As it progresses, people experience changes in memory, daily living skills, communication, and mood. Dementia is progressive, and currently, there is no cure. Each person living with dementia is unique. Getting to know each participant as an individual is paramount in your work.

While dementia can have many significant impacts on a person's life and ability, many strengths remain. Some forms of memory, particularly memories formed earlier in life, creativity, and the ability and desire to communicate are all present far into a person's journey with dementia. This is why this work is so important—to provide opportunities for connection and to make the most of each person's abilities and interests. As a museum, you have the opportunity to positively impact a person's quality of life by offering programs that reinforce those strengths, empower their sense of purpose, and offer meaningful opportunities to connect, contribute, and engage. You will learn more about dementia in part II.

GROWING IMPACT OF DEMENTIA

The impacts of dementia are significant worldwide and with an aging population in many countries the numbers will continue to rise. According to Alzheimer's Disease International, an estimated fifty-five million people worldwide are living with dementia in 2024. These figures are projected to rise to 139 million by 2050. This translates to "a new case of dementia arising somewhere in the world every three seconds."[1] In our region, approximately one in eleven people over the age of sixty-five are living with dementia today.[2] Besides raising awareness, these statistics help to encourage education, action, and program development across all sectors.

Beyond the immediate impact of a personal diagnosis, we know that family and friends of a person living with dementia are affected in many ways. The Alzheimer's Society has found that as many as one in five Canadians have experienced caring for someone living with dementia,[3] and we expect similar statistics worldwide. "Over 50% of carers globally say their health has suffered as a result of their caring responsibilities even whilst expressing positive sentiments about their role."[4]

The numbers are significant. Our purpose in sharing them here is to raise awareness of the prevalence of people living with dementia in every community. Where previously many people felt they needed to keep their diagnosis private, we hope to encourage more understanding and empowerment for people to continue to participate in community life long after being diagnosed. Some museums may wonder if there is a need for a dementia-focused program in their community. The answer is a resounding YES.

Your Museum Audience

For an understanding of the potential impact of your program, you can apply a sampling of the statistics (1/11 people over 65) to your annual number of visitors. Multiply your annual visitors by the percentage who are over sixty-five. Then divide by eleven for the average number of people over sixty-five living with dementia. For an even closer look, divide that by the number of days you are open annually and you will also see your average daily visitation by people living with dementia. It is likely higher than you think.

STIGMA AND UNCONSCIOUS BIAS

Our beliefs, attitudes, and actions toward people with dementia significantly impact their well-being, influencing how they see themselves and how others perceive them. Further, they can impact their ability to engage in their communities, participate in daily life, and access necessary services and support.

According to the Alzheimer's Society, stigma is a major barrier preventing people living with dementia from experiencing fulfilling lives with dignity and respect.[5] According to Sara Evans Lacko, Associate Professorial Research Fellow at CPEC, "people often describe the consequences of stigma as being as challenging as the condition itself."[6]

We define stigma as any negative attitude toward, or social disapproval of, a person based solely on their diagnosis.[7] A common form of stigma, unconscious biases are social stereotypes that we adopt without realizing it. They happen when we make quick judgments based on appearance, behavior, personal background, past experiences, or common stereotypes. As you read this, you may be carrying some unconscious biases about people living with dementia. These may manifest as fear or nervousness, assumptions that you make about ability or interest, or many other ideas and actions, and they may result in consequences you do not intend.

We can think of stigma as problems of knowledge (ignorance), problems of attitudes (prejudice), and problems of behavior (discrimination).[8] When we do not understand dementia, when we carry negative ideas, unfounded fears, and negative stereotypes, we act (or fail to act), we make decisions, and we create barriers.

Stigma leads to the negative reception of a person through purposeful acts of discrimination, systemic barriers, and unconscious bias. These harmful actions and attitudes can also carry over to the families and friends of a person living with dementia, affecting them as well. When a condition is as prevalent as dementia but largely misunderstood, it is easy for stigma and unconscious bias to spread.

Institutionally, your museum may unintentionally have policies, procedures, or other systems that exclude people from participating. Stigma and bias can affect the degree to which your organization is aware, welcoming, accessible, and supportive of people living with dementia—from the mandate through exhibitions, programming, fees, and right down to the sense of welcome from frontline staff. On both a personal and institutional level, it is important to reflect on your ideas and attitudes before you begin this work, to identify, shift, and correct unconscious biases that you may be carrying.

The Impact of Stigma

The impact of stigma on a person living with dementia and their family or friends is significant and far-reaching. Stigma runs so deep that many people who have no lived experience of dementia carry entrenched fears and negative attitudes about how they would live if they were diagnosed. In a survey conducted by the Alzheimer's Society, more than half of respondents did not believe they could live well with dementia, with one quarter stating that "life would be over."[9] Advocates working with people living with dementia are trying to educate the public about the harmful impacts of microaggressions, incorrect assumptions, and beliefs at all levels of experience—personal, community-based, and systemic barriers. "At the individual level, stigma can undermine life goals, reduce participation in meaningful life activities, and worsen a person's quality of life. At the societal level, it can influence policy and reduce funding allocated to care and support."[10]

According to a study conducted in the UK, one in three people are afraid of talking to someone with dementia and one in five say they do not understand the symptoms and would be fearful of meeting someone with dementia. A survey conducted by the AGH of museum professionals found similar reservations. Fear experienced by most professionals is not the result of overtly negative stereotypes or attitudes. These reservations stem from uncertainty about what to expect when interacting with a person living with dementia and concern about whether they will know what to do or how to respond. The fear comes from the idea that a person with dementia is different or unknown.

Stigma can be imposed by others but it can also be self-imposed leading to experiences of unfair treatment, isolation, and feelings of shame. For someone experiencing signs of dementia, stigma can lead to delays in seeking diagnosis and treatment, hiding dementia from others, and retreating from social life. The survey mentioned previously found that one in five people would avoid seeking help for as long as possible if they were experiencing symptoms that might be dementia-related,[11] and over a third of carers across the world said that they have hidden the diagnosis of dementia of a family member.[12]

People who have experienced stigma against dementia share that lack of awareness can cause family and friends to feel intimidated or unable to connect with them after learning of a diagnosis. Stigma can discourage support from others—one survey found that two out of three caregivers find caring for someone with dementia to be isolating and only 39 percent of people would offer support for family or friends who were open about their diagnosis. Only 5 percent said that they would learn more about dementia if someone close to them were diagnosed.[13]

Stigma can lead to unfair treatment based on incorrect assumptions about the abilities of a person living with dementia, leading to them being ignored or dismissed. Negative language, jokes, and stereotypes focus on weaknesses rather than supporting abilities and personhood. Stigma erodes self-image, confidence, and independence.

Stigma and Social Isolation

Social isolation can be part of the reality of living with dementia. The Alzheimer's Society in the UK held in-depth interviews with people with dementia and their carers in their report, *Turning Up the Volume: Unheard Voices of People with Dementia,* and found that "living with dementia and dealing with society's view of the condition often means people lose confidence, independence, and the ability to live the life they want. It can feel like the physical world around them becomes smaller as they lose touch with people and activities close to their hearts."[14] People living with dementia have reported that their circle of friends shrinks once others learn of their diagnosis, and that for many, stigma or fear further shrinks their social connectedness. Caregivers are also at risk of social isolation due to the same fears and because of the competing demands of caregiving, work, and family.

In a recent survey conducted by the Hamilton Council on Aging, only 20 percent of people surveyed said that people living with dementia feel like they are a valuable part of the community. Further, 47 percent of the respondents felt that there were no opportunities for people living with dementia to engage in community activities in the region.[15] While this survey is specific to one region, it is easy to imagine similar feelings in every community.

To combat this, it is a shared responsibility for every community organization to build inclusive opportunities for connection, support, and engagement. For us, *Artful Moments* is a step toward this.

Combating Stigma

How can a museum program reduce stigma? Everyone has a role to play. The best ways to fight against stigma are to think of the person first, to model positive attitudes and actions, to encourage and celebrate participation, and to amplify the lived experiences of people living with dementia.

When people living with dementia feel understood, supported, and included, they participate in their community. Seeing themselves as active participants in museum programs or as regular visitors can change their own sense of ability and inclusion as well as the perception that others have of them. When organizations become educated about dementia, they are able to create opportunities for participation and inclusion. When they center the experiences of people with dementia in their mandates, operations, and activities they become inclusive.

When members of the public see people living with dementia as active members of a community, the public's preconceptions change, and stigma-based ideas are reduced. Here's how you can be welcoming to people living with dementia:

- Embrace the idea and work at building "dementia-friendly" spaces and communities.
- Train staff to better understand and respond to the needs of people living with dementia.
- Make your exhibitions and programs as accessible as possible.
- Adjust communications, signage, and processes to accommodate those with different needs and abilities with dignity, respect, and independence in mind.
- Offer specialized programs and also make regular programming more inclusive.

There is a saying used across many inclusive practices, "never about us, without us." People living with dementia must have a voice to share their lived experiences, to inform decisions and designs about and for them, to teach others, and to inform our understanding of their interests and needs. You can:

- Use focus groups to understand and improve your programs.
- Create advisory opportunities to inform decisions and questions.
- Listen to your participants (and those who do not currently participate) and ask what they want to see and do in your institution.
- Adjust language and processes to support positive attitudes and environments.
- Create opportunities to participate in the planning and facilitation of programs.

THE POWER OF MUSEUMS

Museums, with their unique potential and resources, can empower and provide meaningful experiences for audiences with diverse abilities. This can lead to improved well-being and quality of life.

In its 2016 report, the Canadian Index of Wellbeing cites that "time spent in leisure and culture is often when our lives are most fulfilling, when we can really be ourselves with friends, family, and people in the community."[16] This report cites cultural participation as one of the "most important social determinants of our health."

Museums have long existed as repositories of objects and histories held for the public trust. Today we see foundational shifts in public mandates, awareness of audiences and communities, and the perception of what museums can and should do in a social context. Unfortunately, museums have not always been inclusive or comfortable for large sections of the population to enter. For the person living with dementia who is already beginning to feel uncertain in their abilities or the family member or friend who is afraid of what might happen with their loved one in a public setting, the barriers to cultural participation are often insurmountable.

Figure 2.1 Bringing People Together. Museums have an important role to play as a social space—welcoming people into shared experiences, reducing stigma and celebrating strengths at all stages of life. *Source*: Art Gallery of Hamilton.

In John Falk's research into visitor motivations, he reminds us that "to be perceived as truly fundamental to their communities, museums will need to rewrite their mission and impact statements to more directly align with the identity-related visit motivations of their visitors."[17] Museums must align themselves with the needs, abilities, and interests of their visitors so they can exercise a purpose that is relevant, supportive, and meaningful to these visitors.

Encouragingly, museums are more aware of the barriers to access and visitation than ever before and are taking steps to overcome them. They cultivate their value as an important social space using their capacity to engage, empower, and include larger and more diverse audiences. They assert themselves as vital tools for the well-being of the communities in which they are situated.[18]

An Aesthetic Experience

In general terms, experiences with museum objects can facilitate experiences for participants no matter their level of subject knowledge, their abilities, or their personal circumstances. They do this in many ways—by appealing to our sense of wonder, imagination, history, identity, place, and process.

An aesthetic experience—that is focusing on something that is experienced through the senses, often with ideas of beauty or appreciation—is something that happens without us even trying. During the aesthetic experience, people will experience a state of intense attention, engagement, and awareness. They will find themselves "focused on and fascinated with a particular object," while their awareness of their surroundings or sense of time retreats.[19] Parallels may be drawn to Maslow's concept of peak experience or Csikszentmihalyi's concept of flow. Attention is fully engaged effortlessly on an object or pursuit.[20]

We are constantly bombarded with visual stimuli and our reactions are almost instant. If you see something, you can quickly feel that you like it or you do not and your impressions evolve from there. Anyone can have an aesthetic experience regardless of their abilities.

For a person living with dementia, engagement with museum objects can be very powerful—triggering memories and ideas that may not be easily accessed in other circumstances. This can help to connect them with emotions, thoughts, and ways to communicate that go beyond verbal skills or daily routines.

A Shared Experience

Communication can happen with words, gestures, body language, art-making, and/or writing. Museum experiences informed by a knowledge of dementia can remove some of the barriers that are caused by changes in language or speaking abilities. They can also offer a powerful countering of the social isolation described in the previous section.

The value of shared experience and social connection is one of the most significant lessons learned from our first program. We started by focusing on the person living with dementia and how to facilitate an experience for them. Initially including a family member or friend as a program partner was a way of managing some of the accommodations needed to complete activities. However, the inclusion of a family member or friend revealed something much more significant.

As family dynamics and friendships shift from partnership to caregiving, relationships inevitably change. Museum programs designed for both the person living with dementia and their partner enable both individuals to work together, share an experience, and rediscover each other. They may see themselves and the person living with dementia in a new light, witnessing abilities they never knew existed.

In addition, there are positive benefits for family and friends who participate or accompany the person living with dementia. They are able to experience their loved one engaging, expressing themselves, and enjoying the activity in a safe, comfortable environment. As well, they can experience and appreciate the experience themselves, socializing, and sharing time with others. A growing body of research confirms the anecdotal evidence that the arts can improve quality of life, reduce stress, and allow the person to better connect to the world.

Museum programs are ideal to support the abilities and interests of the participants. These programs facilitate an exchange of ideas, they make connections between the participants and the world at large, and they spark connections to personal experiences and long-term memories. And, most importantly, everyone participates in a meaningful and enjoyable activity.

NOTES

1. "Dementia Facts and Figures," *Alzheimer's Disease International*, accessed March 2024, https://www.alzint.org/about/dementia-facts-figures/.
2. "Dementia Friendly Canada," *Alzheimer Society of Canada*, accessed January 2024, https://alzheimer.ca/en/take-action/become-dementia-friendly/dementia-friendly-canada.
3. "How Canadians Perceive Dementia," *Alzheimer Society of Canada*, accessed March 2023, https://alzheimer.ca/en/about-dementia/stigma-against-dementia/how-canadians-perceive-dementia.
4. "Dementia Facts and Figures," *Alzheimer's Disease International*.
5. "How Canadians Perceive Dementia," *Alzheimer Society of Canada*.
6. "As Many as 84 Percent of People Living with Dementia Report Experiencing Discrimination - New Toolkit Aims to Reduce stigma," *The London School of Economics and Political Science*, October 7, 2022, https://www.lse.ac.uk/News/Latest-news-from-LSE/2022/j-October-22/.
7. Magdalena Rewerska-Juśko and Konrad Rejdak, "Social Stigma of People with Dementia," *Journal of Alzheimer's Disease* 78, no. 4 (December 2020): 1339.
8. "Don't Forget I'm Human: Stopping Dementia Stigma," *Stride,* 2, accessed April 2024, https://stride-dementia.turtl.co/story/anti-stigma-toolkit.
9. "How Canadians Perceive Dementia," *Alzheimer Society of Canada*.
10. "Don't Forget I'm Human: Stopping Dementia Stigma," *Stride*, 2.
11. "How Canadians Perceive Dementia," *Alzheimer Society of Canada*.
12. "Dementia Facts and Figures," *Alzheimer's Disease International*.
13. The full Alzheimer's Society of Canada survey can be found at: https://alzheimer.ca/en/about-dementia/stigma-against-dementia/how-canadians-perceive-dementia.
14. "Turning Up the Volume," *Alzheimer's Society (UK)*, 14.

15. Hamilton Council on Aging, "What We Heard Report: Empowering Dementia-Friendly Communities Project" (Hamilton & Haldimand, 2021), 12, 14.
16. *Canadian Index of Wellbeing* (University of Waterloo, 2016), 80.
17. John H. Falk, *Identity and the Museum Visitor Experience* (Walnut Creek: Left Coast Press, 2009), 239.
18. Lois H. Silverman, *The Social Work of Museums* (New York: Routledge, 2010), 13, 21.
19. Slobodan Marković, "Components of Aesthetic Experience: Aesthetic Fascination, Aesthetic Appraisal, and Aesthetic Emotion," *Iperception* 3, no. 1 (2012): 3.
20. Marković, "Components," 2.

Message for Success

The *Artful Moments* Philosophy

Museums can be places filled with meaning in myriad ways. Experiences within a museum can reach people and can draw them out of their everyday, regardless of their level of subject knowledge or ability. When the collections of objects held within a museum are activated in a purposeful, individualized, and responsive way they offer access points for enjoyment, engagement, and connection that can enhance a person's quality of life. To achieve this, the philosophy that guides our methodology and design is simple:

- Programs are person-centered and participant-led. We encourage and support participants to explore museum experiences in ways that are meaningful to them.
- Participants are individuals to be valued and empowered. We strive to understand them as people first, and then in the context of their personal circumstances, to better adapt and respond to their needs and strengths.
- Shared experiences and social connection are a priority.
- Participants have strengths, interests, and abilities at any stage in their journey with dementia. We seek to amplify strengths and adapt our programs to capitalize on their abilities.
- The experience itself and the process of engagement are prized over specific learning goals or production.

We use museum collections and activities to enhance the strengths of the participants. We uphold the rigor expected of museum programs in our activities while maintaining accessibility and centering the person in our design. We meet the needs of the participants by adapting the environment, approach, and activity. Through this method participants will be engaged in the experience, fostering improved well-being characterized by self-esteem, social connectedness, and positivity.

Part II
The Participant

Centering the Person, Not the Diagnosis

When designing museum programs for people living with dementia, it is necessary to understand how the progressive changes in the brain that are caused by dementia may impact the person and affect their participation. This knowledge will allow the facilitator to plan and deliver a program that focuses on the abilities and strengths of each participant while also supporting areas of need.

Learning about dementia, as outlined in this section, will inform your practice, but it is the relationship that develops with each person in your program that is of utmost importance. You must always see the person as a whole, not as defined by their diagnosis.

3

A Person-Centered Mindset

As a person living with dementia experiences progressive changes, it is important to recognize and acknowledge that they have been and remain a unique, valued individual with their own history and hopes. They continue to hold many relationships and roles including friend, loved one, colleague, caregiver, leader, and creative person. People with dementia have much to share and experience throughout their journey.

Although the diseases that are included under the umbrella of dementia can cause many changes, they cannot erase the person's accomplishments, experiences, or personhood. We must always remember that the person with dementia is a person first. We must not fall into thinking of them only in relation to their diagnosis or the changes that they are experiencing.

Keep this focus in mind as you begin the following chapters where we describe the impact that dementia has on the person. In our work, we have found that a solid knowledge base means that we are better equipped to plan, to adapt on the fly, and to respond effectively to each interaction we have. The information presented in this chapter is based on information from current resources and literature in the field, and informed by the experience of the co-authors in their work with people living with dementia, as well as their contributions to *Artful Moments*. For those who are new to this audience, it may feel daunting to remember and apply all of the information presented. Please know that your understanding will grow with application. Knowledge of dementia is an essential tool in your toolkit, but it is only one part of a flexible program. Don't get lost in the details.

As you move through this section, be sure to take the time to hear the stories of our participants. Each person is so much more than their diagnosis, and you must always keep that at the forefront of your thoughts and at the heart of your program.

WHO ARE THE PARTICIPANTS?

Museums have many unique audiences who visit and participate in programs. Each audience and each individual comes with different interests, levels of experience, and abilities. Visitors come to museums for many different reasons and take home many different outcomes in their experiences, but all hope to find something of themselves reflected and supported there. Unfortunately, we know that some do not. This can be the case for people living with dementia. As their abilities change, their confidence in participating in activities may diminish. As dementia progresses, the person, or their family members or friends may begin to feel that participation in museum activities is less possible, safe, or relevant. Our work with *Artful Moments* demonstrates that this is simply not true.

As museum professionals, we know that even people with little or no artistic background can be inspired by a painting that evokes an emotion or sensation. Historical or natural objects can do the same, inspiring curiosity, reflection, conversation, and reminiscence. If you work with people in your museum, you have likely seen this happen countless times. Engaging with art, historical objects, or natural settings, as well as other related experiences can be meaningful for any person, including those with dementia, regardless of their prior experience or current level of ability. It does not matter if they have previously enjoyed museums. When designed with the participant in mind, your programs can have a positive impact on anyone.

Because of the abilities that remain long after a diagnosis of dementia, many activities can be profoundly meaningful and can enable a means for self-expression, shared experience, and joy.

Participants in the *Artful Moments* program range from those in the early stage of dementia to those in the late stages. Participants in earlier stages often live in their homes or community settings and may attend the program independently or with a family member or friend. Participants in the later stages will attend with a caregiver and may reside at home with support or in a hospital setting such as a long-term care facility. With the necessary adaptations to accommodate a range of changing abilities, programs like this can work for everyone.

Selecting Your Participants

When developing a program for people living with dementia, consider the following factors to help determine your target audience. Understanding your target audience is an important step in planning the rest of your program.

- Will you build a program for people living at home in the community, or will you partner with a retirement home or care facility?
- Will you work with people who have been recently diagnosed, or will you connect through an organization that serves people in the later stages?
- Look around your community to see what programs already exist for people living with dementia and what service gaps you can fill.
- What supports exist that you can align yourself with to help?
- What does your community need, and who are you prepared to support?

Including Family and Friends

In our early work, the program design focused exclusively on the person living with dementia. Our pilot program took place in collaboration with a hospital where patients with advanced dementia resided full-time. These patients had significant changes in their abilities. We thought about their ability to engage with the activities and how to achieve the greatest "success" for each person. For most, this meant having someone accompany them who could offer a pair of hands for support where needed. While the experience of family and friends was considered, it was mostly based on the support they could provide. Their engagement was secondary to our vision.

To our pleasant surprise, rather than just providing support, we observed family and friends connecting with their loved ones in a shared experience outside of their routines related to dementia and caregiving needs.

Bill and Suri were among the first group of participants in our program. Bill's dementia was in the later stages and he required total assistance for his care. Suri visited daily but often found Bill to be frustrated by daily activities. In their lives together neither had been museum visitors. When the program was posted, Suri was skeptical but decided to try it. As the facilitators developed a connection with them we saw their participation blossom. With English as their second language, we often found them chatting together in their native tongue about what they saw in the paintings, often relating them to experiences from their lives. Suri would sometimes translate the facilitator's words when Bill had difficulty understanding. In one session, Bill remembered a large vegetable garden they had once and they laughed and laughed together, and made a collage of that garden. In a letter to us later she wrote:

If a year ago I had been told that my husband and I would get involved with art and art galleries I would have laughed and my husband would have been very upset, thinking that someone was making fun of him. Neither he nor I had ever displayed any interest in art.

Then we had several experiences together. . . . I can't explain how this made me feel. I could have cried at seeing him getting joy at doing something so totally foreign to him. The [experience] has overwhelmed me and I can't tell you how strongly I feel about this incredible initiative.[1]

This was the catalyst for us to begin focusing on social connections, as well as engagement. *Artful Moments* opened up new possibilities for family and friends by encouraging them to see the creative, capable side of their loved one. By working together, participants and the person accompanying them were able to spend time together and to engage in activities they both enjoyed. This helped to strengthen the relationship between the participants and their family members or friends. It also provided wonderful memories for the family members and friends and a temporary relief from the weight of caregiving.

In a later experience at the Gallery, a mother and daughter participated together. The daughter described her love of the program as her chance to have an outing with her mom that they both thoroughly enjoyed. She explained that this experience gave them an opportunity to connect in a meaningful way, "like they used to."

For clarity in this book, we use the term "participant" to specifically refer to the person living with dementia who joins a program. We use "person living with dementia" more broadly when we are speaking in general terms. And we use "family member or friend" to denote the partner that a participant chooses to attend a program with them. Originating in a healthcare setting, much of our earlier writing tended toward clinical terms like "patient," "person(s) with dementia," "support person," "caregiver," or "care partner." Over time and through consultations with participants we have been actively working to reduce or eliminate clinical language in our work, focusing on the person, not the diagnosis in our language.

In our research into museum programs internationally, we have found many different ways to include a family member or friend in program activities. This, like many other aspects of your program design, will ultimately be determined by your facilitation style, the needs of your participants, and by a process of trial and error to see what works best. Some museums require that a participant must attend with a partner (this may be reflective of the level of abilities of the participants), while others make it optional. Some programs arrange their groups so that the participants all sit in the front

Figure 3.1 Including Family and Friends. Participating in a program together provides benefits for everyone involved. Participants enjoy time with their loved ones and others, family and friends may build new friendships and they see their person through a lens of strength, creativity, and success. *Source*: istock.com/loonger.

with family members or friends remaining in the back. This arrangement may be used to center the program and the opportunities for speaking and contributing on the participants themselves, ensuring that their partners do not become too central in the conversations. There can be benefits, in both the facilitation style and the perception to this approach, though, partners may have less opportunity to build connections with their loved one during the program.

We actively encourage participants to attend with a family member or friend, if they wish, whether or not the changes in their abilities require it. We have couples, adult children, friends, and other pairs who join us, along with participants who choose to attend on their own. Our belief in empowering participants in their own choices leads us to invite but not require a partner. Our inclusion of a family member or friend is now part of the social vision of our programs, rather than being seen just as a "helper."

We include both the participant and their chosen partner in conversations throughout a program as a way of fostering relationships and engagement, though we do work to prioritize our participants first. With smaller groups, it is easier to balance conversation among everyone present. With larger groups our approach shifts to ensure that the participants are given ample opportunities to engage first and most often.

The family members and friends who join in often get as much out of the program as the participant does. They share in the joy of their loved one, they talk and laugh together. They can also help to support participation, as a pair of hands, a voice, and a co-creator for activities and questions. For programs that include pairs, this is a relationship to embrace.

THE PERSON COMES FIRST

Much of the content you will read in the next chapter will delve into the changes that occur as a result of dementia. Knowing how dementia impacts the person and their abilities is essential to understanding how to adapt your program. This knowledge helps you to accommodate these changes. However, this is not the whole story.

There is a saying, "if you have met one person with dementia, then you have met one person with dementia." Each person is a unique individual with a lifetime of experiences. Changes that occur in the brain from dementia do not change this. Each person will progress through their journey with dementia in their own way. Our goal is to support each person "in the moment," allowing them to continue to participate and build further life experiences with the support they need at the time.

Always remember that each participant has a life story full of experiences, relationships, and knowledge gained over a lifetime. It is important to keep this at the forefront of any interactions. Everyone will bring their own ideas and interpretations to a work of art, a museum collection, or an outdoor space. Museum programs have the unique privilege of connecting with each person's story through conversation and hands-on activities.

Dementia does not change a person's need and desire to connect with others, to communicate, to feel a sense of belonging, and to share love and friendship. Every participant wants to feel hopeful, to feel valued and respected, and to feel understood. Each participant wants to be productive in a meaningful way, to be useful and successful, to contribute, and to be inspired.

Program Participation and Sense of Purpose

In the previous chapter, we discussed the impact of stigma and isolation that is often experienced by people living with dementia (and their family member or friend). We also shared some of the ways that participation in museum programs and other aspects of community life can combat negative experiences. Another positive outcome of these kinds of programs is the assertion of a sense of purpose, at least "in the moment" for participants.

In a study of age-related sense of purpose in seniors, researchers found that as people age, retire, experience change or loss in their families and close relations, or find that their abilities change, their perceived quality of life can decline.[2] This is further exacerbated for people whose living arrangements change or as they require more support for daily living.

For a person living with dementia, similar feelings be experienced as they begin to depend on others for more of their daily activities or when they become uncertain about navigating experiences that were once managed independently. The same study found that participating in activities, particularly those that promote social connection and meaningful contribution, is an important source of purpose and meaning. A program participant in *Artful Moments* describes her experience:

> Looking at the art and talking about it. . . . When everybody contributes and you're listening to what they're seeing and thinking, it inspires you to see more than you would have seen and to feel more confident. It was the sharing that really attracted me. Of course, the social elements were very pleasant. I looked forward very much to these afternoons—a real highlight.
>
> It stays with you after you've participated. It's not a single afternoon experience that fades away, there's a real deep participation. It can be very satisfying to learn and to produce a small piece of art. You can be yourself in the kind of ambiance that is created there.[3]

We will delve further into the impact that programs can have on a person's overall well-being later, but you can hear in this participant's words the impact of a program that focuses on her—her ideas, her strengths, and the group's interests.

Providing purposeful or meaningful opportunities that encourage and validate the voices and experiences of the participants is different from "busywork" that just fills time. When a person living with dementia is really heard and seen, when their contributions are validated by others, and when connections with other participants and with their family or friends are made, their sense of purpose and their quality of life improve. A thoughtfully designed program that is centered on the person can make significant strides toward this goal.

Leaving Dementia at the Door

In our initial program design, an in-depth learning process about the participants helped us better understand them. Learning about dementia and the adaptations that helped support their abilities allowed us to develop and present the most effective program possible for each participant. Once these adaptations were made, the person's diagnosis was no longer front of mind. It became background information to be drawn upon as needed for planning, delivery, and troubleshooting. By applying your knowledge of dementia as one of many tools in your facilitator's toolkit, you will be better prepared to plan activities, identify potential areas of adjustment, and know what to do if or when someone might benefit from supportive strategies.

Within our team, we use the expression "leave dementia at the door." During a program we do not talk about dementia or talk about the changes that participants may be experiencing (unless they bring it up). We talk about the museum collections in a way that works best for each person in the room. We simply have a group of participants with us who we will engage in a creative program. We focus on being supportive, responsive, and encouraging just as we would with any other group.

A program like *Artful Moments* differs from a therapeutically-driven activity whether that be art therapy, occupational therapy, or a support group. Our focus is on the person and the experience, not the condition or resulting deficits. With their collections and activities, museums are uniquely positioned to offer meaningful experiences that focus on the person and their interests, knowledge, and curiosity, as well as their ability to connect and share with others. Museums can change the narrative of a person with dementia by providing a supportive, person-centered framework where the changes they experience remain in the background and the facilitator's knowledge of dementia is present only to support their facilitation techniques.

Artful Moments maintains a strong focus on empowering participants to experience creative, social experiences. It is about engagement and well-being, separate from a more medical model of care. As two researchers, Mitchell and Jonas-Simpson, wrote in 2019, "the intent of the arts-based activities is not to provide therapy or diversion—instead it is initiated to present opportunities for participants to more fully express themselves in the moment with others."[4] And Clarke-Vivier et al. documented in a 2017 article that "self-esteem related goals are supported by offering programming that can sustain interest and engagement but does not have the disease or its symptoms at the center."[5]

As facilitators, we learn about dementia so that we don't have to talk about it. We bring people together to enjoy meaningful activity and the company of others, and we adapt our program to ensure everyone can take part in their own way.

CHANGING ABILITIES RELATED TO AGING

Dementia is not a part of healthy aging, and the next chapter will explore the effects caused by dementia. In a program for people living with dementia, you may find people whose abilities are also changing naturally with age, other health conditions, or injuries. This will have an impact on how a person engages apart from their diagnosis. Before examining the impact of dementia specifically, consider some of the changes that occur as people age.

Memory and Thinking

In a typical aging process, the brain undergoes changes that may have minor effects on memory or thinking skills. For example, a healthy older adult might forget familiar names or words, or they may find it more difficult to multitask. The person may express some concern about memory loss, but, generally, memory is not significantly impaired and the memory loss is not progressive.

Changes to the Senses

With age, vision changes may make it more difficult to see things up close including small print on paper and screens and to distinguish between things with low contrast such as white paper on a white table. Peripheral vision declines, so it is harder to see things off to the side like the person sitting beside you. Older eyes can require more time to adjust to changing light levels, such as walking into a dim room after being in the sun. Many also have less tolerance for glare from shiny surfaces, like glass on pictures. There is also an increased risk of conditions such as cataracts or macular degeneration.

Aging can cause our senses to become less acute, including smell, taste, touch, and hearing. Many people experience hearing loss for higher-frequency sounds, such as a woman's voice. They may also find it hard to participate in conversation where there is background noise.

Physical Changes

With age, bones and muscles can lose strength, endurance, and flexibility—factors that can affect stamina, stability, and balance. Additional changes may occur due to diseases that change the physical body, affecting fine motor skills and dexterity.

STRENGTHS

Before delving into some of the changes that can impact the brain and affect the person living with dementia, it is important to be aware that many abilities that remain long into a person's journey with dementia. By emphasizing these strengths, we can foster engagement, participation, and positive feelings. We can help the participant to engage in a program in a way that honors their personhood and individuality and makes the most of their abilities, interests, and contributions.

Long-Term Memory

Memories from the distant past are often preserved longer than recent or short-term memories. Drawing on these long-term memories provides the person with an opportunity to engage with others and build relationships. Memories of moments from earlier in their life can provide great conversation between participants, their family and friends, and among the group.

Museum programs have a wonderful opportunity to connect with memories from the past. Objects from an earlier time, artworks that show familiar places and activities, and music from a person's younger days—these can spark memories and offer opportunities to share knowledge and personal. Tapping into a person's knowledge empowers them to lead a conversation and to take pride in their contributions. They become an active and valued member of a group.

Visual Memory

Visual memories that have been stored are more vivid and more easily stimulated compared to verbal memories. This may explain why looking at a museum object may suddenly stimulate a visual memory from the participant's past which then fosters the participant's engagement in the conversation about the object.

Procedural Memory

Part of long-term memory is the memory for motor and cognitive skills that do not require conscious thought—things like brushing your hair, making a bed, or shaking hands. By incorporating these kinds of skills and habits along with incorporating familiar tools and repetitive tasks into the program, the participant will have an easier time engaging in an activity.

Recognition Memory

A general feeling that a person or place is familiar remains longer than a person's ability to remember specific information. For example, the participant may not remember your name, but they may sense that you are familiar or that they have been to the museum before. This type of memory speaks to the importance of always being positive and creating a positive environment and experience for the participant. It also supports the importance of consistency of staff, program spaces, and routines.

Emotional Memory

Memories that stir an emotional response or have a strong emotional connection for the person living with dementia are retained well. Music and smells can be useful in helping participants recall these memories and emotions. For example, baking fresh bread may stir up childhood memories of baking with their grandmother or a song may stimulate the happiness they felt on their wedding day. When these types of memories are stimulated, it may help the participant access previous experiences and emotions that they can then share with others.

Social Skills

Social skills are those highly familiar verbal and nonverbal skills we use to connect with others and maintain dignity. Some examples include smiling, nodding your head, shaking hands, waving goodbye, and greeting someone when they pass. By encouraging these skills when a participant arrives and departs, we help to engage the participant in connecting with others.

Emotional Awareness

Emotional awareness is being able to feel emotion and to be aware of the emotional state of others. This awareness allows the participant to read the nonverbal messages communicated through facial expression, body position, body tension, tone of voice, and mood. If the facilitator is smiling, happy, and relaxed, this will send a more positive message to the participant than if the facilitator appears nervous, anxious, rushed, or upset. As a facilitator, it is important to be aware of your nonverbal messaging at all times as the participant's emotional awareness is well retained.

You can also use emotional awareness to model, emphasize, and extend what you are saying. This is helpful for participants whose receptive language has been impacted.

Sense of Humor

Even though the person with dementia may have difficulty with the abstract thought needed to understand humor, they can socially respond to the lightheartedness of the situation when others are laughing and will often join in the laughter.

Reading

When reading material is modified to be more easily seen and understood, a person with dementia retains the ability to read into the later stages of the disease. This can mean larger font size, high contrast print, extra spacing, and shorter sentences. Modifying reading material also enables the person to better understand what they are reading. Using printed materials to supplement spoken instructions or ideas can be useful in extending a participant's ability to do things themselves rather than needing help from someone else. Independence is important in building confidence and can empower greater participation.

Physical Ability

A person with dementia typically retains the larger movements of the body like using their arms and legs. Fine hand movements usually remain until the latter part of the disease, although tasks like writing or drawing may become more difficult especially if participants have other underlying diseases such as arthritis involved. By being aware of these problems and either modifying the activity or compensating for the problem by the use of adaptive you will design a more inclusive program.

Music Appreciation

Musical aptitude and music appreciation remain. Many people with dementia can recall the tune and the words of songs from when they were younger.

Creativity

Researchers believe that as a brain is being progressively affected by dementia an individual can still experience the drive to be creative. Participating in creative activities may also offer unique ways for a person to connect with visual, emotional, and physical memories, even after other abilities have begun to change.[6] Strategies that may already be familiar to museum facilitators, including visual thinking and visual literacy, can be activated to offer communication and hands-on interventions that support the strengths and abilities of participants.

Well-known benefits of museum experiences such as stress relief, building resilience, and new forms of expression suggest a link between social and creative activities, as well as the preservation of cognitive functions.

Creative activities are not only beneficial for the person engaging in them, they are social activities that strengthen social ties among participants. From offering opportunities for self-expression to the joy of partaking in meaningful activities and creating work of their own, creative experiences can be empowering and enjoyable.

WHAT THIS MEANS

Each person's abilities are unique to that person, and it is vital to promote the continued use of these abilities rather than focus on the changes that occur. By providing opportunities to use these strengths and to adapt to support any changes in their abilities, we create the conditions for engagement.

Strengths remain in all areas of ability including cognition, language, perception, mood, and physical abilities. Changes will occur at different times and in different combinations for each person. With a basic understanding of dementia and its impact, a facilitator will learn to recognize each participant's strengths and abilities.

Our experience and previous research have shown that *Artful Moments* works to create meaningful engagement for people living with dementia across the disease trajectory. Participants who are in the later stage of the disease can also effectively engage and participate.

NOTES

1. Facilitator's account of program session, followed by a letter from the spouse of a participant, 2012. Names have been changed to respect privacy.
2. R. Owen, K. Berry, and L.J.E. Brown, "'I Like to Feel Needed, You Know?': A Qualitative Examination of Sense of Purpose in Older Care Home Residents," *Aging & Mental Health* 27, no. 2 (2023): 236.
3. Artful Moments participant interview, 2022. Names have been changed to respect privacy.
4. G.J. Mitchell, C. Jonas-Simpson, J. Richards, S. Brown, and V. Bitove, "Creating a Relational Arts-based Academy for Persons Living with Dementia (Innovative Practice)," *Dementia* 20, no. 3 (2019): 1148.
5. Sara Clarke-Vivier, Corie Lyford, and Lynn Thomson, "Strengths and Challenges of Arts-based Programming for Individuals with Alzheimer's and Related Dementias," *LEARNing Landscapes* 10, no. 2 (2017): 98.
6. Hannah Zeilig, John Killick, and Chris Fox, "The Participative Arts for People Living with a Dementia: A Critical Review," *International Journal of Ageing and Later Life* 9, no. 1 (2014): 24.

4

What Is Dementia?

Dementia is not a single disease. It is an umbrella term used to describe a collection of symptoms resulting from a number of diseases. In each case, abnormal changes to the brain occur that in turn cause changes in how a person functions in their daily life.[1] Dementia is a progressive disease with the symptoms gradually getting worse over time as more of the brain becomes damaged.

Dementia is often referred to as an invisible disease because the physical changes occur inside the brain while the person's outer appearance is unaffected. Not everyone will experience the same symptoms or progress at the same rate because the damage that has occurred in the brain and the resulting impacts are specific to the person. A person's symptoms may also fluctuate throughout the day or over a period of time for many reasons.

While there is currently no cure for dementia, a person's quality of life can be significantly enhanced by continuing to be active and socially engaged. This is where programs like *Artful Moments* can play a valuable role.

The brain controls everything a person does. In dementia, many areas of the brain are affected and this impacts how the person thinks, communicates, sees the world, feels, and does things. As a facilitator, you need to have a basic understanding of some of the changes that may occur in the brain and how these changes can affect a participant's ability to engage. Remember that it is not important for you to label the changes in abilities but rather to understand and recognize them so that you can apply a strategy to help the person engage. Abilities are organized into five categories:

- **Cognition** refers to the underlying brain skills that make it possible for us to acquire and use information so that we can adapt to our environment.
- **Language** refers to the understanding and/or use of a spoken, written, or other communication system.
- **Perception** refers to the ability to take in and interpret messages from our body and our environment.
- **Mood and emotions** refer to how we are feeling "in the moment" and over time.
- **Physical ability** refers to our ability to carry out body movement.

Although they have been delineated here for the purposes of definition and understanding, each of these areas interconnect, overlap, and affect each other. This chapter will describe the impacts that dementia can have on a person. This is referred to broadly as "knowledge of dementia." It frames the content in the context of museum programs. Subsequent chapters will explore how to apply this knowledge in your program design—in relation to the environment, approach, and activities.

UNDERSTANDING COGNITION

"Cognition" is a term that refers to the underlying brain skills that make it possible for a person to acquire and use information so they can adapt and respond to their environment. Cognitive skills are interconnected and most of our functions depend on several of these skills working together. Changes in cognition also affect other areas of function such as language, perception, mood and emotion, and physical ability.

As a very complex and multifaceted area of ability, cognition can be broken down into several distinct components. These components interact so changes in one area can affect others. The changes can affect one or more components at different times and at different degrees of severity.

Stories from the Museum: Mai

Mai is a regular participant in our programs. We know that she really enjoys her time at the museum since her son tells us about the conversations they share on the drive home. Often, she asks him why the "museum people" were so happy to see her that day. We greet her by name each week but also make sure to introduce ourselves by name every time and we wear name tags. Her son also told us that the previous week she said, "I am not sure what I said today, but they really seemed to like it" and she felt very proud. When she was younger, Mai was very skilled at sewing clothing and told us all about the different kinds of stitching in an historical garment in the exhibition. With her in the group, all of us learned something![2]

Attention

"Attention" is the ability to focus on something specific. Attention is important because it is the first step that occurs as our brains work to remember things. By focusing attention, the brain registers, processes, and then stores the information for recall later. Important aspects of attention include:

- Being able to focus on one thing at a time.
- Dividing attention between two or more things.
- Maintaining attention over a long period of time.
- Shifting attention between several things.
- Remaining focused to complete a task.

Dementia often affects the area of the brain that is responsible for attention. The participant may have difficulty focusing their attention on the object being discussed during a tour. They may have trouble paying attention to more than one speaker during a conversation or maintaining their attention for the duration of the program. It can be hard to shift their attention from one activity to another or to perform one task while listening to the next step at the same time. They may find it hard to ignore distractions like background music, other conversations, or irrelevant noises.

Memory

"Memory" is the ability to collect, process, store, and recall visual and verbal information from the environment. The larger concept of memory can be broken down into smaller types: short-term, long-term, procedural, and emotional memory. An understanding of the impact dementia may have on each type of memory can help a facilitator adapt their program to draw on the participants' strengths, thus maximizing engagement.

Short-term memory allows us to remember small amounts of information for a short period of time. Changes in a person's short-term memory often begin early in the progression of dementia. In a museum setting the participant might have difficulty remembering small bits of information such as the first step of a three-step activity, the name of the artwork they just saw, or the facilitator's name.

This is important to understand because you can adjust the kinds of questions you ask and the way you present information so that each participant can engage in conversations and activities.

Long-term memory refers to information and memories collected and remembered over a person's lifetime. This includes being able to remember specific events that happened in the person's life, as well as facts and concepts that give us general knowledge of the world. Although long-term memory usually declines as dementia progresses, this typically happens later in the disease. Earlier memories generally are better preserved than short-term memory.

Experiences with museum collections can draw upon participants' earlier memories, encouraging recollections of past experiences, and can be a great way to connect with other participants, family members, and friends. Triggering long-term memory can also be a way to draw out knowledge acquired over a lifetime that can be very empowering for the participant.

When the areas of the brain that are responsible for long-term memory are impacted, the participant may mix up timelines in their personal history. They may have trouble remembering previously known facts or answering questions related to factual knowledge. Again, adapting the style and content of your program will allow participants to share their experiences even when memory has been affected.

Procedural memory and **emotional memory** are part of long-term memory though these two types of memory do not require conscious thought. Procedural skills are skills and habits such as brushing teeth or making coffee, and emotional memories are responses caused by certain stimuli like being happy when a special song comes on the radio or seeing a beloved family member. Typically, procedural and emotional memory are retained until the later stages of dementia and can be drawn upon to foster engagement during a program.

New Learning

"New learning" requires a person to attend to and then store information into short-term memory to be recalled later. Since attention and short-term memory are usually affected early in the disease, the participant may have trouble learning new things. In a program like *Artful Moments*, a participant may benefit from support with new activities like mixing colors, learning the names of other participants, or using a computer for virtual classes.

Facilitators can present new activities in a way that supports participants and allows them to enjoy their experience. Rather than relying on a participant having learned how to do something, facilitators can repeat names or the steps of activities each time as a natural part of their demonstration or introduction. This also includes introducing yourself or wearing a name tag as a standard procedure. You can consider it a kind of "recap" to make sure everyone is prepared.

"In the Moment"

It is important to focus on "in the moment" experiences. While participants might not retain all the information or skills learned, the act of sharing and exploring new knowledge "in the moment" can be enriching and empowering. For example, during discussions, we may start by looking at and discussing an artwork. We often bring in relevant factual information about the artwork, artist, or historical context as the conversation flows. While some participants might not remember these details later, they contribute to a richer appreciation of the experience "in the moment."

Planning

"Planning" allows us to manage tasks that need to be done now or in the future by setting goals and then determining the steps needed to finish the task. Setting priorities and doing tasks in the right order are part of this process and are important every time a new plan is being made. For instance, if something is spilled the participant may have difficulty formulating a plan to clean up.

Having a well-thought-out plan, carefully arranged spaces and materials, and a streamlined process will provide a comfortable experience for participants so that changes in their abilities will not affect their participation.

Organization

"Organization" refers to the way a person keeps track of the information or materials needed to finish the task. During a program, the participant may have difficulty gathering art supplies from a common area or their workspace may become very messy.

As a facilitator, good planning and setup can help to ensure participants have what they need for their activity and eliminate any excess items that might be distracting or confusing. During a program, facilitators can also help to reorganize a cluttered workspace like removing excess scrap paper or too many pencils.

Sequencing

"Sequencing" is the ability to complete the steps of a task in a logical order. In a museum program, the participant may try to paint before applying paint to the brush or may start to put the paint away when they have not yet begun painting.

Facilitators can support participants by demonstrating activities one step at a time and leaving time to work in between, rather than presenting a full demonstration and then relying on them to work through steps on their own.

Initiation

"Initiation" is the ability to start something in a timely manner without needing a prompt or cue. The participant may not respond when asked a question in conversation. They may have difficulty picking up a workshop tool even after being asked and others have already begun, or they may appear unmotivated.

Adjusting our facilitation can overcome many difficulties with initiation. We can help a participant join a conversation by calling them by name. This prompt is often enough to help the participant join in. If needed, we can also model ways to respond. In a hands-on activity, we can offer individual support by demonstrating the first step beside the participant's work so they can see how to start or we could offer support by handing them a tool.

Processing Speed

"Processing speed" refers to the amount of time required for a person to make sense of verbal or visual information and then respond to it. You may notice that during a museum tour, the participant takes time to respond to your questions. There may be a delay between being directed to paint and the participant starting to paint. The person will need time to process and understand what they have heard and will then need to formulate a response or action.

Understanding processing speed and planning for it is something that a facilitator should actively and consciously act on throughout a program. Remembering to speak a little slower and to leave space for answers and activity will make a big difference for many participants. Remember to always speak with an adult tone, with natural volume, and a natural flow of speech, just a bit slower. You will learn to be comfortable with a few moments of silence. If you give participants time to process and respond rather than jumping in to fill a silence, it will empower them to comfortably contribute to conversations.

Problem-Solving

"Problem-solving" is being able to adapt and think differently to unexpected situations. Judgment and insight are two of the many parts of this process. The participant may have difficulty figuring out an alternative if the paint color they want to use is not available or make a poor decision to solve a problem such as using a shirt to wipe spilled paint.

By observing your participants during a program, you will be able to see when a participant is having difficulties problem-solving and can step in with suggestions on how to proceed or to assist when needed. Supporting changes in problem-solving can be a delicate balance between empowering with cues and redirection or discouraging by removing agency, their sense of feeling control over their decisions and actions.

Stories from the Museum: Lucy

Once a month I bring a group of people from the retirement home where I work to the Gallery. I am always really pleased to see how comfortable the staff are with my group. In the Gallery, the facilitator seems to stand in just the right place to keep everyone from getting too close to the art even though one person often wants to touch it.

I notice that she makes sure that everyone gets a chance to participate. Sometimes our participants interrupt or speak over each other. She listens and suggests politely that she will come back to one person as she listens to another without putting anyone on the spot. She also makes sure to invite anyone who hasn't shared into the conversation, even with just a "thumbs up."

She just took it in stride when one of the people in the group pinched her and reached out to hold her hand. She gently redirected this person without seeming bothered at all and didn't even pause in her talk. My group felt very comfortable even though a few of the family members who came along were nervous about the trip before we got there.[3]

Judgment

"Judgment" is a process where options are considered, a conclusion is drawn, and a decision is made. In a museum, the participant may make poor judgments such as attempting to touch objects in an exhibition or deciding to leave the program alone before their ride arrives.

As a facilitator, the safety of participants and your museum objects is paramount. Be observant and have support available as needed. Be prepared with strategies to intervene.

Insight

"Insight" refers to the person being aware of their abilities, actions, and behaviors, and of the impact they may have on others and the environment. Insight is needed to evaluate a situation, engage in problem-solving, and receive feedback to adjust what they are doing. When a person has poor insight, the person may have difficulty accepting or understanding the feedback.

During a museum tour, the participant may be unaware that they have said something offensive. They may not understand why others are concerned about their safety or they may have difficulty accepting feedback from others. As a facilitator, you will need to use your knowledge and judgment to choose when to intervene and when not to intervene. Is the situation unsafe? Offensive? Inappropriate? Do you need to redirect the conversation? Are the words and actions outside of social norms but will not cause harm?

Self-regulation

Self-regulation includes being able to adjust and manage emotional and verbal responses and follow social norms. It also includes being able to complete tasks when difficulties are experienced. Changes in self-regulation may be seen in the museum setting during a tour when a participant may talk over another person because they are excited that they know the answer to a question. The participant may be overly friendly, flirtatious with others, use offensive language, or initiate unwelcome physical contact. They may also show frustration if they are not happy with their results.

As a facilitator you can adjust your reactions to your participants' words and actions, remembering that changes in their brain can cause them to act in unexpected ways. You can then choose when and if to respond to the situation as appropriate.

UNDERSTANDING LANGUAGE

"Language" refers to the understanding and use of a spoken, written, or other system of communication. It enables us to express ourselves and understand others. Effective communication involves taking information "in" which is called "receptive language" and getting information "out," called "expressive language." There are several different areas of the brain involved in language. Dementia may impact a person's ability to get the information "in," get the information "out," or both. Some of the changes in language are specific to the type of dementia the person has—language is well preserved in some cases, while in others it is more significantly impaired earlier in the disease. As dementia progresses, changes in other areas of ability can also have an impact on language.

Stories from the Museum: Fatima and Max

In a recent program, I had two participants whose language abilities had been affected by dementia. We had a great time together, but I had to make some adjustments in the way I conversed with them.

Fatima does not speak. I learned from her husband that she has [expressive] aphasia, which affects her speech but not her understanding of what she hears. I noticed that she smiles and nods as I talk, so we tried using gestures to communicate together—thumbs up for "yes" and thumbs down for "no." We also used a tilting hand to mean "maybe"'or "a little bit." Once I adjusted my questions to be answered like this, everything went really well. We even got to compare a painting that she liked a lot but her husband did not.

Max took a bit more time to figure out. He seems to listen intently and will respond enthusiastically and often at length when given the opportunity. He uses lots of words and sounds, but I can't really understand most of what he tells me. I make sure to listen and make eye contact while Max is speaking and I nod to encourage him. I pay attention to where he points and listen for words that I can understand to try to draw out what he is saying. I try to paraphrase what I understand to see if I am getting the right idea. I am not yet sure how much of what I say he understands—he nods a lot when I ask him questions. I will usually try "yes" or "no" questions to help him communicate and this seems to make him happy.[4]

Receptive Language

"Receptive language" is the ability to understand information that is being taken in—the meaning of what is being said to an individual or of what they read. This includes understanding when they hear or read numbers, words, phrases, sentences, and paragraphs. For example, reading this book is receptive language.

Dementia can affect a person's ability to understand language so they may have trouble making sense of what is said to them or what they read. The following situations can make understanding more difficult:

- Speaking quickly to the person.
- Conversation when more than one person is speaking.
- Speaking in long or complex sentences.
- Giving more than one direction at a time.
- Using a pronoun instead of the actual name of the person or object being referred to.
- Using figurative speech, idioms, sayings, or abstract concepts.
- Using indirect language, relying on the participant to infer or interpret what you are saying.

Expressive Language

"Expressive language" is the ability to express ourselves through speech or writing. Telling someone how your day was, sending an email or text are all expressive language.

Dementia may affect a person's ability to express themselves or to get their message "out." They may have trouble with speaking, writing, texting, or typing. In a program, the participant may:

- Have difficulty finding the right word or feeling the word they want "is on the tip of their tongue."
- Make sound or word errors. They may use words that are related by meaning or sound similar, or they may use a nonsense word.
- Speak with slower or hesitant speech.
- Give little or vague details in what they say.
- Make spelling errors or be unable to write words and messages.
- Make errors in saying or writing numbers, dates, amounts of money, phone numbers.
- Have reduced confidence speaking or answering questions.
- If they are a multi-lingual speaker, use their first language more often—a person's first language is often less impacted.

Language in Combination with Other Abilities

When we consider language in combination with cognition, dementia can affect a person's abilities in many ways. Some cognitive changes can further impact a person's ability to understand and express themselves. In a program, a participant may:

- Need more time to process information and/or more time to respond.
- Not follow along, or not participate as much when there are distractions (visual, sound, or internal thoughts).
- Have difficulty finding the words they want.
- Not remember what had been said or what they wanted to say.
- Go off-topic when speaking.
- Sound disorganized or have a line of thought that is hard to follow.
- Have less awareness that their message may be hard for another person to follow.
- Have less social conversation skills—they may interrupt, speak out of turn, or speak over others.

As a facilitator, keeping this in mind will allow you to communicate more effectively. By adjusting your rate or level of speech, remembering to pause and give the participant time for processing, eliminating distractions, and working to be clear and concise in language choices, you will support your participants and their ability to take part in a program.

UNDERSTANDING PERCEPTION

"Perception" refers to the ability of the brain to take in and interpret messages from the body and the environment. Changes in perception affect the way a person with dementia understands and navigates the space and objects around them. Three key concepts of perception are important in museum programs—spatial awareness, recognition of objects, and mind–body coordination.

Stories from the Museum: Morris and Jane

I took my wife to a program at the art gallery today and I learned some tricks to help her make art. She used to love to paint but lately hasn't been able to. When we sat at the table and we saw the paint, I wasn't sure what to expect. She looked at the paintbrush but wasn't sure what to do with it. I handed it to her but she just put it back on the table.

The artist came over and showed us how to get started—he dipped the brush into the paint, then handed it to Jane, and pointed to the paper, suggesting that there was a good place to start. I watched and she started to paint! The artist explained that sometimes it just takes the right cue or a familiar action. Once she started I could see how happy she was. She kept going, using lots of different colors and lines. Even though her work looked different from what she used to do, it was great to see her taking pleasure in painting again![5]

Spatial Awareness

"Spatial awareness" encompasses several concepts that have a common thread of understanding the relationship between objects in space and the relationship between the person and other objects. This includes:

- **Figure/ground:** knowing what is in front and what is behind. It can be hard to distinguish a white sheet of paper on a white table, to find a paintbrush on a cluttered table, or to draw one object in front of another.
- **Position-in-space:** knowing relational concepts such as up and down, in and out, over and under, front and behind. The participant may have difficulty following directional instructions during an activity using spatial language.
- **Topographical orientation:** knowing where one place is in relation to another and being able to navigate between them. For example, the participant may have difficulty navigating through the museum or locating the washroom.
- **Depth and distance:** our three-dimensional understanding of the world and the distance between objects. A participant may put a jar of water too close to the edge of the table, over- or under-reach for an object, or misjudge the depth of the stair and fall. They also may avoid walking on shiny floors as the floor appears wet or take a high step where the floor color changes from light to dark as the dark area seems to have depth.
- **Spatial relations:** knowing where we are in relation to other objects. The participant may stand too close to an art exhibit or bump into an object on display because they do not know how close they are to it or they may miss the chair seat when attempting to sit.

Considering perception enables facilitators to adjust the space in which a program takes place and tailoring language and instructions to help support participants.

Recognition (Agnosia)

With agnosia, the person has difficulty recognizing familiar objects they see, touch, smell, or hear. This can occur despite any physical impairment of their senses. Although they may not recognize a familiar object with one sense (such as vision), they may recognize it if a different sense (like touch) is used. In a museum setting, the participant may put non-edible items like clay or a paintbrush in their mouth, or drink from a cup used to rinse paintbrushes. They may not recognize how to use a paintbrush or pencil that is needed for the activity. Further, they may not recognize they are in a museum, the person who brought them to the program, or even themselves when looking in a mirror.

Safety concerns may arise when familiar objects are no longer recognized and may be used incorrectly. As a facilitator, it is important to observe participants carefully to see when safety concerns may arise and address situations where you can step in to assist.

Mind–Body Coordination (Motor Apraxia)

With motor apraxia, the person may be unable to carry out or coordinate the action they were asked to do even though they understand what you want them and have the physical ability to do the action. Providing an environmental cue and/or modeling or demonstrating may help the participant initiate the action.

Motor apraxia may be inconsistent so that sometimes the person may do the action spontaneously but other times they benefit from cueing and assistance. In a museum setting, a participant may be unable to wash their hands when asked. However, later upon seeing a sink (or in the presence of a sink), they may turn on the tap and wash their hands spontaneously. Similarly, when asked to paint, the participant may need a demonstration to start or may need you to place the brush in their hand. However, at another time they may independently pick up the paintbrush and paint.

As a facilitator you can use your knowledge of dementia and your observations to know when and how to best support your participants. Over a few sessions, you will get to know your participants, and will have a better understanding of how you can best assist them. There are many different ways to accommodate a participant's abilities, it just takes practice to find the right way to work.

UNDERSTANDING MOOD AND EMOTIONS

"Mood and emotions" refer to how a person feels. Mood is a general feeling or state that lasts for a longer period, while emotions are specific feelings experienced at a particular time. People living with dementia may experience depression, anxiety, and intense or rapid changes in their emotional responses. These can lead to social withdrawal, apathy, loneliness, social isolation, and a loss of self-esteem. Additionally, some displays of emotions may change. Smiling and laughter can decrease over time.

Stories from the Museum: George and Min

I had a great moment in my gallery conversation today. There is a man named George in my group who usually seems uninterested in the program. He does not smile at all but his wife keeps bringing him back and she seems to have a nice time. I am used to groups who smile and put up their hands, talk, and even laugh at my jokes a bit, so this participant has been hard to read. I know that even though he does not show enjoyment, it does not mean he is unengaged, so I pay close attention each week to get to know him better. Today I talked about a painting of a backyard garden and George told us about the vegetables he used to grow in his own garden, and how much he enjoyed it. It was great to see the connection!

In another program, a participant named Min and her daughter were both engrossed in a conversation about historical kitchen tools and recalled memories of baking bread together. When we switched to the activity, making biscuits in the kitchen, Min became distressed and frustrated. She had trouble following the recipe and started to cry. After a short break, her daughter suggested that they share one bowl and work together, and things went better after that.[6]

In a museum program, the participant may lack facial expression and may not smile at humorous comments. They may watch other participants and the facilitator but have trouble actively engaging in the activity themselves. They might be disinterested in the activity, withdraw from group conversation, or they may worry about how well they are doing or be critical of their work. Some may show unexpected emotions such as crying for unknown reasons.

As a facilitator, you are used to reading a group's engagement based on their participation, body language, facial expression, and emotional displays. When facilitating a group of participants living with dementia, your usual methods of reading whether participants are engaged may need adjustment. Consider your knowledge of dementia and the unique needs of those in your program. You might see less outward participation, body language cues, or facial expressions. Unexpected emotions may arise. By understanding your participants, you can identify and promote enjoyment and participation throughout the program.

UNDERSTANDING PHYSICAL ABILITIES

"Physical abilities" refers to the ability to carry out large and small body movements. In the early stages of dementia, a person may experience mild changes in coordination or fine movements such as drawing or using art tools. In the middle stages when cognitive and perceptual problems become more apparent, the person has more safety risks such falling. In the late stages of the disease large body movements decline leading to problems walking safely or sitting without support. The person can also lose strength, making moving and engaging in art-making activities difficult. In addition to the dementia and age-related changes, they may also have medical conditions that may further affect their physical abilities.

Stories from the Museum: Lydia and Her Mother

Every week I take my mom to the museum for an arts program. I worried at first because her balance is not very good and she gets tired easily. Lately, her hands have been shaky too—she said that she didn't want to do the art because hers would be "no good." The museum is a large building and I was concerned she wouldn't be able to keep up.

The facilitators, though, had thought of everything. When we went into the room with the art there were chairs already set up for us, and when we moved to the other side of the room there was another set of chairs ready too. The facilitator had planned a lovely talk about several paintings that were all in the same room. When we started a hands-on activity, the artist talked about the way that everyone made lines in their own way—straight, wavy, or even scribbled and that they were all great ways to have your own style. My mom felt better knowing that she didn't have to worry about her hands. They even had a special grip on her pencil to make it easier to hold. We had a great time and my mom wants to go back next week.[7]

In a museum program, some participants may experience changes that will affect their participation. Walking or standing, especially for a long time, may be hard, and a person may hold onto furniture or a wall for support. Their hands might be shaky when using tools. They may have reduced sensation, dexterity, and coordination in their hands. They may also be more sensitive to loud noises, have difficulty bending down or reaching up for objects due to stiffness or restricted movement, or they may stop an activity due to pain or limited endurance.

As you plan and deliver a program, you should consider both safety and ability when selecting locations, materials, tools, and activities. Considerations such as seating and movement in museum spaces as well as tips regarding tools and materials will be discussed in subsequent chapters.

STAGES OF DEMENTIA

Dementia is progressive, meaning symptoms gradually worsen and are not reversible. While the experience varies between individuals and depends on many factors, including the type of dementia and the affected areas of the brain, change is inevitable. However, with proper care and engaging activities, a person's quality of life can be improved throughout their journey with dementia.

The progression of dementia is often described in three stages: early, middle, and late. While individuals' experiences vary, each stage shares some commonalities. This section will include a description of the typical abilities and the impact at each stage.

Please note that this information is not meant for you to apply or label your participants, or as admission criteria for your program. Its purpose is to help you organize your observations and reflections about your experiences with participants and to understand how to respond to what you see.

Early (Mild) Stage

In the early stage, people living with dementia may experience some combination of symptoms including mild forgetfulness, difficulty navigating in the community, and following fast-paced discussions. The changes are subtle at first, but over time, the person or those around them begins to notice these changes occurring more frequently.[8] Eliminating background noise and allowing extra time to answer questions are examples of strategies that may be effective for someone in the early stage.

Frank is a regular participant in virtual programs. He loves art and really likes to talk about it too. He has great insights into the artworks we look at and tells the occasional joke too. With Frank, we don't see a lot of evidence of changes in his abilities. Occasionally we have seen a slight delay in his ability to formulate comments and he may make comments about his own perceived changes in abilities. Little adaptation is required most of the time, other than leaving a bit more time for him to process his thoughts. It can be easy to forget that Frank might benefit from supportive adjustments.[9]

With participants like Frank, we must watch closely as it is easy to make assumptions about their abilities and not modify the program to maximize their engagement. It is important to carefully monitor your observations about each participant so that you continue to offer the right amount of support and challenge.

Middle (Moderate) Stage

A person in the middle stage may have more difficulty with certain everyday tasks, their memory may be more impacted, problems with perception may emerge, and their ability to participate in conversations may need more support. They may also experience some changes in their mood.[10] During the middle stage of the disease, participants can benefit from additional support in programs, especially adjusting how you ask questions and provide instructions.

Alfred was reserved at first and before they started the program he told his brother that he would not say anything, just listen. He has become much more comfortable over time. He answers questions when asked although he doesn't volunteer ideas without being prompted. Alfred's first language is French and sometimes asks his in French for help with finding the right word.

Alfred sometimes takes time to find the right words but with guided questions is able to participate. On occasion, his answers don't completely relate to the question, but other times he has great insight. Each week he loses attention around the 45-60-minute mark and wanders away when the hands-on activity starts, and sometimes earlier if distracted by other family members.[11]

For Alfred, we remember to always pause and wait a little bit longer so that he can process his thoughts. If he seems to be having difficulty after a few moments, we can try to rephrase or simplify the question. If a comment does not relate to the conversation, we try to connect something he said back to the discussion to help him re-engage. We also know not to worry if he moves on from the program early.

Late (Severe) Stage

Late-stage dementia significantly impacts all aspects of a person's abilities including memory and other cognitive functions. Language abilities may also decline, making communication challenging.[12] Adjusting your approach is key including how you ask questions and the types of activities you offer. Engagement may appear different from other groups. Look for nonverbal responses such as thumbs up/down and eye contact. Engagement and the benefits that come from it are still very powerful.

> *Kelly is in the later stages of dementia. She lives in long-term care and has lots of help with everyday activities. At the museum she listens to the conversation and nods or signals when we ask questions. She paints with us every week but needs some help getting paint on her paintbrush. She and her husband usually make artwork together with her pointing to tell him where to put the colors. Sometimes she does it herself too. Her paintings don't look like the steps we demonstrated but she is really happy with her work. Her husband is also really happy to see how engaged she is in the conversations and hands-on activities, and enjoys the time they spend working together.*[13]

When working with participants who are in the late stage of dementia, you will need to develop a good sense of each participant's abilities and adapt your approach, as well as your activities. There are a lot of strategies for participants whose cognitive, perceptual, verbal, or physical abilities have changed. The way you plan, present, and offer support in these instances is different it is an amazing opportunity for enjoyment and engagement "in the moment."

Why Is This Important?

The progression from one stage of dementia to the next may sound daunting when you imagine designing a program to support the changing needs and abilities of participants, especially in the later stages. While it does require careful planning, ongoing reflection and adaptation, and great sensitivity to the participants, you can create an engaging and meaningful program for people in any stage of dementia. At the AGH, *Artful Moments* began in a hospital setting with people in the late stages of dementia, while our current programs are offered more often for people in the early and middle stages of dementia.

Our success is based on understanding each participant, not just their dementia diagnosis. As facilitators, we tailor strategies based on individual abilities. Remember, everyone experiences dementia differently.

When considering your participants and their abilities, it is a good idea to think about how much access and adaptation you are able to apply. We have learned that groups combining participants at very different stages are not always as successful. Feedback from participants has led us to understand that some participants are more comfortable with others who are at similar stages.

One reason for this is practical—the approach and activities are quite different as abilities change and as a facilitator it becomes difficult to balance significant differences in one presentation.

The second reason is related to the preferences of the participants themselves. For those who are in the early stages or who may have been recently diagnosed, adjusting to their prognosis can lead to discomfort or fear. Joining a program with those in the later stages has caused those feelings to grow for some of our participants. For them, the sense of connection with people in similar circumstances builds comfort, acceptance, and social support. This social connection is an important part of the program. In the later stages of dementia, there is less awareness by the person with dementia of the changes in their abilities, leaving them more comfortable with or less aware of the changes taking place in the others around them.

It can be difficult to screen participants based on what stage they are at in their journey with dementia. In communication materials, you can carefully address more specific abilities in your participants. Individual conversations with participants and/or their family members or friends as part of your intake process can help to identify those who might be better suited for a different program.

APPLYING KNOWLEDGE OF DEMENTIA

The previous chapter explored the strengths that are preserved well into a person's journey with dementia and the importance of focusing on a positive understanding of your participants. With a mindset of supporting abilities rather than dwelling on impairments, we put the person first and create an empowering experience.

Your understanding of dementia informs program planning, guiding the ways that programs, spaces, and delivery are adapted to suit your audience. This knowledge serves as a foundation to guide your understanding of the observations and experiences you have with your participants, and to identify strategies for support if and as needed. There is no "formula" but rather an ongoing application of knowledge, balanced by experience and a personal touch that grows with every interaction.

When and How Much to Adapt

Knowing when and how much to adjust your program is an important consideration. By understanding the impact that dementia can have on a person's abilities, a facilitator may be tempted to make broad and sweeping changes to ensure that all needs that may occur have been addressed. However, consider this—is this decision based on a well-intentioned goal of making sure each person's needs have been met or is it based on an unintentional bias leading to a belief that your participants cannot participate in activities like other people? Being person-centered means adapting to the person and their specific needs "in the moment." Do not make assumptions.

Figure 4.1 Gentle Support for Strengths and Participation. When facilitators provide small cues to encourage participation and observe carefully where there are difficulties, they can activate a person to continue working. *Source*: Art Gallery of Hamilton.

Without careful attention and observations of participants there can be a risk of over-simplifying your program. This is a common experience for many people living with dementia and one that we are working to change. An online project called *Dementia in a New Light* offers real-life examples of both negative attitudes and experiences coupled with insights from people living with dementia themselves. One person writes,

> People assume that learning new stuff would be very difficult for me. This makes me feel that I may have some limitations but that doesn't mean that my life has to stop with the diagnosis. . . . Too many professionals try to take too many things away too quickly. Not asking or testing me for my ability to do activities.[14]

The next chapters will explore at length the adaptations that can and should be made in your program design following the *Model for Successful Engagement*. Your knowledge of dementia should guide your environmental setup, facilitation style, and selection of activities. These choices should always be carefully and continually tailored to the needs and strengths of your participants. Some key points:

- Design programs that are flexible and focus on strengths. Think about what a person is able to do and look for ways to capitalize on that.
- Create programs that allow for independence and dignity. What people can do they should do themselves. There are many ways to communicate, create, and contribute.
- Know that some adaptations will be advantageous to most members of your group while some will be applicable to just a few. Find ways to shift between approaches that suit each person individually but include everyone at their own level.

The best approach is to change only as much as you have to so you can support a positive experience and facilitate each person's participation. With practice, it will become your standard working style. You will even find that techniques that you apply in your specialized program will also be effective in many of your other programs.

SCOPE OF PRACTICE

Scope of Practice is a term from the medical field and refers to the activities that a person is authorized to perform, usually based on education, clinical training, and often licensing by professional colleges.[15] The information presented in this chapter is a compilation of current research and resources from a range of resources including international support and educational organizations, medical and occupational therapy literature, and peer-reviewed articles, all of which can be found in the bibliography for readers who wish to learn more. With the expertise of the authors who have experience either in museum education or in clinical practice, we have filtered this knowledge through the lens of museum programs to provide comprehensive and relevant information that will support facilitators in their work.

The information in this chapter will serve you in understanding your participants and identifying some of the ways you can plan for and support their experiences in your museum. It will help you understand your observations in your programs. It is not intended to equip you with the skills to identify whether a person has dementia or not, or offer clinical or therapeutic supports or advice—there are many professionals in your community that can provide those services.

The field of dementia care is broad and there are many practitioners who can support your work at all stages. *Artful Moments* began as a museum/clinical partnership and the combination of different areas of expertise has been exceedingly beneficial to our progress. Seeking out supports in your community will only improve your learning and the experiences that you can offer to your participants.

Where the needs of these participants may exceed your scope of practice, a network of services can fill the gap.

NOTES

1. "What Is Dementia," *Alzheimer's Association*, accessed December 2023, https://www.alz.org/alzheimers-dementia/what-is-dementia.
2. Facilitator's account of program, 2013. Names have been changed to respect privacy.
3. Community service organization facilitator's account of program, 2017. Names have been changed to respect privacy.
4. Facilitator's account of program, 2021. Names have been changed to respect privacy.
5. Spouse of a participant's account of program, 2019. Names have been changed to respect privacy.
6. Facilitator's account of program, 2022. Names have been changed to respect privacy.
7. Adult child of a participant's account of program, 2018. Names have been changed to respect privacy.
8. "Early Stages of Dementia," *Alzheimer's Society UK*, accessed December 2023, https://www.alzheimers.org.uk/about-dementia/symptoms-and-diagnosis/how-dementia-progresses/early-stages-dementia#content-start.
9. Facilitator's account of program, 2021. Names have been changed to respect privacy.
10. "Middle Stages of Dementia," *Alzheimer's Society UK*, accessed December 2023, https://www.alzheimers.org.uk/about-dementia/symptoms-and-diagnosis/how-dementia-progresses/middle-stage-dementia#content-start.
11. Facilitator's account of program, 2019. Names have been changed to respect privacy.
12. "Late Stages of Dementia," *Alzheimer's Society UK*, accessed December 2023, https://www.alzheimers.org.uk/about-dementia/symptoms-and-diagnosis/how-dementia-progresses/later-stages-dementia#content-start.
13. Facilitator's account of program, 2018. Names have been changed to respect privacy.
14. "Stereotypes," *Dementia in a New Light*, accessed December 2023, https://dementiainnewlight.com/content/stigma/stereotypes.
15. "What is Scope of Practice," *American Medical Association*, May 2022 https://www.ama-assn.org/practice-management/scope-practice/what-scope-practice.

Message for Success

Making the Most of Abilities

Creativity. Sense of humor. Long-term memory. As strengths, these are the ingredients of a shared experience that is meaningful, enjoyable, and socially connective for everyone. Through a journey with dementia, a person's experience of their world changes but a need to connect persists, and the potential for improved quality of life in the moment exists for everyone.

This is the opportunity for museum programs to make a difference for people living with dementia—to make the most of the abilities that are present. Museum collections offer opportunities to tap into personal connections for participants. They provide sensory enjoyment and opportunities to experience new and interesting things. They facilitate communication in many forms and personal reflection and self-expressions. Sharing these moments encourages social experiences and allows for many different forms of expression regardless of level of ability, prior experiences with museums, or diagnosis.

Part III

The Environment

Navigating the Museum Site

Museum spaces offer unique opportunities for programs but also present some challenges. This section will explore both aspects to help you incorporate your knowledge of dementia when creating an optimal program environment. The goal is to design a space that maximizes safety, accessibility, and comfort for participants and facilitators, and that successfully fosters engagement and well-being.

It is important to remember that within each environment there are many factors to consider that are unique to your site. In some areas, you will find opportunities to make changes to your environment to better suit the needs and abilities of your participants, but there will also be elements that you cannot change. In these instances, you will instead adapt your program design and presentation to accommodate the needs of your participants within the existing conditions.

The *Model for Successful Engagement* informs all aspects of program design, delivery, and evaluation. In Part III, we examine exhibition spaces, activity spaces, and pre-program spaces where your program will take place. We will also discuss the essential components of the social environment, and the unique circumstances implicit in programs with a virtual environment. Much of your program design and facilitation will depend on the opportunities and limitations of your environment. Just as with other "pillars," if your environment is not supportive of engagement for the participant, their experience in your program will be negatively impacted.

Part III is built upon a strong understanding of the participant and your knowledge of dementia. That foundation will guide your work.

5

Understanding the Environment

In its most basic sense, an "environment" is the surroundings or conditions in which a person exists. We all live, work, learn, and play in different environments. The conditions around us in each place have significant impacts on our ability to function, to be comfortable, to be well, and to engage. We may overlook how the design and objects in our surroundings influence us until they cause problems.

Here we define the environment as the overall museum site that participants experience from the time they arrive at the entrance (or the parking area) until the time they leave and all of the circumstances that exist in between. In each museum site, there will be multiple smaller environments including exhibition and activity spaces and the main entrance or greeting area. Each has its own conditions and accommodations to be considered. We will also consider the environment in four categories: physical, sensory, social, and the uniqueness of the virtual setting.

WHY IS THE ENVIRONMENT SO IMPORTANT?

A program's environment, whether thoughtfully designed or not, significantly impacts the participant's experience and engagement. When the environment is set up to support each participant's abilities, activities will be more comfortable and enjoyable, fostering natural interactions and social connection. To encourage and facilitate this, your environment should foster:

- *Social interaction*, among participants, family and friends who may attend with them, and program facilitators.
- *Independence*, making it possible to navigate the activities and to participate with limited or no additional support. A person who does not need to ask for help feels empowered.
- *Dignity*, ensuring that participants, family and friends, and facilitators feel valued, confident, and respected.
- A sense of *well-being*, knowing that they, the participants, are supported and safe, and in an enjoyable and meaningful experience where they are valued and appreciated.

These factors are essential in any museum program though the way to achieve them may be different depending on the abilities of your participants. To guide your planning of the program environment, we will refer back to previously discussed changes in the brain to inform how we plan and adapt our environment for individuals with dementia.

How Does the Environment Affect Participants?

As we explore the impact of the environment on participants we return to the importance of focusing on strengths and the person. The way we design the environment has the potential to facilitate positive engagement and empowerment or to close off opportunities for participation.

Here we pause to consider the literature about disability. In the medical model of disability, the focus is on "fixing" an impairment. The disability lies with the person. In contrast, the social model of disability moves the focus away from the person's differences and onto the barriers that prevent access. As an example, if a building has accessible entry features and elevators, then differences in mobility are not limiting.[1] We adjust our environments to suit our participants and by doing so we mitigate or remove the impact of some of the changes in abilities they experience. When considered in this way, it is easy to see the importance of a carefully planned environment guided by informed actions.

Expanding our investigation of environmental impacts, we move to the theory of salutogenesis. This theory holds that good health is not merely the absence of disease but rather a purposeful action of engaging in and expanding on positive experiences. It focuses on strengthening the positive aspects of life and engagement, rather than on preventing or treating disease. In doing so, it encourages a focus on maximizing strengths not on "fixing" illness or disability.[2]

We have found resonance with the ideas and application of this idea in our work. Salutogenesis is a broad field applied in many different areas of healthcare and well-being practices, but it has also become widely used in architecture, supported by the idea that, when designed within the right framework, "the built and natural environments can help people live life meaningfully and with a true sense of agency."[3]

Salutogenic theory describes tools or resources that support a person's positive capacity in three domains—intellectual (comprehensibility), physical (manageability), and affective (meaningfulness).[4] Environments should be easy to understand and navigate, accessible and comfortable for people with a range of abilities, and offer opportunities to engage in personally meaningful experiences. Studies have shown that rich and stimulating environments have a positive impact on health, and applying the practices of salutogenesis leads to improved health outcomes, moods, and sense of self.[5] By this description, museums are ideal venues. In your program planning, you cannot change your building but you can make informed adjustments to your spaces to foster positive experiences.

FOUR KINDS OF ENVIRONMENTS

As you explore the participant's experience of your museum site there are many aspects and locations to consider. As your program may take place in various of rooms or locations you will need to consider each space separately.

Later in this chapter, we introduce the idea of an assessment of the environment to better understand your site. To organize this process, we have broken the environment into four distinct categories. These will guide you in thinking about the full experience of your museum through the lens of your knowledge of dementia. The four categories of the environment include physical, sensory, virtual, and social. Although we touch on all four categories, in this chapter we will delve more deeply into the social environment and cover the physical, sensory, and virtual environments in greater depth in the next chapter.

Physical Environment

The physical environment refers to the material surroundings or components of a place—the building or outdoor space of the museum. We consider every area that a participant needs to travel through, move, or touch, including rooms, doors, walkways, floors, and furniture. Physical accessibility is a crucial piece to consider. This includes everything from how your participants get into your site to the ways they navigate through exhibitions and activity spaces.

Within a physical environment, there are many changes that you can make to suit the specific abilities and needs of your participants, but there are also aspects of your environment that cannot be changed—the architecture of your building, the layout or lighting of an exhibition space, or the location of your activity space. These are the things that you will have to have a plan to work around during your program to ensure that you meet each participant's needs.

Within the physical environment, we must also consider a participant's experience over time. A participant's stamina and strength may wane over time so accommodating the need for rest also becomes part of your adjustments.

Sensory Environment

The sensory environment comprises everything a participant perceives through sight, hearing, touch, and smell. In museums, this includes not only the obvious sights and sounds of exhibits but also the subtler elements that can influence a visitor's experience. For example, consider:

- **Active sensory experiences:** People moving and talking within the space.
- **Passive sensory elements:** Room layout (cluttered vs. open), changes in lighting or color between rooms, and background sounds like ventilation or traffic.

As a person's dementia progresses, focusing on a specific activity can become more challenging with increased sensory distractions. Museums present two primary sensory challenges: comfort and distraction. Comfort factors include:

- **Ambient temperature:** Is it too hot or cold in the space?
- **Seating options:** Are there comfortable and accessible places to rest?
- **Lighting:** Is the lighting harsh or glaring? Are there sudden changes in light levels between spaces?

Distractions can arise from:

- **Sounds:** Noise from exhibits, other visitors, or building systems.
- **Visual clutter:** Galleries packed with objects or activity spaces with too much visual information.

By being mindful of these sensory considerations, we can create a more welcoming and engaging environment for visitors with dementia through adaptations to the museum and/or to the way we plan a program.

Virtual Environment

The virtual environment refers to how participants experience the environment when they join programs online, by phone, or perhaps asynchronously. Virtual environments offer many specific conditions to consider that are related to physical, sensory, and social impacts. It is important to think about both sides of the experience —the environmental conditions that you, as a facilitator, control in your space and the conditions experienced by the participant in their space, some of which you can help to improve and others you cannot control.

Virtual programs provide engagement and connection from the comfort of home. Programs may take place online with screen-based platforms for sharing images of objects and activity demonstrations. Programs can also be offered by phone using conference call technology and printed resources. Virtual programs can eliminate barriers such as accessibility and travel while also adding unique opportunities like connecting people over great distances. We will explore the physical, sensory, and social environments in virtual programs in the next chapter.

Social Environment

Environment extends beyond the physical structure of your site to the social environment. This refers to how the participant feels in the museum and in a group of participants. The participant's perception of how welcome or capable they feel, the attitudes and communication they experience from staff and other guests, and the degree to which they feel their needs and abilities have been considered all have an impact. In addition, the degree to which social interaction is prioritized in all aspects of a program has a huge impact on the success of that program.

The social environment is about the connections between participants, between participants and facilitators, and other museum staff, and the style and content of communication. Institutional attitudes and practices are important in the social environment.

In Part I, we talked about the importance of positive perceptions and attitudes, of building a person-centered practice, of addressing bias, and focusing on strengths, not challenges. These considerations all affect the social environment and are an important part of making a museum dementia-friendly.

WHAT DOES IT MEAN TO BE DEMENTIA-FRIENDLY?

A Dementia-Friendly Community is a place where people living with dementia are understood, respected, and supported.[6] It is a community where they feel confident in their abilities to participate in and contribute to community life, are included in conversations and experiences, and have choices and control over their day-to-day lives. Further to this, Alzheimer's Disease International's website tells us that:

> At one level the concept of dementia-friendly is simple—to work for the common goal of a better life for people with dementia and their families. But it is much more than this. The framework of dementia-friendly has the power to change the way we think about living with dementia. It extends to areas such as language, improvements in social support, health and dementia services, and the physical environment.[7]

We can apply this thinking to museums as we strive to create a dementia-friendly environment within our spaces including physical factors, the social and organizational culture, and the way we set up programs. We also accomplish this by including the voices, opinions, and advice of people with lived experience of dementia in our design and planning, decision-making, evaluation, and presentation.

Within the scope of the programs described in this book, we focus on participants' experiences as part of a specifically designed program for a specialized audience. While this is an important aspect of becoming dementia-friendly, it should not be the only work undertaken to build inclusion within your museum. For some of our participants, *Artful Moments* is a program to join because they appreciate knowing they will be supported in their experience and that they will find others "like them' with whom to share the experience. However, many people will also visit on their own, and join other programs, especially after a positive initial experience attending a program. To be a truly "dementia-friendly museum," a person should know that regardless of when they visit, they are welcome, that they will find the support they need (if or when they need it), and that the staff there understand them.

Your experience and learning from this book offer knowledge and strategies that can be broadly applied to your entire organization. There are also many resources available in your community, including online information, training programs, and other support to move you toward becoming a dementia-friendly museum.

Take a moment to think about what being "Dementia-Friendly" means to you. Is your museum dementia-friendly? What examples of being dementia-friendly do you see now and what changes can be made?

SOCIAL CONNECTIONS

It is Monday afternoon, and Stella is on her way to the local museum with her daughter just as she has done every week for the past six months. She is excited to see "her ladies'" today, although she is less certain of her destination. She will spend time chatting about the things at the museum with a group of people with similar diagnoses and their family and friends, followed by a session in the workshop room creating a hands-on artwork inspired by what she has just seen. She looks forward to this enjoyable activity and the connections with the other participants, and her daughter looks forward to the shared experience with her mom each week, taking a break from the caregiving or support roles she may play outside of the program. She calls these outings a "date" with her mom.[8]

Our goal with all programs is for our participants to feel welcome, valued, and included. In *Artful Moments*, the social connections provided in the program are among the most valuable outcomes and the social environment plays a significant role in achieving this. It is essential to create a welcoming and supportive atmosphere that goes well beyond the physical considerations for safety. The social environment must foster relationship building between participants and their family or friends, between participants and facilitators, and among the participants themselves.

When we consider the social environment that we have created for *Artful Moments*, we ensure that our participants feel supported, welcome, and that they have a personal connection with us. Our work reflects this through the way we learn and train, the ways we connect with participants and their family and friends, our priority to foster social connection within a group, and the organizational attitudes we hold.

Education and Training

When we began, we spent a lot of time on training that was provided by our clinical partners. Our education in understanding dementia was extensive and is ongoing. As we learned the facts, we were reminded to keep the participant at the center of our work, and that while knowledge of dementia formed the background of our planning and presentation, once we engaged with the participants we did not talk about dementia (unless a participant brought it up), or use complex terminology. We

Figure 5.1 Shared Moments. Programs offer opportunities for both facilitated and individual connections. This image shows a moment following a more formal group conversation where a participant and his daughter stopped to look more closely and talk about what they saw. *Source*: Art Gallery of Hamilton.

learned how to deliver a program, and how to communicate and support our participants in a positive way. We also extended training and education to our other program and frontline staff to build capacity for the whole institution.

Recommendations

- Provide facilitators with training about dementia so that they are able to understand each participant and recognize the various levels of ability within the group.
- Train facilitators in strategies for interacting effectively with people living with dementia so they understand how to be inclusive during group conversations especially when participants may communicate in different ways. Teach them how to adapt their communication to suit each person individually.
- Ensure facilitators know the importance of using sensitive language and how to "leave dementia at the door" so that a safe, inclusive, and stigma-free environment is provided.
- Provide general education to all staff on how to respond to participants in a supportive and reassuring manner, communicating clearly and simply, and interacting respectfully.

Personal Connections

Before the start of the program, the program lead or facilitator contacts each participant to introduce themselves. We often include the participant's family or friend in the conversation, provide directions, explain the program, and answer any questions. Some participants benefit from the support of having their family or friend included.

This step is important in getting to know everyone and making them feel comfortable. We also plan for consistent staff through the program, to allow everyone to become familiar with each other.

On the day of the program, we make sure there is someone present to greet participants as they arrive. This helps with any difficulties with accessing the building but it also adds to the sense of welcome. We ensure that our front desk and security team know the details of the program and how to find us if someone is late.

Recommendations

- Ensure the greeter is knowledgeable about dementia and the program and is familiar with the participants and the building. This will help the participants feel safe and confident on arrival and departure.
- Ensure a calm and welcoming atmosphere. Staff can foster social interaction by encouraging the use of the participant's social skills including introducing themselves, acknowledging the person by name, making eye contact, saying hello, and following up with simple social conversation if appropriate such as asking the person how they are or what the weather is like outside.
- Set a positive tone within the environment—be warm, welcoming, respectful, and inclusive.

Fostering Social Connection and Relationship Building

Providing a calm and organized environment is key to fostering relationships. Using quiet, non-public hours, and ensuring everyone on site is aware of the program is essential. Focusing on each participant as an individual is the first step in relationship building. It starts with a facilitator-to-participant connection, but over time can shift to a participant-to-participant relationship. A smile and a positive demeanor go a long way particularly because the participant's ability to read nonverbal messages remains after other abilities have changed.

We encourage everyone to share their names or introduce themselves including facilitators and other helpers who are present, letting everyone know their name and their role. Name tags are an effective tool to help support memory changes. Reading ability remains after other verbal abilities have changed. Knowing and using someone's name is an important social connector.

The setup of your environment plays an important role in this too. In the exhibition spaces, we arrange chairs in a half-circle or a curved group in both the gallery and the studio to ensure the participants can see the objects and interact with each other.

Recommendations

- Have everyone wear nametags and repeat introductions each week as a consistent practice to support social communication.
- Arrange seating in activity spaces to encourage connection—so that participants can see and hear each other, as well as the objects being discussed.

Organizational Attitudes and Growth

Artful Moments began as a single program that happened off-site more than half the time. It was a small program with only two or three staff members and volunteers involved. It was a new kind of program with different goals, presentation styles, and participants than what we were used to. We offered introductory training to program staff and guides who worked with the public to begin to build understanding and engagement with our larger team. We shared the positive evaluation results that we had found and we saw a growing awareness of the importance of this work. Open communication, active evaluation and sharing, and finding ways to include the voices of those with lived experience of dementia are all important steps to building inclusion.

When we consider stigma in museums, it often stems from a lack of knowledge and experience with dementia coupled with an earnest sensitivity to making a mistake and causing harm, rather than the presence of overt negative attitudes toward people living with dementia. This is why providing education to all of the staff is so important. Sharing knowledge breaks down those barriers and opens individuals and organizations to the benefits and potential of these kinds of programs.

Recommendations

- Share knowledge, training, experience, and success with everyone.
- Build on success; include more voices such as facilitators, participants, and the community.
- Do the work and see where it goes. Be open, observant, and responsive. Learn as you go.

What starts as small, insular programs can, when shared institutionally, make major shifts in organizational culture and mandate. *Doing the work makes us better.*

Group Size and Participation

Programs like *Artful Moments* are centered on social connection and interaction. We ask and answer questions, we share opinions, and we remember to relate what we see to our own lives. This requires trust, camaraderie, and time for everyone to speak.

Your goals for your program will influence your decision on how big or small your group should be. Are you looking for a modified tour experience that will simply offer visitors opportunities to engage with art and museum objects? Or do you hope to build community, social connection, and friendship? For a very connected, relationship-building program, smaller is better.

The platform you use for programs can affect your group size as well. In-person programs allow greater opportunities for camaraderie, simply by being physically together. Individuals are easier to observe, and there are many opportunities for interactions between participants during programs in a more informal way—the facilitation style may be more casual. In online programs, interactions are more controlled and measured, and while everyone can see each other, familiarity and social connection takes longer to build. With phone programs, most social cues for relationship building are not present—there are no visual cues or opportunities for nonverbal communication. Familiarity comes from hearing each other's voices and names. It is quite possible to build relationships over the phone—participants hear what each other thinks and feels, and can still ask and respond to questions from each other.

Finally, participants' abilities will have an impact. Programs with people in the earlier stages of dementia will often experience fewer changes to their abilities. You will be able to converse easily, ask many questions, and share longer responses. There will be less need to focus on "yes" and "no," or choice questions. People may talk more and may need less support from the facilitator. In addition, you may be able to move, physically and conversationally, more quickly. People who have experienced more changes in their abilities will need more time for processing information along with other supports.

Recommendations

Using our methodology and goals for social connection, it is essential that each participant in a group has ample opportunities to speak and be heard throughout a program. We encourage participants to interact with the facilitator and with each other to create a community of friends. This requires lots of time for participants to talk and to get to know each other.

The facilitator must be skilled in drawing out ideas from a diverse group, and in balancing multiple people's voices, modes of communication, ideas, and levels of knowledge. To make all of this work, having a small and closely knit group is most effective. The ideal number of people can vary from one organization to another and from one platform to another, but in all cases, too many people will cause the level of engagement to decrease. In our programs, we have worked with groups as small as three and as large as twenty. Our recommendations are based on those experiences with our social goals in mind.

Figure 5.2　Fostering Connection. The tone of your program is set right from the start. Participants gather together in comfortable seating before the program to hear about the plan for the day. Name tags help everyone feel connected. *Source*: Art Gallery of Hamilton.

For optimal engagement and social connection, we have found that an ideal program group size is four to eight participants, plus their family member or friend. In-person programs allow a slightly larger group to interact comfortably—for instance, a total group size of fifteen, while virtual programs are best with about eight. As your group size increases, carefully consider how you balance your focus between the person with dementia and their friend or family member. In smaller groups, it is easy to engage everyone equally, but as group size increases, we tend to focus more on the participant with the family and friends taking on more of a supportive role.

START WITH AN ASSESSMENT

The first step in setting up an appropriate and supportive environment is to see what you have to work with. As a museum facilitator, you will be very familiar with many of your site's "problem areas"—those areas that may have caused complications with other programs in the past. Museums can have many challenges when it comes to accessibility. The next chapter will further explore many of those factors. You cannot change your building, floors, access to an elevator, or even the arrangements of objects within your exhibitions. When you layer in the knowledge of dementia and the participant, museum environments can seem daunting to overcome. While you may have more flexibility in activity spaces they can also present challenges.

In contrast, the design of the program is in your control. In some cases, you will be able to make environmental changes to suit the needs and abilities of your participants and, in others, you will need to be creative in adapting your activities to suit your space. This is where an assessment is an essential step to help you identify aspects of your environment that work as they are now, that can be changed, and that you will need to work around.

Environment Assessment Template

The first step in program design is to be aware of the conditions present in your environment. Assessing your space is your first opportunity to apply what you have learned about dementia abilities in many ways, across various situations.

We suggest that your assessment considers the ideas presented in this section, looking at the physical and sensory environments first, followed by the social and virtual environments. Even when you know your site well, take the time to walk around and reflect on the space. Analyzing the space with a colleague or community advisor can provide other meaningful perspectives.

The next chapter will introduce the different zones in a typical museum experience—pre-program spaces, exhibition, and activity spaces. In any kind of museum, you will find a version of each of these zones. Because of the differences in how each zone is used, it is a good idea to assess them separately. If you are a larger museum, you may want to break your assessment down further, considering each room individually. When exhibitions change, it is also a good idea to do a new assessment of the exhibition that reflects any changes in accessibility or function.

As you work through each space, you will begin to find solutions to some areas to address. For example, to facilitate comfort add temporary seating; for navigation consider additional signage and staff support. Options to shift your environment toward becoming more dementia-friendly can be temporary or long-term. We cannot change our architecture and often we are unable to make changes to the content or arrangement of an exhibition. In cases where there are challenges that cannot be addressed directly, be creative. Can you focus on smaller areas for your program? Are you able to provide reproductions for small or hard-to-see items? Can you temporarily bring objects to a different space for viewing?

Sample Environment Assessment

	No Changes	Change Needed	Adapt Program	Notes/Improvements or Adaptions needed
Is the exhibition space close to the gathering space?	X			Tour starts just to the right of the entrance.
Is travel between exhibition spaces (doorways) unobstructed?			X	Heavy doors – prop open before program starts or have volunteer to assist with holding doors.
Are there flooring elements that could pose a tripping/falls risk?		X		Remember to walk thru space before program to adjust or remove floor mats.
Are there areas of concern related to vision? (glass walls, high or low obstacles or displays)		X	X	Plan tour to avoid objects in display case OR have selected object removed from case for viewing during session.

Figure 5.3 Environment Assessment. To set up an effective program environment it is important to consider every aspect of your site through the lens of the participant. This sample demonstrates how to get started. *Source*: Art Gallery of Hamilton.

We have created an *Environment Assessment Template* to help you identify the common areas to consider. The template focuses on the physical and sensory aspects of the physical museum environment—social and virtual environments can be considered separately. It is part of a full workbook to guide your program planning. Figure 5.3 provides a sample of the template to show you how it may be used. The full template can be downloaded from www.artfulmoments.ca.

It is a tool to help you experience your space from the perspective of your participants. We recommend filling it out while walking through each of the spaces that you will use. Make notes about your observations, reflections, and thoughts on how to improve your environment. The template is divided into sections that address everything from the time a participant arrives until they leave. That said, we know that each museum is unique. Not every item will apply. Your site might offer notable items that we have not included. Edit the document to suit your needs. We ask a series of questions that you can answer under one of three categories:

- **No changes:** meaning that you are ready to go, with no areas of concern.
- **Change needed:** this indicates an area that does not suit the needs of your participants and that you can change to improve it. This could be as simple as adding signage or seats, or more complex like adjusting the furniture arrangement. Make notes about the area of concern and then note what you will do on a program day to improve it.
- **Adapt program:** this indicates an area of concern that you cannot easily fix. In this case, you will need to change your plans to accommodate or avoid the problem. This could be a space with lots of noise that you cannot change and means that you will avoid it during a program.

With this guide in hand consider each program area. Walk through each room or space where your participants will spend time (including entry and gathering areas) and use the template to help you identify factors that may affect your participants' experiences. Keep your knowledge of dementia in mind as you work through this process, and add any other observations or questions that may come up.

NOTES

1. Amanda Leduc, *Disfigured: On Fairy Tales, Disability and Making Space* (Toronto: Coach House Books, 2020), 36–7.
2. Jan Golembiewski and John Zeisel, "Salutogenic Approaches to Dementia Care," in *The Handbook of Salutogenesis*, ed. M.B. Mittelmark et al. (2022): 513.
3. Golembiewski and Zeisel, "Salutogenic Approaches," 515.
4. Golembiewski and Zeisel, "Salutogenic Approaches," 514.
5. Golembiewski and Zeisel, "Salutogenic Approaches," 530.
6. "Dementia-friendly Communities," *Alzheimer Society of Canada*, accessed January 15, 2024, https://alzheimer.ca/on/en/take-action/become-dementia-friendly/dementia-friendly-communities-ontario.
7. Alzheimer's Disease International, "Dementia-friendly Communities."
8. Facilitator's account of program, 2018. Names have been changed to respect privacy.

6

Examining Museum Spaces

In this chapter, we will take you through the three key "zones" of a typical museum program. As you work through your space, imagine yourself in the place of one of your participants. Stand, walk, and sit where they would. Pay extra attention to the sounds, sights, and experiences that you might not normally notice. Think about experiences (and challenges) you have with other programs but remember that the ideal circumstances may not be the same from one program to another.

PRE-PROGRAM SPACES: ENTRY, LOBBY, AND PARKING

In the context of a visitor's or a participant's experience, your environment is not just the indoor spaces your site occupies—it is the full experience from the time they arrive until they leave and every interaction in between. Therefore, we begin with your "pre-program spaces"—the entrance, lobby, gathering site, and even the drop-off or parking areas, as the first zone to consider. While they are a small part of your actual program, these spaces can be very complex to navigate and can affect the rest of the participant's experience and their perceptions of their visit. This is an area of "first impressions" influencing whether participants may feel comfortable and safe or whether they may become unsettled or anxious. Be sure to consider all aspects of your participant's arrival including:

- Where will the participant park or be dropped off?
- Is the main entrance clearly marked and easy to find?
- Is there a process to get in the door (particularly during non-public hours)?
- What do they need to do once they come through the doors?

When it comes to your pre-program environment, remember that a person living with dementia may be experiencing changes in their abilities such as:

- ***Changes in memory and new learning.*** Are there cues about how to enter your site and what to do once they are inside?
- ***Age-related vision changes or difficulty understanding written words.*** Following signage or directions may be difficult. Is there someone to greet and direct them? Instructions may need to be supplemented by staff to assist, especially if the program is run during non-public hours.
- ***Changes to spatial awareness.*** A participant's ability to navigate from the entrance to the main desk area or gathering spot may be impacted.
- ***Changes in-depth perception.*** Safety on stairs, crossing thresholds into elevators, or managing patterned floors may be more difficult.
- ***Age-related changes in physical mobility.*** A participant may have more difficulty managing stairs or long walks, sometimes requiring assistive devices. This can change the accessibility of a site.

- **Heightened moods or emotions** can lead to feelings of anxiety or overstimulation during the process of getting to the museum itself. This can be mitigated by a helpful assistant, a friendly greeting, and time to rest and compose themselves before beginning a program.

Sharing Our Experiences: Pre-Program Spaces

The AGH is a downtown gallery with underground parking. We have two entrances on street level, though during days that we are closed one door is always locked and the other door has a small intercom used to reach the security desk. There is a long, marble staircase up to the main level where all program participants gather. The space is brightly lit with floor-to-ceiling windows and a marble floor. Next, we have a large lobby with a counter, a coat room with lockers, a gift shop, the entrance to the exhibition space, a main elevator, and more. There is a lot going on. To help the participants successfully navigate the many challenges of this space, we implement several preparations:

- We send instructions in advance, including where to park and which door to use.
- We request that the elevator be turned on in advance of the arrival time, as many participants like to come early to ensure they arrive on time.
- We post a staff member at the entrance to greet participants as they arrive, open the doors for them, and help with the elevator and wayfinding.
- We inform security to know that people will be coming up so that they can further direct them as needed.

A facilitator warmly greets participants by name as they get out of the elevator and shows them where to hang their coats, the location of the washroom, and where they can sit and rest while they wait for the program to begin. We ensure there are enough places to sit, hand out nametags, and have casual conversations until everyone arrives. This is also where we begin our program with introductions and a description of what the day holds. We hand out any necessary materials for the exhibition portion of the program or the facilitator carries them until needed.

After many years of public programming, some of these challenges (and the solutions to them) were very familiar. Other challenges that are more specific to our participants with dementia were less obvious until we physically walked through the site from the parking lot to the lobby. Our assessment template will highlight many areas of this process for you but there will likely be others unique to your location. Take some time to walk through your "pre-program" spaces with the assessment and make notes as you go. You will begin to envision solutions as we continue through this chapter.

Advantages:

- Seating and a central gathering space are already present in a prominent location.
- Accessibility features including elevators and push-button doors are in place.

Challenges:

- Our building is large with multiple entrances and potentially confusing directions.
- Entry process is complicated during non-public hours when the programs take place.
- Accessibility related to a large staircase, heavy doors, and long hallways.

Recommendations for Safety and Accessibility

Assess entrance, lobby, and gathering areas for accessibility and safety paying attention to issues related to lighting, glare, and flooring surfaces. Adjust where necessary and possible.

- Complete any necessary safety modifications to the environment before the program starts—this includes adjusting floor mats, wet floors, seating, and signage.
- Identify those areas that cannot be modified but remain a potential safety or accessibility concern. This may include things, like heavy doors with no automated options, places where participants could become lost or disoriented, and patterned tile floors with light and dark transitions that may be hard to see or understand and may cause challenges while walking.
- Highlight those concerns to frontline and program staff as areas to pay careful attention to. Point out areas of concern to participants to help them navigate.
- Depending on the concern, you may also appoint a staff person to assist participants navigate the space if they would like help.
- To improve the readability of signs, simplify instructions to just a few words. Use enlarged fonts such as Arial Bold, capitalizing the first letter of each word. Use a matte surface to reduce glare and good contrast between background and text.

Recommendations before the Programs Begin

Communication is the key to preparing participants and their family members and friends. The aim is to ensure the participant has clear directions before their arrival so they can be confident and relaxed.

- Provide a simple one-page set of instructions describing the program.
- Include the address and phone number, the dates and times of the program, and where to park, enter, and gather.
- Indicate where a greeter will be available.
- Be clear and concise and include pictures where useful.

Recommendations for Program Days

Have a person wearing a clearly visible name tag to greet each participant upon arrival. Try to have the same person greeting participants each time to build familiarity. Participants should be escorted to a consistent departure area as well at the end of the program. Having a consistent person and process will reduce the stress and potential difficulty for the participants to find their way to the program. This will also promote a sense of safety, and help save their energy for actively engaging in the program.

- Have a consistent gathering space near the entrance for arriving and departing, ideally with comfortable chairs and tables for belongings.
- Have signage in simple language for wayfinding but have greeters also show everyone when they arrive.
- Have payments and other administration done in advance to reduce the need for the participant to provide their personal information do financial.
- Have everyone wear name tags. This will help facilitators, especially early in the program, and will foster social connection among participants, helping them address each other by name if they are so inclined.

With changes in short-term memory and new learning for some participants, familiar routines can help develop a sense of familiarity. Start in your parking lot and walk through the path of travel from parking to gathering for a program to identify any areas of concern. Make it as detailed as possible as this will help you later.

EXHIBITIONS AND DISPLAYS

Exhibitions and displays are where most of your public programming probably takes place. This is likely also the environment that is the least flexible and where you will need to adapt your program to suit what you have, rather than the other way around. An assessment of your exhibition spaces is more about identifying the areas of concern and building a plan for how to work within them.

Whether indoors or outside, exhibitions often cover large areas and can require a lot of walking and standing. Objects on display may be spread out, requiring time and effort to travel between them. Indoor challenges may include complicated wayfinding between exhibition spaces or with stairs, elevators, and narrow hallways. If your site includes outdoors, traveling over outdoor terrain such as uneven ground is more difficult for those with balance issues or who are using mobility devices.

Objects may be small, far away, or otherwise hard to see. Glare on glass or display cases may affect visibility, and/or there may be dim or difficult lighting conditions. There may be complex or crowded display areas, ambient or exhibition-specific noise, or other sensory distractions. To better understand the challenges of your space, ask yourself some questions:

- What can I see, hear, smell?
- Where can I sit?
- How easy or hard is it to get around on foot? To find my way back?
- How easy or hard is it to navigate in a wheelchair? With a cane?
- How comfortable am I?
- Does the exhibition or display strategy make it easy to focus on specific objects or is it a very busy visual space?

In these spaces, many of the same physical and sensory considerations that we addressed in the previous section are important to remember. Be sure to consider:

- **Physical changes** related to mobility, the need for rest, and the proximity of washroom facilities.
- **Vision changes** related to lighting, glare, and changing lighting conditions.
- **Hearing changes** related to background noise in the space and, ability to hear the presenter and other participants.
- **Changes in cognition** and **perception** may affect orientation and wayfinding, the ability to filter out distractions, judgment, and safety.

Social connection and engagement will increase or decrease based on how you physically arrange your program environment and how you approach facilitation. The space will affect how easily the group can engage with the objects or activities, connect, and express and validate ideas, opinions, and observations.

With this in mind, take a walk through your exhibition spaces to identify areas of difficulty. Begin to notice how objects and artworks are arranged within this environment. Notice lighting, ambient sound, and the way that talking sounds in large and small spaces. Pay attention to doors, stairs, the location of furniture, display cases, and existing seating. How many times does your path of travel turn or change? How easy or difficult is it for a participant to navigate back to the entrance or the washrooms?

Sharing Our Experiences: Exhibition Spaces

Every museum will have its challenges and opportunities when it comes to programs like *Artful Moments*. Your existing tour programs will be a great place to start thinking about how to use the spaces but it is equally important to see them with fresh eyes. Where we regularly plan tours that cover a lot of ground, we realized early on that we needed to change this approach to our exhibitions.

Our exhibitions cover two floors, multiple rooms, and changing wall colors, lighting, and contents. The floor plan is complex, with multiple entry/exit points from each room, and requires a lot of walking. Art in different sizes, styles, and media is hung on walls at standing eye level, or in groupings of multiple artworks hung closely together. Sometimes the art has glass or shiny surfaces. Sculpture is displayed at different heights, some in plexiglass cases and others freestanding. The safety of visitors and the art is an ongoing concern.

There is a central staircase and an elevator to the second level. Some areas have glass walls with automatic sliding doors while others have an open doorway. There is seating in many spaces, and portable stools are available to carry from space to space. While many rooms share a similar level of light with no natural light, there is one space on the second level with floor-to-ceiling windows that can seem blinding when entering from a darker space, especially on a sunny day. From an accessibility perspective, based on our knowledge of dementia, there is a lot to contend with.

Advantages:

- There is a lot of variety available for program content
- With many rooms and thematically organized areas, it is easy to break a large exhibition experience into smaller chunks.
- Accessibility features have been built into most areas.
- Two days of non-public hours and a later opening time allow us to offer programs when other visitors are not in the space.
- Automatic doors are a recent improvement that has solved a long-standing problem of heavy doors that some visitors had difficulty opening.

Challenges:

- During public hours, the Gallery can be busy (and noisy) with visitors, school tours, and other programs.
- There is a lot of travel involved in seeing the exhibitions. If you are used to touring through large floor plans, it may be an adjustment to think of your site in smaller sections.
- Glass walls and glass doors can be difficult to see for people with low vision and those who are not familiar with the space.
- Some rooms have a lower light level with lighting directed toward the artworks rather than generally illuminating the space.
- Some objects are on stands within the room at various heights and others directly on the floor—these can be difficult for people who use large mobility devices.
- Some exhibitions have an audio or video component that can be disorienting or loud with sound carrying into other rooms.

When planning every session of each program we walk through the space to remind ourselves of any challenges. We plan which objects we will discuss based on theme, visibility, proximity to other selections, and how much travel is required within the program. We look for groupings of objects for each session's "content" to avoid too much travel in between. Using this plan, we determine resources that are needed and we plan seating. To avoid unnecessary activity, we arrange seating for participants at every tour stop in advance. We do not want to move chairs unless it is just a small distance within a room. Between rooms, a typical tour of four to six artworks can have up to four or six separate sets of chairs. Figure 6.1 shows a gallery space with seating arranged in two locations at once.

By becoming aware of the factors that affect your participants' ability to experience, interact, and succeed in your space, you will be better equipped to create an activity plan. In some instances, the presence of difficult conditions might lead you to avoid certain objects or locations, but in others, you may be able to modify your plans to allow you to include them effectively. You will find that many

Figure 6.1 Pre-Arranged Seating. To minimize distraction from rearranging seating, we set up chairs at every stop in our conversation plan. *Source*: Art Gallery of Hamilton.

objects can still be used, as long as you consider how the physical, cognitive, and perceptual changes that occur due to age and dementia may affect the person.

Recommendations for Program Time and Location

- Offer programs during non-public hours if possible or at times when the museum is less busy. During public hours, avoid using crowded areas. This will reduce noise and distractions and help the participants focus their attention.
- Where possible, consider turning the sound off (or down) to eliminate distracting noise.
- Be aware of the accessibility of the site for participants. Consider those who use mobility devices or who tire easily. Reflect on participants having to climb stairs, open heavy doors, or navigate around furniture, displays, or uneven ground. Adjust your plan as needed and consider alternatives.
- Consider your path and distance of travel between objects and overall. Try to move in a predictable path avoiding too many turns and backtracking.
- Think about ways to focus a session on a small section or single room for one week's program and another section on a different day, rather than trying to see everything at once.

Recommendations for Space and Social Considerations

- Consider the group size and how to seat people to encourage social interaction. Participants must be able to see the object you are talking about and will feel more connected if they can also see each other. Chairs set in a half-circle allow for visibility.
- Ensure exhibition spaces have sufficient space for people with mobility aids such as wheelchairs, walkers, or canes to move easily and that objects are not too close together for participants to navigate.
- Along with the physical accessibility issues, consider those who may have trouble with spatial awareness causing them to bump into objects if they are too close together.
- Be aware of the proximity of washrooms to exhibition spaces. Let people know if the washroom is located on another floor, and repeat this information during your program.
- Consider whether contact with the artworks will pose any concerns to the gallery or pose safety concerns to the participant should anyone exercise poor judgment.

- As a facilitator, positioning yourself next to an object or between the object and the group can help if you need to intervene.
- Use visible markings, physical barriers, or signs to let participants know how close they can be to an object or display.

Recommendations for Sound and Hearing

- Turn off or turn down unnecessary noise wherever possible including sound components of exhibitions to reduce distraction.
- Consider the acoustics in the exhibition space, especially if you are outdoors or competing with other environmental noise like wind. These may cause problems for those with hearing aids and be difficult for others to tune out.
- In loud environments, consider using an appropriate voice amplifier to project your voice. In addition, you could consider the selective use of individual listening devices for participants, to enhance their hearing and/or their ability to focus.
- Be aware that some audio devices may not be ideal—when only the facilitator's voice is amplified it can reduce social interaction and increase feelings of social isolation. Conversation may become more one-directional. Individual hearing amplifier devices could also cause irritation or discomfort for some participants. Observe and change plans as needed.

Recommendations for Changes in Vision

- Be aware of difficult lighting such as glare on objects, reflections on display cases, overly dim or bright light, or where there will be a transition from one lighting condition to the next. This may impact the person's ability to see others and objects. Age-related visual changes, as well as perceptual problems, may cause objects to be misidentified because they cannot be seen clearly. Objects with a lot of glare are best to avoid using for conversation topics.
- Consider the location of the objects in your exhibitions when choosing your subjects. Age-related physical difficulties such as range restrictions of the head and neck may make it challenging for persons to look up high or low. Use artwork at seated eye level whenever possible.
- Look carefully at the objects for detail, contrast, and size. Small objects, those with fine detail, or objects with very little contrast may be more difficult for the aging eye to see. Very visually busy objects may be challenging for those with perceptual problems.

Adapting to Challenging Sites

Regardless of location or type of museum, exhibitions can be difficult to access for people who cannot easily climb stairs, travel long distances, manage rough terrain, or for those who use mobility devices. For small museums with more intimate exhibition spaces, building multi-week programs with fresh content may offer another kind of challenge.

Accessibility challenges can feel like a barrier to program development but there are many ways to proceed. You are likely already working through similar barriers in other programs. For programs for people living with dementia, think about your existing strategies and see what applies or can be adapted to suit. Think creatively about your space and your collections. Ask yourself as many questions as you can and be curious about the challenges.

- If the exhibition space is not accessible, is there an activity space or another building that is?
- If you cannot access the collection in the museum itself, can you bring selected objects to a more accessible location or room?
- Do you have a teaching or handling collection?
- Do you have digital options?
- How can you supplement what you have in your exhibition space to add to the experience?

Inaccessible Historical House Museum

In this example, we visit a beautiful but inaccessible building from the early nineteenth century. It has a grand front staircase, historically designated grounds, and no elevators or ramps. It has exhibitions on three levels with many stairs. There is no way for anyone who uses a mobility aid to enter the home at all. How can this site offer a program?

It was not possible to bring participants who used mobility devices into the home but there is a converted outbuilding at the back of the house with its own access from street level and with a drive-way where people could be dropped off. It also opens into the gardens with a view of part of the home.

The collection includes selected objects or replicas that can be moved to this outbuilding for participants to view and handle, and the conversation can be supplemented by digital images of the interior of the house with the objects in their regular setting. The facilitator had a small budget to shop for specific accessories, fabrics, and small items that were period-appropriate, and she found a collection of journals and photos. On a sunny day, we held a session on the paved areas of the garden, focusing on the plant species and the overall design of the space. We served tea and time was spent listening to the birds and smelling plants in the gardens.

Even though some of the content was presented virtually and some objects were replicas or inexpensive substitutions, there was still a great deal of value in the social context of being together and sharing conversation in person. Much of the program focused on the idea of "home." By combining real artifacts and digital images, the facilitator was able to present a lively and rich conversation, that was further developed with a hands-on domestic object-making activity that was themed to the time and place.

Botanical Garden and Conservation Center

Here we encountered a wonderfully scenic area filled with plant and tree specimens, but also lengthy trails, uneven terrain, and limited rest points. For participants whose physical abilities have changed the site is inaccessible.

Some outdoor sites may have tour buses or trolleys that can tour larger outdoor sites. If your site is one like that, you can apply the techniques and adaptations we have already described to your plans and lead a conversation on the move. We recommend smaller numbers and perhaps an adjusted route. Pay careful attention to speakers and volume and consider stopping the vehicle to talk rather than the added sensory interference of noise and movement.

To complement this experience, you could use an accessible activity space like an outdoor gazebo or patio for your program, bringing in samples of plants and materials to see, touch, and smell. Hands-on activities like planting seedlings, or drawing or photographing samples will add to the experience.

Small Community Art Gallery

Though in a recently constructed building, this gallery was part of a larger complex. There was a single room for exhibitions that often focused on only one or two artists at a time. Planning a program in this space was a different experience from what we were used to. In a larger space, you can plan a multi-week program by visiting a new room each time, but in this case, we worked with a single room.

We focused on smaller themed sections of the exhibition in each session. The first week we focused on color and the natural environment where the artists lived and worked. We encouraged lots of sharing of memories and used color wheels and fabric swatches to think about color combinations.

For the next session, we focused on texture and technique—carved wood and rough painting surfaces. We found new ways to experience the same artists with pieces of wood and carving tools (safely handled). And in the third session, we moved to works on paper and talked about drawing. Options for planning multi-session programs in a setting like this require creative thinking.

- Supplement some sessions with virtual content
- Pull objects from the Collection that are not on display
- Bring in related objects and focus on one artwork each time
- Spread out a program to every other week to allow exhibition changes to provide new content

Every site offers its own challenges and will require its own solutions. There are always ways to adapt while maintaining the core of your program—social connection, appreciation of collections and exhibitions, curiosity, and hands-on fun.

STUDIOS AND WORKSHOPS

The third zone to consider is your activity space. This may be a studio, a workshop, a kitchen or a lab, or any number of other spaces where people can make things or try their hands at an interactive, exploratory activity. Some museums may even lead hands-on activities within their exhibition spaces or in a different building altogether. Hands-on activities as a response to conversations about our exhibitions have always been an essential part of *Artful Moments*. The two types of activities together offer participants a fulsome opportunity to use their strengths and abilities and to share enjoyable experiences with family and friends.

Depending on the museum, activity spaces are often very different from exhibition spaces in function, restrictions, appearance, and even location. Activity spaces are where participants may work but they are often also the place where tools and materials are used, demonstrated, and stored. These are where participants are provided with opportunities to touch things and explore materials, and where the social atmosphere can be more casual.

In activity spaces many of the same concerns that have been discussed previously are present. Can participants see and hear the facilitator and each other? Can the facilitator see and hear them? Is the facilitator freely able to move around the group to speak with people individually as well as in the group? Are participants comfortable? And are they safe?

As with other spaces, spend some time in your own activity space. Sit where a participant would sit and also stand where the facilitator would be. Move around the space as you would while teaching and ask yourself some questions:

- What can I see, hear, smell? Is the space filled with clutter and visual distractions? Is it sterile and uninspiring?
- Where will I sit? Are the chairs comfortable and is the table at the right height to accommodate the varying needs of participants?
- When seated can I see where a facilitator would stand and demonstrate?
- Do I have enough table space to work?
- As a facilitator can I move around easily to connect with everyone in the room?
- How will I clean up? Can I wash my hands in the room?
- How close is the washroom?
- How easy or hard is it to navigate in a wheelchair? With a cane? With a walker?
- How long does it take to travel from the exhibition space to the activity space?
- How comfortable am I?

The studio or activity space can be a more flexible environment in which to design and present activities but is also one where careful consideration of abilities, accessibility, and safety must be prioritized. Consider:

- *Physical ability and comfort*—things like seating, tables, access to materials, and the accessibility of the space to people with mobility needs.
- *Sensory changes*—sensitivity to light, sound, smells, clutter, and other distractions.
- *Safety*—with tools and materials, and as a space with potentially more clutter and obstacles.

With this in mind, look at your potential activity spaces to determine what changes might be useful in supporting your new program. Consider whether your usual activity space is the best option for a program like this or whether you have other options on your site that could be used.

Sharing Our Experiences: Activity Spaces

In our program planning, we had to consider carefully the best location and setup for our hands-on activities. First, our exhibition spaces do not permit hands-on activities beyond pencils and sketchbooks. In addition to the restrictions for the protection of artworks, the spaces do not have adequate seating, lighting, or space for tables. Therefore, we had to make other plans. This may or may not be a similar challenge in your space.

We have several potential workspaces to choose from though only one formal studio. Each has advantages and challenges. Choosing between these options is often based on many factors including the availability of the spaces, the convenience (or difficulty) of elevator and mobility-related access, and the abilities and comfort of each group of participants.

Studio Classroom

Our dedicated activity space is fully equipped with tables and chairs for up to thirty-five, a sink, and supply storage. This is where our school programs, public art classes, and camps take place. It is located on the third level, requiring elevator access. The many tables and chairs mean access with mobility devices is awkward without careful rearranging. And, it is full of visual distractions and "creative mess."

Advantages:

- The Studio is a large space that can accommodate easy mobility once extra tables and chairs have been removed.
- There is a washroom nearby, and the room is in a quiet area of the gallery so that noise and distraction are reduced.
- The facilitator has easy access to supplies and a sink, making setup and working easy.
- The room is well-lit with natural light.

Challenges:

- To get to this room requires using an elevator. This is time-consuming as the elevator only holds a few people at a time.
- It is far from the entrance.
- There is a lot of "stuff" in the room which can be visually distracting for some. Others like the "creative feel" of the room with all of its environmental cues about the activities that take place there.
- The studio tables and chairs can appear dirty which is distracting for some.

Community Gallery

This multi-use space is used for a variety of functions from classes, camps, and artist talks to small receptions. It also has an exhibition space for community groups. The space is located at the end of our lobby, with sliding glass doors to cut down on some sound from the lobby. It has two levels, natural lighting, and adequate space for a group of 15–50 seated. Stairs are used to access each level, making physical access difficult for some participants. There is a small elevator that takes one participant at a time and requires a staff person with a key for use. There is a washroom nearby, but it requires stairs or elevator access to use it. Instructors also must bring supplies and water into the space for programs.

Advantages:

- This space is close to the exhibition spaces and the lobby so travel time is reduced.
- It is spacious and brightly lit by natural light.
- It is clean and free of distracting clutter and is an attractive space to spend time in.

Challenges:

- With stair or elevator access, many participants require assistance, affecting their independence.
- This is of particular concern for those who need to use the washroom.

Pavilion

This is a large multi-use space at the far end of the building used for large events and public programs. With floor-to-ceiling windows, it is filled with natural light (often to the point of being too bright). It is on ground level with no stairs and has washrooms nearby. It is a huge space with nothing on the walls so there is little visual distraction, though the size of the room can be intimidating. The sound is affected by the size of the empty room as well, which can be distracting for some. It is a long walk for participants depending on which exhibition space they have been in to view the art, but there are no other mobility-related difficulties.

Advantages:

- This space is large, well-lit, and free of distractions.
- We can set it up in various ways so it is very flexible.
- The room is located at one end of the exhibition spaces so access from the first level is easy to plan for and there are no stairs to worry about.
- Washrooms are located just outside the doors.

Challenges:

- The space is large which can dwarf a small program and feel intimidating.
- Depending on where your time in the exhibitions finishes there can be a lot of travel to get there. There is little visual stimulation.
- Facilitators must relocate their supplies from the studio which means more setup and cleanup time.

We use all of these spaces regularly. From the description, you will have identified some of the potential challenges present in each space. Our activities and the availability of the space are often the deciding factors, and we adapt our plans to suit the space.

Recommendations for Activity Spaces

Once we set the program location, we plan the room setup. Tables are set for each participant and their family member or friend to allow lots of room to work, or we will seat two solo participants together. Tables are arranged in a large horseshoe to make it easier for everyone to see and converse with each other. Where the exhibition conversation tends to be more directed, in the activity space the group often chats about their lives, their interests, and the activity they are working on. Everyone sits on one side of the table so the facilitator is easy to see.

One easel shows finished activity examples and a second easel is used for demonstrations. We put only the supplies needed at the time on the table to reduce distraction, clutter, or confusion. We hand out further supplies as needed. The facilitator often uses small bins or baskets to pre-arrange supplies for each table so that handing them out is faster. We try to keep the space quiet from outside noise, although in some cases we play soft background music, but at a low volume so as not to be distracting.

- Choose an activity space that is large enough for participants to move and accommodate any mobility issues.
- Choose a quiet space, and turn off extraneous noise such as a radio (unless being incorporated into the activity) to reduce distractions, accommodate age-related hearing loss, and assist with participants maintaining focus.
- Where possible, use a space with natural lighting or a well-lit area to accommodate age-related vision changes and reduce glare.
- Try to use a consistent activity space each week. While changes in short-term memory might affect whether a participant remembers the room from one week to the next, a consistent room can build a sense of familiarity and comfort.
- Ensure that washrooms are close by and easy to access.
- Prepare everything in advance including tables, chairs, and the demonstration to avoid moving furniture around. This can be irritating and distracting. Ensure the participants have a clear view of the demonstration.
- If possible, try setting up tables in a horseshoe shape to help participants see everyone, as shown in figure 6.2.
- Use chairs with armrests and back supports to provide comfort and promote safety when rising or sitting.
- Adjust the height of the work surface to accommodate participants who are exceptionally tall or short or those who use a wheelchair—furniture risers can be purchased or built to change the height of tables. Set the table height to support a participant's arms on the table so their arm and hand are stable for using art tools.
- Adjust the room to a comfortable temperature.
- Establish a "just right" environment—balance between having too much going on and not enough, to help maintain attention and avoid over- and under-stimulation.

VIRTUAL EXPERIENCES

On Tuesday morning, Lucy sits down at her dining table, and with her daughter's help, she gets out her laptop. She has carefully set up her watercolor paints and paper, a pencil and eraser, and a permanent marker. At the appointed time, she joins an online meeting where she is greeted by a facilitator and several other

Figure 6.2 Socially Oriented Hands-On Spaces. To achieve social connection and engagement, the way a space is arranged is important. We use a U-shaped arrangement of tables so everyone can see each other, and place only the materials needed at the time on tables. Other things are handed out as needed later. *Source*: Art Gallery of Hamilton.

participants, some with a friend or family member beside them. One of the participant's sons signs in from London, much to the delight of his mom. The group chats about a selection of artworks as they appear on their screens and, at the end, they have a lively debate about which piece they would like to take home. Next, they get out their art supplies and create a painting inspired by the work they have seen. The facilitator shows them a step at a time and they follow along (or work in their own way if they wish). Lucy shares a beautiful portrait she has made of the facilitator and comments on the work of the other participants.[1]

Virtual museum programs for people living with dementia offer opportunities for engagement and connection from the comfort of participants' homes. They can eliminate barriers such as accessibility and distance, while also adding unique opportunities like connecting people over great distances using technology. We have had families share in a program from the opposite side of the country, as well as participants from well outside of our community.

Many aspects of the physical, sensory, and social environments that have already been discussed still apply to the virtual environment. As a facilitator, you will need to focus on your environment and on the conditions that you project through the presentation—things such as distractions of noise and background, the organization of content and workspace, the appearance of your screen, and the logistics of getting each person into the program. While each participant will be in their own environment at home, there are some ways to help themprepare for the programs to improve their experience. Once the modifications have been made, virtual programs can be highly engaging, social, and fun to present!

When planning your virtual environment, remember to consider your knowledge of dementia, particularly age-related changes such as vision, hearing, and comfort, and changes in cognition that may impact learning new technologies.

The Shift to Virtual Programs

For our expansion to include virtual programming, we began with our in-person programs to determine which elements to maintain and how to transfer them into a virtual version. This meant combining highly interactive conversations about works from our collection and meaningful hands-on activities, with a facilitation style that was responsive, supportive of abilities, and informed by our knowledge of dementia. We also identified the adjustments needed to suit a virtual platform. These included both the perspective of the participant and the facilitator.

To be engaged, participants must:

- See the artwork and the hands-on activity demonstration.
- Hear the facilitator and the other participants clearly to foster the same social connection we had seen in the in-person programs.
- Have reference materials for the objects and activities to help them prepare and participate.
- Have the same activity supplies as the facilitator to ensure clear instruction and easy access to the correct materials.
- Feel supported and confident in how to participate.
- Have access to technology, such as the internet, laptop, tablet, or phone.

To be successful as facilitators, we must:

- Be able to see and/or hear participants.
- Have access to digital reproductions of works from our collection.
- Be comfortable facilitating an interactive conversation (not just a lecture!) virtually.
- Be able to demonstrate or guide a hands-on program for participants.
- Encourage participants to join the conversations and to connect with each other.
- Be able to support and adapt our facilitation on the fly, based on each participant's needs.
- Be able to troubleshoot programs with technology connections, interaction, and hands-on difficulties.

Recommendations for Technology Solutions

The next step is to determine the platforms to use for virtual programs. We considered the available technology and what our participants would be comfortable using. We also considered different ways of sharing content, either synchronous (live) or asynchronous (pre-recorded). We have asynchronous material available on our website for general use, but for *Artful Moments* we offer exclusively synchronous programs in light of our mandate for social connection and the reduction of social isolation.

Online Programs

Programs delivered through video conferencing platforms offer many advantages. Participants and facilitators can see and hear each other, they have additional options for communication like Chat functions, screen annotation, and screen sharing. There are also many services available to use at no cost to participants.

The most important factor in choosing a platform is the ease of use for participants. This means the fewest steps to join a program, and wherever possible, no passcodes or other complications. Other priorities include:

- Using high-quality reproductions for objects at full-screen size to ensure visibility for participants.
- Adding extra slides with graphics, arrows, and other details to help direct attention, but used sparingly to avoid too much distraction.
- Having a second camera set up for the hands-on activity allows participants to watch your demonstrations step-by-step, as well as to see what they are expected to accomplish at each step. Having two cameras allows you to switch between the desktop and face-to-face views easily.
- Using headphones with a good microphone for better sound.

- Encouraging participants to have their cameras on for increased social connection and to help the facilitator observe for engagement or difficulties (but respecting the wishes of those who prefer not to).
- In some cases, using the chat functions to add extra prompts to help participants or to connect one-to-one as needed.

Phone-Based Programs

For some participants, online programs do not work. Potential participants may not have access to devices or the internet, or they may not be comfortable with this format. We encourage you to consider phone-based programs as a very viable option, especially if you have already made the transition from in-person to online.

On Wednesday afternoon, Lee sits in a comfortable chair and waits for his phone to ring. He has a binder of full-color images in front of him and some drawing materials nearby. When the phone rings, he is greeted by a facilitator who tells him about the day's program and then he is entered into a conference call to share an hour of lively conversation about the artworks in his binder. It takes John a few moments to find the right words to share his ideas, but his participation in the program is active and thoughtful. Later in the week, he may return to his binder to look at the artwork and show his daughter his drawing when she visits.[2]

While an open-air conference call system can work for a phone-based program, we have found better success using a more sophisticated system that includes facilitator controls. We recommend conference call systems that support features such as adjusting volume, calling participants directly or inviting them to join the call, and muting individual participants or removing participants from the call if needed. As with virtual programs, it is important to choose a system that is user-friendly for participants. Other important elements of phone-based programs include:

- Visual references for the objects being discussed such as a booklet with numbered pages with all of the objects, close-ups, and reference images. This is an essential component and will allow for an experience similar to an online program.
- Activity outlines and step-by-step images of the hands-on activity.
- Use of headphones with a good microphone for better sound.

Planning a Virtual Program

While virtual programs offer greater control over your presentation environment, success hinges on careful planning and execution. As participants will be remote and potentially unfamiliar with the format, it is imperative to consider every detail. Careful planning helps to ensure that your program will maximize both engagement and social connection. Your preparation should include:

- Organizing all images and reference materials in an activity package. This includes the objects or artworks for discussion, the steps to follow in a hands-on activity, lists of materials, and any other relevant materials. Create all of the resources you will need including slideshows and program kits.
- Send clear instructions for how to join a virtual program. Include this information in the packages with a contact number or email for problems, as well as any access codes or other details needed. Have all of this information at the front of the kit, clearly marked.
- For online programs—send a welcome email with program links a few days before the start date of the program.
- On the day of each session, send an email with the meeting link, supplies needed, images of the day's supply setup, and images of the objects for discussion or the hands-on activity if relevant.
- For phone programs—include phone numbers and access codes for each week in the binder. Where possible use a system that allows you to call the participants.

Your planning should continue into how you set up on the day of a program. Being well prepared and organized is an essential element for a successful and engaging program. Your organization and demeanor will have an effect on the participants' engagement. Ensure that you:

- Have your slide show loaded and ready to go, and test your screen-sharing and second camera.
- Have your list of works or objects and any notes you need to guide your discussion on hand.
- Have a completed sample of your hands-on activity, as well as all of the tools and supplies ready to go before you start. You can use your setup as an on-screen image to help participants get ready.
- Have a class list handy so you can address everyone by name, with any relevant notes you may need. For larger groups, you can use your list to track when people are asked questions to ensure you include everyone regularly.
- Have any co-facilitators join you on screen about ten minutes in advance to complete any discussions that are needed and to ensure everyone knows their roles.

As a facilitator, your location is also important. Being comfortable, organized, and well-set-up ensures that your presentation is engaging and not distracting. Ensure that you:

- Sit in a comfortable chair with good support and room to move around when needed.
- Eliminate background noise in your space and use headphones to improve sound quality.
- Have everything at hand so you do not have to shuffle papers or supplies, or cause delays.
- Have a clock nearby to help keep track of your time. Check the time regularly.
- Choose a well-lit location to present, preferably with natural light. Check that you are not back-lit and turn off any lights that may create glare or bright spots for your participants.
- Look at your background and work area to remove any unnecessary clutter that can be distracting
- Make sure your first name and the first name of others are displayed to aid social connection
- For phone programs, organization and sound are key.

Figure 6.3 Clear Instructions and Images. As you prepare for a virtual program, be sure to include concise instructions and clear, organized images to support preparations at home. If participants are unfamiliar with a material, a photo will help them. *Source*: Art Gallery of Hamilton.

Supporting Participants in a Virtual Program

Some participants may be unfamiliar with a virtual program format, and/or unsure how to prepare. Additionally, participants may struggle to filter out background noise or distractions they are accustomed to at home. To address these concerns, consider including the following recommendations in your information packages:

Getting ready for a program:

- Choose a well-lit space.
- Turn off your TV and radio.
- Sit in a comfortable chair.
- Sit at a table with space to work.
- Set up materials ahead of time—only what you need today.
- The setup photo will help you choose the right tools and materials.
- Remove any clutter in your workspace so that it will be easier to work.
- If you have problems connecting, call this number. . . .
- If you are unable to attend, please let us know at this email/number. . . .

For those joining an online program:

- Set up your screen so you can see it clearly and do not have to hold it.
- Have your camera angled so we can see you.
- Make sure you are plugged in or have a full battery on your device.

For those joining a phone program:

- If possible, use headphones for better sound.
- Make sure you are plugged in or have a full battery on your phone.
- Make sure you have your booklet of images with you for the discussion.

AFTER AN ASSESSMENT

This chapter has given you an overview of considerations that we have experienced and examples of how we adapted to them. The Environment Assessment Template offers an extensive list of questions to help guide you through your museum environment with fresh eyes, informed by the knowledge of dementia that you have acquired in earlier chapters. Like any program plan, this one is a work in progress—you will learn as you go. With new people joining your programs, the specific needs for your environment adaptation will likely change too. Preparing well and applying your knowledge and growing experience will allow you to be flexible and responsive to each new situation.

With a full assessment of your museum in hand, you will have a list of things to do. Divide your notes into two lists—the things you can change, (like adding signage or seating) and the things you have to work around. With these items organized, you will be prepared to start the next phase of your program planning. An excellent step forward in becoming more dementia-friendly is if you can make permanent changes to your environment—this will increase your capacity and institutional impact. If any of your spaces change dramatically, be sure to refresh your assessment to reflect the new advantages and challenges.

There are resources available in your community and many service organizations to help you better understand and apply accessibility best practices to your site. They may also provide a practitioner

Figure 6.4 Virtual Programs. Your instructions about how to prepare at home will help ensure a good experience. A participant and his wife are working with salt-dough that they made at home using prepared materials and following a demo online. *Source*: Art Gallery of Hamilton.

with experience to help complete an assessment with or for you. If you have a local college or university, this might be a great opportunity to engage a student or emerging professional to help you conduct your assessment. Occupational therapists, students, or other community service providers may be able to lend their experience and expertise and you may make an important connection for future projects. Consulting with people with the lived experience of dementia—the people who will be directly affected by your work is another key step in ensuring that you have met the needs of your participants.

NOTES

1. Facilitator's account of program, 2020. Names have been changed to respect privacy.
2. Facilitator's account of program, 2021. Names have been changed to respect privacy.

Message for Success

Many Ways to Adapt

Museum spaces present both challenges and opportunities for creating an inclusive environment that supports a participant's engagement. Museums have responsibilities to the objects they collect, the exhibitions they present, and the range of programs and audiences with whom they work. As facilitators, we are faced with buildings that can be challenging to navigate due to their location, architecture, and layout. There is a lot to contend with when planning a program for participants whose success will be directly affected by the environment. A well-planned environment is critical to an effective program. It is a continuous learning process—you will discover new ways to optimize the space as you go.

The good news is that however flexible or inflexible, accessible or barrier-filled your physical environment may be, there are many different ways to solve the challenges that the environment may present. A well-planned environment is one of three important pillars, informed by your knowledge of dementia that will support the engagement of your participants. You have seen your museum with fresh eyes and are beginning to see the exciting possibilities to come. Keep tweaking until you get it right. There is always a solution—or many.

Part IV
The Approach

Tailoring Interactions

Individuality Matters

Interpersonal communication is the process of exchanging ideas, information, feelings, and intentions with another person. It can take place verbally or nonverbally through body language, gestures, tone of voice, and facial expression, and it includes expressing and listening/observing. A person's communication is a demonstration of their individuality, through the messages they share, their style of communication, and their process of expression. This will be reflected through your approach as a facilitator and in the participation of each member of your group.

When working with people living with dementia, the way you interact with participants is extremely important, resulting in either an engaged participant who feels empowered to contribute or one who disconnects. Planning effective interactions with participants means considering several factors:

- **Dementia-related changes:** Each participant experiences dementia differently, so understanding their specific abilities is crucial.
- **Comfort and familiarity:** Consider their comfort level with museums in general and your specific museum layout.
- **Planned activities:** Tailor your approach to the type of activities you have planned.
- **Individual preferences and communication styles:** Respect each participant's unique preferences and how they best communicate.

Approach is the second pillar in the *Model for Successful Engagement*. The ways that you communicate, plan, and adapt your interactions with your participants will make or break your program. A successful approach will need to be nimble, individualized, and well-informed by your knowledge of your participant to suit the needs and circumstances of the moment.

The Golden Rule: *focus on the individual*. Above all, remember that each person is unique, and your method of connecting with them should be too. By keeping this at the forefront of your interactions you can ensure a more engaging and personalized experience.

7

Understanding Approach

Approach refers to a way of doing or thinking about something—the way we communicate, facilitate, demonstrate, and plan. Because of the changes in abilities that a person with dementia may experience, an informed and responsive approach is essential to ensure participation, comfort, and engagement in the activities.

By applying your understanding of dementia to each participant, you can create a positive and personalized experience. Consider the five key areas affected by dementia: cognition, language, perception, mood, and physical abilities. This supportive communication and facilitation approach aims to foster confidence in:

- *Participation*—How can you ensure each participant enjoys and contributes comfortably?
- *Understanding*—What communication strategies best support their cognitive abilities?
- *Self-expression*—How can you best support both verbal and nonverbal communication?
- *Social Connection*—How can you facilitate positive relationships between facilitators, participants, and their loved ones?

WHY IS APPROACH SO IMPORTANT?

A thoughtful and responsive approach is the key to connecting with participants. Communicating with them in a variety of ways that best suit them, offering responsive and individualized cues to support participation, and applying your knowledge of dementia in each step and interaction will ensure that each participant is supported and has an enjoyable experience. To encourage and facilitate a positive experience and engagement your approach should foster:

- *Independence:* making it possible to participate without additional interventions as much as possible.
- *Dignity:* ensuring that participants, family members and friends who join them, and facilitators feel valued, confident, and respected.
- *Social interaction:* connections among program facilitators, participants, and family and friends.
- *A sense of well-being:* letting participants know that they are valued, supported, safe, and in a place that provides an enjoyable experience.

These four concepts are essential. This chapter outlines the skills necessary to lead a program that achieves engagement with each participant, enabling them to express themselves and to connect socially.

What Is a Person-Centered Approach?

A "person-centered" approach places the participant first in every aspect of the program from design through presentation and even evaluation. A person-centered approach means focusing on each person's individuality, interests, histories, preferences, and abilities rather than on their diagnosis and the changes and losses that result from it. It also means that the way you approach one person is not necessarily the way you connect with another. Being person-centered means being attentive, and responsive and using individualized strategies for each participant in a manner that supports their unique strengths.

While we have spent a great deal of time learning about dementia, once you have that knowledge to guide you, your approach and the focus of the program shifts to the individual in that moment. The key points of a person-centered approach include:

- Treating the person with dignity and respect.
- Understanding that each participant has their own history, lifestyle, culture, preferences, likes, dislikes, hobbies, and interests. It is important to get to know them as a whole person, not simply a person with a diagnosis.
- Looking at situations from the point of view of the participant.
- Providing opportunities for the person to have conversations and relationships with other people.
- Ensuring the person has the chance to try new things or take part in activities they enjoy.

Take a moment to think of a time you felt "centered" versus "irrelevant" as a participant in a conversation or program.

- What did the facilitator do or not do to make you feel that way?
- How can you apply or improve your approach based on your reflection?

The Benefits of a Person-Centered Approach

The positive impact of using person-centered principles has been well documented in care settings. We can extrapolate this success to apply it to museum settings. Any organization that provides programs and services for people living with dementia is encouraged to adopt person-centered principles as a way of reducing stigma and exclusion. By appreciating and understanding the person we connect with them rather than their diagnosis.

By placing the participant at the center of the program—by modifying our program to suit the needs and abilities of each participant individually—we have seen an overall improvement in the experience of each participant and an increase in their enjoyment and satisfaction with the program. This has been evaluated by measuring the engagement of participants. Using person-centered principles will also encourage each person to participate more, and to feel safe and empowered in their own thoughts and actions.

It is important to note that a person-centered lens is not merely used to design and set up a program, but, rather, it informs every interaction from start to finish. Placing the participant at the center of the program means paying attention to each person, assessing their engagement throughout, and adapting to changing circumstances on the fly. It is a delicate balancing act between meeting the needs of several different people at once while also maintaining a cohesive presentation. However, once mastered, this approach will become a key to success in every program or activity you present.

UNDERSTANDING YOUR PRESENCE

Approach begins with you. Moods and emotional states can be contagious. As empathetic beings, we are attuned to the ways that other people present themselves—their body language, facial expression, sense of calm or rush, and general comfort. This awareness can affect the way others in a group feel and act.

A person with dementia retains their emotional awareness, and their ability to be sensitive to and to understand the emotional state of others. This includes being able to read the nonverbal messages communicated through facial expressions, body language, tension, tone of voice, and mood. Your participants will sense if you are rushed, distracted, or stressed. Your demeanor will affect the mood of the program.

Imagine this ...

You are seated in a classroom or a gallery space and the facilitator comes rushing in with a stack of papers, phone in hand, not quite aware of the people they are about to face. They stop, drop their materials on a table, apologize for being late, talk about all the things that have just happened to them, and then rush right into the start of the program. How do you feel?

Like your participants, you will sense rush, anxiety, and ill-preparedness. You will feel uncertain about what is about to happen and if this person even knows what they are doing. You will not have had any time to adjust or transition into the program and will likely adopt a lot of the anxiety and discomfort you have just witnessed.

Now picture an experience where the facilitator is waiting to greet the group, welcoming everyone by name and making small talk as everyone arrives. At the appointed time she asks if everyone is ready to begin (and waits for an answer). She stands and waits until everyone else is standing or ready to move to the activity space, and they travel together. The room is set up when they arrive, and she asks everyone to take a seat. She waits until everyone is settled, encourages everyone to take a breath, and then gently eases into the start of the conversation.

From these two descriptions, it is easy to sense the difference, and participants will too. No matter what has happened in your day, always stop and take a moment to compose yourself. Never rush through your introductions or any of the first steps. Start by introducing yourself, welcoming everyone (by name), and ensuring that everyone is ready and has what they need. Tell them the agenda for the day and check in with everyone to see how they are feeling. If your program has to be shortened slightly as a result, then do so.

Check Yourself at the Door

Before you begin a program remember to pause and check your own emotional state. Pay attention to your body language, facial expressions, tone of voice, rate of speech, and volume. Take a moment to breathe, and put aside any frustrations, anxiety, or disturbance you may be carrying with you from the previous events of your day. Smile, slow down, and begin in a positive frame of mind.

Remember, it is not just your words that communicate with others—your nonverbal cues convey much more. Use open body language and gestures and take the time to set the right tone.

Be present with your participants, leave other concerns of your day behind, and enjoy your experience. If you can do this your participants will too.

Listen, Observe, Be Interested

Interactions that take place in museum programs are personal and specific. The tour or conversation is not about ensuring that you communicate a set of specific details or facts and it is not primarily about knowledge acquisition (although that can happen). We use museum objects as tools to inspire conversations—memories, opinions, observations, and creative storytelling. Keep in mind that none of your "content" is more important than the introductory framing steps. If you need to trim parts of the session, the content is where to do it.

As a facilitator, your approach must be grounded in paying attention to the participants. Listen to what they say, and watch their nonverbal communication. Body language can tell you far more than words. Is a person making eye contact or looking away? Do they lean in to share connections with their partner or fidget and look ready to leave? Christine Bryden is an author and speaker who was diagnosed with dementia, and she said, "if there was only one thing to say, it would be to listen with your eyes and all your senses."[1] Respond to the specific experience and ideas of each person in your group and build the experience as you go. Be sure you enjoy the experience yourself. As a museum facilitator, what could be more fun than spending time talking to people about the objects that you love?

Some participants may not be able to tell you with words if something is wrong—if they do not understand, if they are having trouble communicating, or if they are uncomfortable or tired. By observing each person's verbal and nonverbal communication (or lack of), physical and emotional state, and comfort in participating, you will be able to adapt to suit their needs. Changes in behavior, shifts in conversation topics, or the emergence of other concerns are signals that something needs to be adjusted.

Be Patient, Flexible, and Responsive

Patience, flexibility, and responsiveness are essential in programs for people living with dementia. Always remember that participants' abilities continue to change over time and potentially during a single session. For some, understanding information and formulating a response (whether verbal or action) can take some time. It is important to be comfortable with silence. Leave time for people to process information. Give them time to act. Learn when to wait and when to gently support them.

Being prepared with a good plan is important but always be prepared to adjust as you go. When working with people living with dementia, things can change quickly. What worked before may not work "in the moment," and your flexibility to adapt your plans can encourage participants to continue. Responding to the conditions "in the moment" with sensitivity and creativity can be the difference between a positive experience and a negative one. The strategies that follow will support you in your adjustments but the first step is with you as the facilitator. Be flexible and be prepared to adjust or abandon plans.

INCLUDE EVERYONE

First and foremost, these are social programs. Participants are sharing an experience with you, a family member or friend, and with other participants. As a facilitator, it is important to find ways to include everyone throughout each session and to seek out and encourage participation. While some people will contribute eagerly, others may hesitate for many reasons—worry about not knowing the answer, feeling self-conscious, difficulty finding the words they want, trouble with understanding, or with expressing their ideas. They may have difficulty knowing how to jump into a conversation. Some will only want (or be able) to participate in nonverbal ways. Ensure everyone has an opportunity to express themselves. Get to know your group and their preferred level and style of participation and be sure to give each person regular opportunities.

Active Participants

Participants may raise their hands or even begin speaking right away. Some participants may also speak over others as their ability to self-regulate or respond to social cues begins to change. In these cases, it is easy to recognize the interest in participating.

Also, look for more subtle signs. A participant might look directly at the facilitator or the object being discussed or they may speak to the family member or friend who joined with them. In the hands-on activity, they may look at the materials or move them around but not take steps to begin working. Try to recognize these indications as well and use facilitation techniques to call them into the conversation when it may be hard for them to initiate participation.

Less Active Participants

You will recognize some signs of not wanting to contribute from other programs you have led. In addition to not raising their hand or beginning to speak, participants might purposely look away, seem nervous, or shake their heads when called upon. A participant may wander away from the group, ask to leave, or disconnect in other ways. In some cases, they may show unexpected emotions or they may fall asleep.

As you learn about dementia, you will begin to understand that the signs listed above may or may not be indicative of a participant's interest in joining in. Initiation is one of the abilities that can be affected by dementia along with reduced social cues. Some participants will benefit from being called upon by name to invite them into the conversation and make space for them to process how they wish to join. If a person truly does not want to participate actively, respect that and accept their choices.

As a facilitator, supporting inclusion while also allowing for an individual's choice takes time to master. This skill comes from knowing the people in your group, and it improves with practice. In-person, it can be straightforward to keep track of each person's level of participation. You will be able to observe the group, registering body language, attention, and interest in contributing. Others can be called upon by name—name tags are important to help you with this.

Depending on your group size you may be able to ask each participant about each object, or you may need to limit questions about each object to a smaller number of people—just be sure you give everyone a chance throughout the session. At times, it can also be useful to make use of "group participation" techniques—hands up to show preference or consensus, or thumbs up or down. Be sure to vary your invitations to participate with a variety of formats to keep things interesting.

Balanced participation during virtual programs can be a bit trickier to navigate. Always remember that technology can be a barrier for some people. We have found it best to avoid reliance on the "hands up" or the chat options on online platforms as it can become an added stress for some, and others will simply not use them. Unless there is a lot of background noise, we avoid turning mics on and off for the same reason. Most of our programs run with cameras and mics on so that we can see everyone and interact with more comfortable in-person cues like physically raising their hand (not the virtual version). The simplest way to manage inclusion in virtual conversations is to develop a routine of calling on participants by name, rotating among your group. As a facilitator, having a list of names beside you is very helpful. You can check off each time you have engaged someone, which helps to ensure that you are including everyone. Be sure to let participants know you will call on them by name, and that they can "pass" at any time. Use similar options for nonverbal participation too.

Meet People Where They Are

Each participant's skills, experience, knowledge, and abilities are unique. Their entry point into this program must also be yours. Do not make assumptions or set expectations in advance but instead spend some time and careful observation to understand each participant's starting point, comfort, abilities, and needs. Be aware that each person's mood or attention may change from day to day or even during a session. It is important to be aware of and adapt to changes as they occur.

A person with dementia may experience a different connection to "where and when" and this may fluctuate from moment to moment. It is important to be sensitive to these changes. For participants in the earlier stages of dementia, a gentle reminder of where they are (in the museum) can be helpful if they have become temporarily confused. In the later stages, it is not always necessary to try to orient them to the present as often it is more comfortable for them if you validate their reality by "joining" them in their place and time.

Embrace the unexpected. Be prepared to adjust plans, conversations, and activities "in the moment" to best engage participants. Flexibility and sensitivity are essential.

SUPPORTING PARTICIPATION

The key to success in your approach is how well you support the participation and ultimately the engagement of each participant in your program. We will explore engagement in more depth in Part VI, but we begin now with a look at participation as a first step. Participation is the act of joining with others in doing something. But what does that look like?

Traditionally, in a museum setting, we may envision lively and interactive programs with animated questioning, dialogue, and even some theatrics on the part of the facilitator or the participants. Simply put, participation is people getting actively involved in the program.

Now let's widen the scope of our thinking. Participation can also be subtle. It may be participants laughing at a funny comment, smiling, or nodding in response to something they have heard. For some, it may just present as them paying attention to the conversation or activity, or raising their hand, or giving a "thumbs up" to something they agree with. It may be listening or taking note of something they have heard or seen. For some, it is simply being present, in the company of others. With your knowledge of dementia in mind, pay careful attention to each participant.

One of our earliest experiences in this work involved a focus group of people in the later stages of dementia. In a group of five people, we saw a wide range of abilities and forms of participation, from one active person who responded to every question, to others who watched but said very little, to a person who did not engage with us at all. There was some banter with those participants who contributed, but we were not sure how to connect with the others. Then all of a sudden, when one painting was introduced, the woman (who we thought had fallen asleep) raised her head and began to recall a memory from earlier in her life. In that instant, she connected fully and we understood that she had been quietly engaged all along. In another case, we saw very little interaction but heard later from a participant's family member that they spoke about the program for the rest of the day after we had gone.

We have learned that for people with dementia, like for any museum visitor, participation can encompass a wide range of actions, both active and subtle. As abilities change, so too does the need to support and observe participation in diverse forms, whether the program be in-person, or virtual.

Figure 7.1 Facilitator Presence. As a facilitator, your presence can have a big impact on participants level of engagement. From gentle support to activate strengths and skills to friendly encouragement and multiple forms of communication, pay attention to each participant's abilities and emotions "in the moment." *Source*: istock.com/monkeybusinessimages.

The social environment plays a pivotal role here as well, as it is important to establish trust, comfort, and a safe space for people to feel comfortable in joining.

Building Relationships

To encourage engagement, personal connections between facilitators and participants are very valuable. Building relationships through individual contact and developing familiarity and trust with each participant fosters successful engagement. Being comfortable together, with the facilitator and with other participants, is an important part of the social connection and overall program success.

We start building relationships before a program begins by calling each participant (or their family member or friend when requested) as part of our intake process. Where family members or friends are involved, they may have questions for you too but wherever possible speak to the participant directly, rather than just speaking about them to their family or friend.

Planning for consistent staffing each week is also important for fostering relationships for both the facilitator and the participants. As a facilitator, you will get to know your participants over time—how they interact with others, what they like and dislike, and the best strategies to support their participation. Participants will feel valued and respected by your connection. The familiarity they develop with you will add to their comfort and enjoyment in the program.

Sharing Expectations

Guiding participants and their loved ones about what they can expect and what they should do during a program is an important step in supporting participants and achieving successful engagement. It can also include setting social norms or creating a social contract. Managing expectations builds comfort, reduces anxiety, and helps to prepare participants before a program starts. There are a few different elements in this development that can be used and shared. These include:

Pre-program information: This can be printed information that is sent by mail or email that informs people in advance what they need to bring or have prepared, what will happen during the program, how to get ready for their experience, and contact information. This can include things like program outlines, instructions, and introductions of facilitators with photos.

Weekly program reminders as described earlier further relationship building and offer ongoing opportunities for dialogue, questions, and sharing of concerns. Individual conversations build rapport between facilitators and participants and make them feel comfortable in sharing their experiences.

At the start of each session: Use the first few moments to welcome everyone by name and share some social exchange. This builds further familiarity and rapport in the group—and validates each person as an interesting and valued individual. It also takes away the feeling of rushing into the program and makes the group more comfortable. Do not count on everyone remembering names or instructions from previous weeks—by restating everything each week you remove the pressure of relying on memory. Name tags are a helpful support for social engagement as well.

Consider a mindful practice to start a program. This can be as simple as a one-word check-in to see how people are feeling to a more elaborate breathing or visualization exercise. A mindful practice should be something that feels authentic to each facilitator. This is a great way to help participants focus on the moment and the experiences that they are having.

Setting Social Norms

Take a moment each session to remind people of the social norms or expected behaviors. There will be some variations between in-person and virtual programs but these should always include treating everyone with respect, being patient and positive, and not speaking over each other.

For all programs: Reminding everyone that they are gathering with the aim of sharing an experience in a positive and supportive way is a good way to set the tone of a program.

- We ask everyone to remember there are many voices and that everyone should try to listen to each other.
- We ask everyone to use appropriate, respectful, and kind language.
- We tell participants that they may stay as long as they like and may leave early if they need to, or take a break if needed. We make sure to let them know where they can go for a rest.
- We make sure that we know how participants will leave safely—whether they will leave on their own, go with a family member or friend, or wait for a ride.
- We encourage everyone to share but tell them that we understand that some people may not feel comfortable right away.
- We show and tell participants how and when to ask and answer questions—this may be different for on-site or virtual programs.

Specific to on-site programs: Set expectations for how people should conduct themselves in the museum. Do not assume that everyone in your group has been to a museum before or understands the norms of museum etiquette.

- Reminders about not touching the museum objects along with any other rules about food, drinks, or photography.
- Reminders to be respectful of everyone's personal space.
- At the start of each session share housekeeping details—locations of bathrooms, exits, and where to go if they need a break.
- Share plans for the day including timing, locations etc.

Specific to virtual: Virtual experiences may be less familiar to some participants. In both your pre-program communications and at the start of each session, review your actions and expectations. Try out any technology details, including screen sharing, annotation, and chats to be sure everyone is prepared.

- Encourage everyone to have cameras and mics turned on, to share together but also let them know that they can choose to turn off their mic and video if they prefer.
- If they choose to turn off their mic, let them know that during the program, you will ask if they would like to share their thoughts, for which they would turn on their microphone. When you call on them later, be prepared to instruct them on how to turn the mic on again if they have difficulties.
- Share the names of everyone present, especially for phone programs where people cannot see each other. This is a good way to check that you know who is there and also to remind others of who is present.
- If necessary, ask participants whose rooms are noisy to turn their mics off and ensure they can turn them back on.
- Practice using mute, turning cameras on and off, and agree on how participants will signal that they would like to ask or answer questions. If you intend to use chat or poll functions review those as well.
- Let everyone know how to get back into the program if they are cut off or need to leave briefly (links or callbacks).
- Encourage everyone to share their created work but also that they can opt not to do so.

Ongoing Check-Ins

Conversations with participants and/or their family and friends can be useful to discuss experiences whether pertaining to a specific session or reflecting on the program as a whole. This is a valuable way to gather feedback for future improvements. From time to time it can also be useful to make individual connections to discuss any feedback, to allow participants to share concerns, or continue relationship building. As with other interactions, wherever possible, speak to the participant themselves when discussing questions or feedback. There will be times when that family or friend's support in this process is needed too, but always aim to include the participant in these discussions as appropriate.

ROUTINES AND LENGTH OF PROGRAMS

Programs are all about connection and trust. We want to make our participants feel as comfortable and safe as possible. Ensuring consistent staff and routines is an important part of this. We have the same staff and volunteers for the full program. This helps participants to be familiar with our team and us with them. This comfort helps participants to engage during the project and also helps us to adjust more easily as needed throughout the program.

We have tried several different program styles—monthly, weekly, and occasional visits—and have found ways to make each successful and meaningful for participants. However, we have found that the best results come through regular programs where participants have the time to become familiar with the routines, staff, and other participants.

For in-person and virtual programs we offer weekly sessions in eight-week blocks. The first week is where we begin with introductions. We meet our participants and build an understanding of their abilities, interests, and personalities. Participants meet the facilitator and see how a program works. They see the other participants and start to understand how to interact. In-person, they see the museum for the first time and learn how to navigate through the space. We keep the first week a bit shorter to allow time for all of this. By the third week, everyone has settled in and have started to know each other. Trust has been established and participants are more comfortable and willing to share and offer opinions. By the sixth or seventh week participants are quite comfortable and seem almost like familiar friends. More recently we have had success in alternating weeks between in-person and virtual sessions, allowing participants to attend one format or both as they prefer.

We follow the same routine each week. We use the same gathering spot before the program starts. We do a warm welcome and then proceed to the exhibitions when in-person or to the virtual tour conversation. We use the same number of objects each time and the same length of time. We follow the same process in the hands-on activity as well. When people know what to expect they feel more at ease and safe. For many of our participants, a close relationship is built with the staff team. A sense of familiarity for people and places is often created even when memory and recognition has been impacted by dementia.

NOTE

1. Christine Bryden is an author and public speaker who was diagnosed with dementia. This quote is from an in-person conversation between Maureen Montemuro and Christine as part of a GPA—Gentle Persuasive Approaches—workshop in Hamilton in 2011.

8

Communication Strategies

Effective communication is a shared responsibility. However, when dementia impacts a person's language skills, the responsibility to keep the conversation flowing shifts to you.[1] As a facilitator, you must modify your communication to maximize the participant's understanding or comprehension and their ability to express themselves. You will "facilitate" the conversation. You are a "ramp," helping and supporting their engagement and participation.

EFFECTIVE COMMUNICATION

Many of the following strategies will apply to any programs you present, but they become even more important when working with participants with dementia. These strategies address changes in abilities related to attention, cognition, and language.

To begin a program or a conversation, be sure you have the participants' attention. Stand so that they see you without having to turn. Begin speaking only when the participants are ready. Make eye contact with everyone in the group to encourage a feeling of inclusion. Remember to stand facing your group with the object for discussion beside or near you (do not turn to face it) so that the participant's attention is not divided between you and the object they are looking at. Point at the object as you introduce it to the group to help further cue their attention, then pause for a moment to give everyone a chance to look and think.

- When providing information, break it into smaller chunks with pauses to allow processing time.
- Call on each participant often to maintain engagement.
- When asking questions, say the participant's name first and make eye contact so you have their attention.
- Be patient and allow silence and extra time for a participant to respond.
- Always show that you are interested, and provide positive and encouraging feedback using words and body language.
- Use nonverbal cues—your facial expression and body language will convey a lot. Use gestures to emphasize or further explain what you are saying but try not to move around too much. Model nonverbal responses like thumbs up and down, hands up, numbers.
- Speak clearly and at a slightly slower pace to allow for the extra processing time that may be needed.
- Use a normal volume level.
- Never use a condescending or patronizing tone. Remember, participants are adults even as dementia may impact some cognitive abilities.

- Avoid phrases like "can you"—this could make participants feel less confident if they cannot do something. Instead, use terms like "try" or simply direct instructions like "draw a circle" or "pick up your brush."

Supporting Changes in Memory

Participants will benefit from including strategies to support changes in memory. By making a routine of repeating important information like names and details in every session you will ensure an inclusive and comfortable experience where participants do not have to rely on remembering.

- Introduce staff and other participants to each other each week as a part of your introduction. Wear name tags to support social connections.
- Tell participants important information such as routines and schedules for the session, the location of important places like washrooms, and how they should act as part of each session so that they do not have to rely on memories of previous experiences.
- If you ask the group a question, repeat it each time you call on a new person.
- Avoid asking if a participant "remembers"—this could make participants less "confident if they cannot remember." Instead of "Remember when we saw this last week?" or "Remember when we sculpted last week?" use direct statements. For example, "Here is a room that we viewed last week' or "I 'enjoyed doing sculpture with you last week.'"
- Avoid asking about facts like names, dates, or historical events that require participants to recall information. When this information is interesting or relevant, simply tell them.

STRATEGIES TO SUPPORT UNDERSTANDING

As a person's abilities change, they will need progressively more support to understand the information they hear. By using strategies to support understanding, you will change the participant's experience from one that may be frustrating, confusing, or less meaningful to one of engagement and enjoyment. Consider the words and phrases you use to communicate information:

- Find clear and concise ways to describe objects and ideas—five- to seven-word phrases are a good limit while you assess your group's abilities.
- Share one idea at a time with a pause to allow for processing. Watch everyone to see how well they are following along. Leave longer pauses or silences than you might in other programs.
- Slow down or add more information or rephrase a statement as appropriate.
- Use familiar words and plain language. Avoid slang, metaphors, and figurative language as these may be misunderstood. The more concrete your statements, the less chance for confusion.
- Use specific nouns for objects, places, and people rather than vague terms like "he," "it," "here." This will ensure everyone knows what you are talking about even if they may have lost track of an earlier part of your presentation.

Clarity and concrete language are important. To wrap up a program, a facilitator once asked, "Which artwork would you like to take home?" intended as a fun way to talk about what painting participants liked best. One participant interpreted this as the facilitator trying to sell her something and became suspicious and distrustful. In a subsequent session, the same facilitator successfully adjusted the question to simply, "Which painting do you like the best?"

Equally important is to consider how you present information and engage participants. Your support of abilities through timing, repetition, and body language will further support understanding, and using multiple strategies at once (words and gestures) can benefit all participants.

- Ask only one question at a time, and wait for the answer before moving on to the next. Repeat the question again for each person you engage. Be prepared to reword the question or offer choices for answers if the participant has difficulty.
- Give instructions in one- or two-step, simple statements, pausing between steps to allow processing time or to complete actions. If participants appear to have difficulties following the instructions, slow down and rephrase.
- Start with one-step instructions. Pause between statements and watch to see how it is going. Shift to two-step directions if appropriate. Shift back to one-step instructions as needed.
- When talking, try to stay relatively still—avoid distracting movements like swaying, fiddling with your hands, or pacing.
- Use purposeful gestures to add emphasis or demonstrations. Your nonverbal communication will help add meaning—facial expression, gestures, visual aids, demonstrations.

For participants who speak a different language than you, be sure to explain carefully in simple terms. Try to use a few words in their language if you can. Ask their family member or friend if attending to assist with interpretation and be sure to leave time for translation. Incorporate nonverbal communication such as gestures, body language, pointing, using objects, pictures.

When Someone Has Difficulty Understanding

There will be times when, despite your best efforts to communicate clearly and thoughtfully, someone will have difficulty understanding you. They may look puzzled, struggle to answer, look to their family or friend for direction, or they may say something that is not related to your question.

Do not take it personally or feel that you have done something wrong, and try not to feel flustered. This is a time to take a moment, breathe, reset, and try again. There are several ways to adjust, depending on the situation:

- If the participant may have missed part of what you said, repeat it using the same wording with a clear voice and a slightly slower rate.
- Try to rephrase using different words. Break the idea into smaller parts and check for understanding as you go.
- Be comfortable with allowing extra time and silence before you repeat or rephrase.
- Maximize gestures, intonation, facial expression.
- Use visuals—point, show, demonstrate.
- If needed, go back to what they had understood, and retry from that point.
- If appropriate, write down a few keywords and refer or even point to the words as you are talking.

Take responsibility for any communication breakdown. While you may feel frustrated or that it is your fault, remember that the participant may feel anxious or frustrated too. If they are still having difficulty you can retry later.

For hands-on activities, you can also offer support. For example, offer to help get their brushes ready, or you can show them the steps on another paper. You can even suggest and model further assistive strategies for the participant and their family member or friend—encouraging them to point or try a technique called "hand-over-hand' that will be described in a moment.

STRATEGIES TO SUPPORT EXPRESSION

Expression refers to how the participant communicates to you. Participants may express themselves verbally or nonverbally. As facilitators, we can adjust our approach to enable participants to have an easier time expressing themselves. A key element is for you, the facilitator, to be patient and show that you are engaged. Even in the later stages of dementia, participants are socially aware and will benefit from your engagement with them. It will help them to feel more relaxed, safe, appreciated, and valued, and that in turn will help enhance their ability to express themselves.

As with any interactive program, it is important to remain relaxed and "in the moment"—the conversation may venture off track and that is fine. Programs like *Artful Moments* are not about knowledge acquisition, but rather they are about connection with the museum objects and with each other. When the conversation goes off on a tangent enjoy the experience and model that openness for others.

Recognize that expression is not only verbal but that eye contact and gaze, facial expressions, tone of voice, and gestures are forms of nonverbal expression. Read the group and offer encouragement if no one is talking. Use a full group invitation such as, "I notice a lot of people smiling, do all of you like this piece?"

As you take the time to get to know your participants you will understand their abilities and preferences. You can adjust your questions to support each participant's level of expression. Two-choice questions or "yes" or "no" questions can be effective for participants who have difficulty composing a comment. Show or demonstrate choices so that the participant may refer to or point to their choice.

Find ways to incorporate a variety of options for expression—hands up to express opinions, thumbs up or down, pointing at things. These are easy and low-risk acts of participation that can engage and include even the more reluctant participants who are nervous about answering questions or volunteering ideas. These easier starts can sometimes lead to longer expressions. These are also great ways to include participants whose speech has been affected by dementia. Ensure everyone has an opportunity to express themselves.

When You Have Difficulty Understanding

Just as your participants will sometimes have difficulty understanding you, you will encounter times when you have trouble understanding what they are trying to express to you. Encourage the participant to continue trying—nod, smile, show that you are interested in what they have to say. Listen carefully and do not interrupt the participant's train of thought as they may have trouble remembering what they were going to say.

- Listen carefully to what the participant is saying and try to find a word or phrase that you can build upon.
- Verify what they have communicated by paraphrasing or repeating what you have heard. If you have not fully understood the person and you think they will be comfortable trying again, try asking them to repeat what they have said, or ask clarifying questions.
- Try to go back to what you last understood, verify that information, and then build forward.
- Pay attention to their body language, facial expression, and intonation for clues.
- If the participant can speak but cannot think of a certain word, ask them to describe it with prompts like asking what it is used for or what it looks like.

If you are still having trouble, acknowledge it. Take responsibility for the communication breakdown using statements like, "I'm sorry, I am not asking the right questions today! I care about what you have to say. Let's try again later." Be empathetic and reassuring, especially if emotions become heightened. Shift the focus away from the participant and use group action such as asking everyone who likes this picture to use a thumbs up or put your hand up. Remember that even if you cannot understand the participant after using all your strategies, the participant will appreciate your effort in trying to understand them.

In some cases, there are participants whom you simply cannot understand. For example, a participant in an early program had very earnest expressions, though we had difficulty understanding more than a few words when he spoke. Gestures were helpful in some cases. And in others, where he had a lot to say we paid close attention, and offered encouragement by smiling and nodding to continue sharing and to value his contribution. We verified his message using the words we had understood. For this participant, he was fully engaged "in the moment,' expressing his ideas in his own way and was valued for it. He enjoyed the program and we enjoyed his presence and engagement.

Challenging Situations

You may encounter situations where someone says or does something uncomfortable or inappropriate. This may be related to cognitive changes in self-regulation and insight. They may not realize that what they said was offensive or may have "lost their filter" and shared opinions that could unintentionally be hurtful to others. Examples include:

- Using language such as swearing, slang, derogatory language, or a racial slur.
- Continuing to speak "on and on" including over others.
- Sharing personal information that may make others uncomfortable.
- Touching artwork, objects, or the facilitator.

If a challenging situation happens, remind yourself of *why* it may have happened. Maintain composure and monitor your emotional reactions. If it is a small slip, you may simply ignore it. In other cases, modeling more appropriate language or actions can improve the situation. When comments are made that could be insensitive or insulting, acknowledge you have heard what was said and then rephrase with terms that are more sensitive language. You may redirect the conversation or if needed, engage the participant in a more suitable activity. If the offensive comment is not addressed, the participant may repeat it, making other participants uncomfortable.

As an example, in one program, we talked about a photograph by an Indigenous artist and a participant repeatedly used the term "Eskimo" and made comments about the clothing in the image that were culturally insensitive or out-of-date. The facilitator restated, using the correct term, to model better language choices for the group. To redirect insensitive comments, she refocused the group on the image and indicated that in this image the clothing in the image had specific names and meanings. She used the opportunity to highlight a more appropriate description using comments like, "From reading more about this artwork from our Inuit collection, I have learned that this woman's coat is called an amauti. Each family or community had specific ways of stitching or shaping the lower hemlines. This can help us know where the artist lived."

Your acknowledgment does not mean that you agree with the participant nor that you agree with their behavior, but it is a step in redirecting the behavior. It is also important if one participant says something to another that is uncomfortable, that you acknowledge it and redirect it so that both feel acknowledged.

Avoid arguing. Some participants will be unable to see other points of view or to understand things that contradict their ideas. Disagreeing or pursuing "being right" can lead to heightened negative emotions and stress. Remember that the cognitive changes that occur in dementia can make it difficult for the person to understand and retain new ideas, to see other perspectives, or to change a set idea.

When participants touch objects or the facilitator, the reasons are similar—changes in the brain can result in reduced inhibitions or self-regulation. Gently but firmly ask them not to touch (you or the object).

FACILITATION AND ASKING QUESTIONS

For many programs, asking questions is a foundational method of encouraging conversation. This strategy is central to our program approach provided that the facilitator pays careful attention to the types of questions they ask and that they closely observe the participants' responses to ensure the question is a good match for their abilities. Questioning is an art form and one that can be developed with practice. Likely, you already use this skill regularly in other programs and that experience will help you here.

- What questions do you ask in other programs?
- What types of responses do they elicit?
- What are different ways to ask for information or ideas from your group?
- What are you hoping to observe?

Create questions for your program in advance, including how the question can be asked in a modified way. This will save you from scrambling on the spot.

De-centering Yourself

The shift from a content-centered approach to one that is person-centered is about more than simply asking questions. Posing questions and encouraging participants to respond does make your program more interactive but to be truly centered on the participant you must do more.

In a traditional learning environment, regardless of our approach, we plan the content delivery to achieve certain goals—we want participants to learn specific things. When we ask questions, they are often designed to lead participants into arriving at a predetermined idea. We may welcome lots of responses and ideas but with gentle guidance, we move participants toward specific answers. In many ways, the facilitator is the center of this kind of discussion. They are the leader, "in charge" of the experience.

This approach is great for learning. Museum objects offer rich opportunities for reflection, connection, and critical thinking. They can teach us a lot, whether in their social/historical/philosophical context, scientific or technical narratives, or aesthetic ideas. Museums are a wealth of educational opportunities.

A person-centered approach is something different. When we center the participant, we de-center the facilitator. Being person-centered is about bringing the participant and the object together and seeing what happens. Everyone is equal in the conversation. We ask questions to ease people into conversations and to encourage them to share their ideas. We follow wherever they lead.

That is not to say that we do not plan content. We research chosen objects and develop questions to help guide us but we use this preparation to have knowledge at hand when or if we need it. Sometimes a conversation may go in another direction entirely. Museum educator Andrew Westover expresses it well when he says, "If I am going in front of a work of art, I want to have as much information as I can, not because I want to spew it out (because ideally, I don't even share 10 percent of that information) but if someone asks, I can give them something tangible that advances [the conversation]."[2]

Part of this approach is remembering our knowledge of dementia, particularly as it relates to supporting changes in memory and new learning. As a person experiences changes in their brain due to dementia, new information may be remembered. As such, our focus is on the experience more than on building new knowledge.

The other part is our focus on the social experience. Conversational programs have the opportunity to tap into long-term memory and other skills as they proceed. When hearing the ideas of others, participants may be reminded of their own experiences and be able to make personal contributions to the conversation. As facilitators, we can encourage this by leaving space and supporting input. As Westover shares in his ideas of value-driven teaching, the nuances in each person's observations and the care that we as facilitators impart to both the participants and the objects become the "connective tissue that propels us forward" in the experience.[3]

The most enjoyable conversations are often the liveliest where everyone can contribute ideas and the talk may travel in unexpected directions. When interest and individual contributions take the lead, participants are empowered in their experience. They feel valued and connected.

Questions to "Get a Sense" of the Participant

Getting to know your participants is essential for a program's success. It is important to have a period and process of observation and "assessment" at the start of each session. This does not mean that you should try to diagnose or label a participant's condition, abilities, or progression but simply use what you see and hear to inform your approach. You can use careful questioning to do this.

Over time you will come to know participants by name, by the ways they typically interact and participate in the program, and what their abilities and mindset are like most times. Because of the changes that happen with dementia, you will see fluctuations in cognition, language and communication, perception, mood, and physical abilities. These fluctuations can occur within a session, from one session to the next, and across a program. This is why careful, ongoing observation is so important.

Start with a direct, but open, question and see how people respond. We often use questions like, "Tell me what you see when you look at this painting" or "What is the first thing that catches your attention?" These questions are not fact-based, can be answered in several ways, and are errorless. Both are also direct in telling participants how to answer. In particular, the second version tells them that they only need to share one thing that they notice. Several different kinds of responses are possible. The participant may:

- Answer with very concrete, simple observations, "I see a dog, and a man and a woman."
- Provide a more complex answer: "A man and a woman are talking on a bridge, and she seems to be telling him something."
- Respond with an unrelated answer, "Today I came on the bus, and I missed my lunch."
- Have difficulty answering at all.

By listening to how each participant responds, you will have many clues as to how to proceed. Based on the kind of answer you hear, ask yourself some questions and use your observations to guide you.

- Did it seem easy or difficult for the participant to compose an answer or initiate speaking?
- Did they speak right away or take time to find the words?
- Was the answer related to the artwork?
- Did they understand the question?
- Did they look to their family member or friend for help or clarification?
- What kinds of words or gestures did they use?

Take note of each participant's response and how they looked and acted. Your approach will likely be different for each person depending on their abilities. When starting a new program, we do this step at the start of every session and at several points during a conversation. It is a good check-in to test how well your approach is working. In every case, always be prepared to adjust—the rate of speech or vocabulary that you use, the length of sentences, the complexity of the questions, and the type of answers that you ask for. Step questions up or down based on replies. Try to adjust your level of vocabulary to match or suit the level used by your participant when possible.

As you facilitate a conversation, be sure to connect with each participant regularly. Use follow-up questions to move the conversation along. If you observe difficulties, ask that participant a related question in a different way. We usually ask several participants the same question in a row, paraphrasing their responses as we go so that each person feels engaged and connected to the group. This helps the participant to maintain attention. Have a plan but always be prepared to adapt on the fly.

The Basics—Five Types of Questions

The types of questions you ask can have a huge impact on participants' engagement and their ability to participate. By selecting different questioning styles, you can adapt your approach to support each participant's abilities, ensuring that everyone is able to contribute to the conversation and feels included and valued. Here are five different types of questions to consider:

1) Open-Ended Questions

Open-ended questions can be answered in a variety of ways and do not have a single, correct answer. They are useful in encouraging people to share in whatever way they are able and put the participant in control of the direction of the conversation. Examples are: *"What do you see?"* or *"What is the first thing that catches your attention?"*

Open-ended questions can be useful to help you decide how to continue the conversation. For the participant who is comfortable responding to open-ended questions with limited support, you may encourage them to share their ideas with similar questions. You may also opt to draw out more using probing questions.

2) Probing Questions

A probe is used to follow-up on a participant's response and encourages further conversation without influencing the answer. You can probe for clarity, to draw out more information, or to encourage further looking. Examples are: "What do you think the object is for?" or "What makes you say that."

Open-ended and probing questions are a great way to empower participants to share and lead their own experiences. However, it can be difficult for some participants to formulate and process a response without support. For participants whose answers are more concrete or those who may have some difficulties, you can shift to more directed questioning styles that help participants know how to answer or what they should look for.

3) Leading Questions

Another option for guiding conversation is to use leading questions where multiple answers will work but participants are guided in the ways that they might answer. You may guide them by the words you use to phrase the question, helping them along the way. For example, you might say: "You might notice that the woman is smiling at the man. The man appears to be holding flowers and he is smiling too. Do you think they know each other?"

4) Closed Questions

For participants who need further support, closed questions have a limited set of possible answers, but suggest a response that is not simply "yes" or "no". Examples are: "What season do you see in this photo?" If needed, you could add a cue, "What season do you think the artist is showing, Winter? Spring? Summer? Or Fall?"

Closed questions are beneficial in helping narrow the possible responses. They support participants with word-finding challenges and those who may have difficulty organizing their responses. Possible answers can also be cued by the facilitator. Try to avoid fact-based questions, as they can cause stress for people who do not know the right answer. If you want participants to know a fact, just tell them, don't make it a question. If you ask a participant to choose between several options, consider a secondary cue like a printed list to support memory changes.

5) Binary Questions

Binary questions offer further support with a targeted answer and can be used for both verbal and nonverbal responses, including nodding, pointing, or thumbs up/down. There are many options for two-choice questions, including sharing opinions and confirming understanding. A yes/no question can be used to open dialogue if either answer is possible and allows space for individual choice or opinion. For example: *Did you notice the dog? Is this a winter scene? Do you think this painting took a few months, or a few years, to complete?*

Supported Questioning

Supported questioning in a group is a way of including everyone in the conversation, by asking for similar information from each participant, but asking in a way that is suitable for the individual. A supported questioning process helps each participant contribute using a communication method that works for them. It provides enough space for individuality but also accommodates different abilities. One person may be asked in a way that accommodates a thumbs up/down response, while another may be asked for a descriptive word or observation.

The types of questions just described present a scale of styles from the least supportive (open-ended) to the most supportive (binary). You can move up and down the scale in your engagement with a single participant as needed or as you engage different members of the group. For example:

"This room includes familiar furniture. (it includes an historical setting with a bed, a dresser, a comfortable chair, and a mirror). Ella, do you think this is a bedroom? Does everyone else see a bedroom too? Arwen, would you like to sleep in this room? Priti, do you think the room was for an adult or a child? Can you tell me why you think so?"

In this example, all of the questions are related to identifying the room as a bedroom but in each case, the participant's abilities are considered. Questions allow for individual responses and a group consensus question to get everyone involved. Some are binary, with cued responses, while the last question offers an open-ended option for a participant who is able to respond in that way. The facilitator switches from one style to another in the natural flow of conversation.

Creating Questions

Each of these types of questions can be useful to support participants and their abilities. The best approach is to vary your question types throughout your conversation and be prepared to adapt them on the fly as you need. It is a good idea to have some pre planned questions in mind before you begin, so take some time to practice. Figure 8.1 shows how to use observations to adapt your questions.

To practice, choose an object from your museum to write questions that will spark conversation with a group. Practice rephrasing them into different question types. This practice will help you become comfortable asking questions in different ways. You will be better able to support your participants' understanding, expression, and engagement. Reflect on what you've written for questions-what types of questions do you favor? Practice expanding how you ask questions. Plan for variety, flexibility, and role play shifting smoothly between question styles.

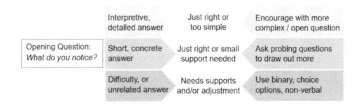

After an opening question, pay attention to the answer. How a participant answers will provide clues about their engagement, understanding and ability to reply. Adjust accordingly for each person, and you will have a connected, engaged group.

Figure 8.1   Adjusting Questions to Support and Engage. Responding to each participant based on their participation helps to improve engagement. This diagram shows how to adjust questions to better support a range of abilities. *Source*: Art Gallery of Hamilton.

An Example of Adjusting Questions

This conversation took place in front of a painting called *Agreeable Meeting* by William Blair Bruce (figure 8.2).

Facilitator: *"Mary, what is the first thing you notice in this painting?"—the answer can be a list of items, a description of the time, place, interaction.... There are LOTS of different ways to answer.*

Mary: *"I see a man and a woman and a dog." The facilitator's follow-up can be something like, "What are the man and woman doing?" OR "Does it seem like they know each other?" Mary can continue to share her ideas for a few moments.*

Facilitator: *"Simon, did you notice what the two people are wearing?"—the answer can be a description of colors, styles, time period, and can be simple or complex BUT it has also given this participant something specific to look at.*

Simon: *"The man is wearing work clothes and the woman is wearing a dress." Follow-up questions can be used to continue or the facilitator can move on to another participant.*

Facilitator: *"Nancy, is the woman happy to see the man? Do you think yes or no?" (while modeling thumbs up or down since she knows that Nancy has difficulty speaking). Nancy gestures "'thumbs up" and smiles.*

In this conversation, the facilitator has included three participants who may have very different abilities in a single conversation. The flow is smooth, and no one seems to be singled out with a specialized approach. Each responds in their own way and contributes to the experience. Each feels validated, included, and pleased to share an experience.

- Mary's question is open—she may choose any aspect of the painting to comment on and can be as concrete or interpretive as she wishes.
- Simon's question is still open but the facilitator has helped a little by focusing on clothing. He may answer in a variety of ways but has a cue about where to start.

Figure 8.2 An Agreeable Meeting. This painting is a popular conversation starter, with many different entry points. Participants may list people and objects they see, discuss the weather or speculate on what the two people are talking about. William Blair Bruce (Canadian 1859–1906) *Agreeable Meeting* 1893 oil on canvas Art Gallery of Hamilton, Bruce Memorial Donation 1914 Photo credit: Art Gallery of Hamilton

- Nancy's question supports her strengths. While she cannot speak she can understand. A binary question is supported and modeled through two choices with hand gestures. Nancy may answer "yes" or "no" based on her own opinion and the facilitator can draw out more ideas with carefully worded follow-up questions.

As the conversation continues, a participant may have difficulty answering:

Facilitator: *"Frances, what season do you see in the painting?" She appears puzzled, as shown by the expression on her face, and she turns to her family member for help. She seems to have difficulty starting an answer.*

Facilitator: *"Frances, this doesn't look like winter, does it?" (Frances shakes her head)—"Do you think it is summer or autumn?"*

Frances: *"I think it is autumn." She may leave it at that or having started, she may be able to elaborate, telling us that she notices there are few leaves on the trees.*

If she still has difficulty, the question could be further adjusted to have a single choice, or a "yes" or "no" answer such as, "I notice that there are not a lot of leaves on the trees—does this look like autumn to you?"

On the other hand, for another participant, asking which season may be too simple a question. You could ask a more complex question like, "What do you notice in the painting that tells you about the season" or simply, "What is the weather like?"

This is our approach to adapting a question—making it more or less complex to match the participant's abilities. Your baseline will be asked at a general level that is open enough to allow for a few different kinds of answers. Based on what you hear and see you will proceed more concretely for a participant who needs more support or a more expansive way for the participant with more to say.

After some time together, you will have a sense of the level of questions that will be successful for each person though you may also need to adjust on the fly when difficulties occur. If asking one way does not work, step back and ask another way.

Practice this approach with the questions you already ask—step up to a more sophisticated question and step down to a two-choice question and a "yes" or "no" question to familiarize yourself with the strategy.

Modifying Your Questions

You already have many great questions in your tool kit—think about your experiences with other tour groups, your planning process, and the kinds of things you want to know. Practice modifying your questions to suit your participants. If you can, have the object or a good reproduction nearby.

Practice by writing several questions that start a conversation or encourage participants to look and think about your object. Use our examples and your knowledge of dementia to adjust them to suit participants with different abilities. In this case, the focus is on progressively adjusting an initial question to offer additional support or stimulation "in the moment" during your conversation.

Responding to Unrelated Answers

In some cases, a participant may respond in an unrelated way. They may have been distracted by something, they may be answering something asked in a previous moment, or they might just be disconnected from the moment. When this happens, there are a few strategies to try:

- Acknowledge what they have said and then repeat yourself and try to redirect or reorient the participant to the activity.

- Ask another question to clarify what they are thinking about or gently guide or lead them back into the conversation—acting as a bridge to get them back on track.
- Leave space for them to express themselves and validate their contribution.

Depending on the person, a combination or sequential use of these strategies can be appropriate. One of our goals in the program is to instill a sense of value and self-esteem in the participants. They want to feel a sense of belonging and by sharing something with the group, that feeling is accomplished. You show respect and inclusion by hearing them, by helping them to respond, and by taking the time to try to understand and guide them closer to the topic of discussion. For a participant who is not answering the question asked, we still show respect by, simply listening and encouraging them to share. Here is an example that occurred while showing a painting of a large waterfall:

Facilitator: *"Joe, have you seen a waterfall as large as this one?"*
Joe: *"I used to go fishing with my brother. He was trouble, that little one. Always trouble (smiling)."*
Facilitator: *"Joe, you mentioned fishing. Does this waterfall remind you of fishing as a boy?"*
Joe: *"So much trouble (laughing). Never stopped, that one."*
Facilitator: *"Joe, it sounds like you've had some adventures with your brother. This scene with so much water helps us think of other places with water. Such a lovely waterfall. Mary, have you seen a waterfall as large as this one?"*

Do's and Don'ts of Effective Questions

Creating the right kinds of questions is essential in your approach. Over time you will adjust the type and level of complexity naturally but when starting out it is a great idea to have a few options preplanned. The way you facilitate those questions is equally important to ensure engagement. Here are a few of the most important tips to keep in mind when delivering your questions to a group of participants:

DO:

- Ask only one question at a time and wait until the answers are given before adding a follow-up.
- Leave space and quiet for participants to process and respond.
- Listen to the answers and offer positive encouragement and feedback.
- Repeat or paraphrase answers to help others hear and understand.
- Adjust questions from one participant to another to match abilities.
- Ask a variety of types of questions with different types of responses.
- Ensure that each person in the group is called upon regularly to ensure attention and engagement.

DON'T:

- Ask fact-based questions or questions with only one correct answer.
- Ask recall questions—whether recalling from previous conversations or past experiences.
- Argue with participants or correct their answers.
- Rush or jump in too quickly to over-explain or fill silences.
- Cut off a participant when their answer seems unrelated to the question.

OFFERING FEEDBACK

Encouragement and validation go a long way in building a participant's confidence, trust, and ability to participate in a program. In all that we do, we aim to facilitate engagement, and social connection, and build self-esteem. A great way to do this is to make the environment a positive and supportive one. The ways we offer feedback and the types of feedback we give can have a big impact on how a participant feels in our programs.

During Conversations

Answering a question or sharing an idea can feel like a big risk. Participants may be reluctant to speak—they may be afraid of making a mistake or they may worry about what others will think about their choice of words or the way they speak. Add to that someone who might feel self-conscious about their abilities or who has difficulties with understanding or expression and participation can be difficult. As facilitators, we can model ways to participate, we can adjust how we ask questions and we can offer feedback.

Engaged listening is when we pay careful attention to what the participant is saying, whether through words or nonverbally. Gestures, eye contact, nodding, or smiling all show that we hear and value the participant's input. This subtle encouragement can help someone to keep trying even when they are having difficulties. It lets them know that you are interested and that what they think matters. Tips to remember:

- Ask questions to further explore and answer
- Rephrase to show understanding
- Thank participants for their contribution
- Make positive comments to acknowledge their participation
- Use what one participant has said as a bridge into the next questions—for example., "Mary shared that she saw that the vase chipped. Felice, what do you see?"

Asking questions to further explore an answer, and rephrasing to show understanding builds on that, as does thanking the participant for their contribution or making other positive comments to acknowledge the participation. We can also acknowledge contributions by using what one person said as a bridge to ask someone else. "Mary shared that she saw the vase was chipped. Felice, what do you see?"

During Hands-On Activities

As participants are working, move around the room. Take time to observe, comment, or ask questions about their activity. This shows your interest in having them there and it allows them to show their enjoyment or to look for further support. It continues the building of relationships and trust.

Sharing work at the end can feel like a big risk. Not everyone will want to share and that is okay. When someone does share, always try to offer positive and authentic feedback. Empty compliments are easy to see through and offer little value in building trust or confidence. When you see a finished activity, look for a detail or an aspect that you can comment on to make your feedback personal and meaningful. You can compliment their creative approach, their color choice, or the subject they have chosen. No matter what the work, you can always find something to be specific and positive about.

NOTES

1. This discussion about who holds the responsibility to continue conversation and engagement was part of a workshop led by Anna Ortigara, a Gerontological Clinical Nurse Specialist, at St. Peter's Hospital, Hamilton, 2004.
2. "Values-Engaged Gallery Teaching with Andrew Westover," *Art Engager Podcast* Episode 102, January 25, 2024, https://thinkingmuseum.com/captivate-podcast/values-engaged-gallery-teaching/.
3. Westover, "Values Engaged Teaching."

9

Working with Family and Friends

For many participants, having family members, friends, or other companions join them in a program is an important part of the experience. Attending with someone can offer participants support in traveling to and from a program, in wayfinding, and even as a helper in conversations or hands-on activities. For virtual programs, they may assist with technology needs as well. While not every participant needs extra support from a companion, for many having a friend or family member join them in a shared experience adds to their success and enjoyment. And for the family and friends, the pleasure of sharing experiences with their loved ones is very meaningful.

Depending on the participant's comfort and ability, some may feel very able and at ease joining a program independently. Attending on their own also enables a participant to take pleasure in both the program activities themselves and the social relationships that develop among the other participants and staff.

HELPING HANDS

In Part I, we described our initial motivation for including a family member or friend: we had hoped that a second set of hands to help with activities and maximize the participant's involvement and enjoyment. While this did occur we also saw so much more. We saw loved ones connecting fondly "in the moment." We saw thoughtful co-creation of artworks. We saw communication that took advantage of the different subjects, materials, and modes of expression that we presented through art. We saw enjoyable moments for the family members and friends that were completely removed from any care-based activity, offering them engagement, respite, and social connection.

Our observations solidified our commitment to a person-centered approach, valuing both the participant and their family member or friend as partners in the program experience. Our goal is to support relationship building and equip caregivers with strategies to enhance their experience. Here are some key considerations:

* How can we ensure both the participant and family member or friend can engage meaningfully?
* What does participation look like for family and friends? This could involve parallel engagement, co-creation, and collaboration, directed creation, or being an engaged observer. Each of these will be explained in a moment.

We can help family and friends manage their expectations and provide them with tools for success. Through our interactions, we can model supportive and assistive strategies for caregivers.

Balancing Engagement

Family members and friends have an important role to play in supporting their loved one in their changing abilities. They are most familiar with the participant—their likes and dislikes, their personal history, their preferred communication style, and their abilities. Family and friends can help both the participant and the facilitator in supporting participation.

One of the first and most comforting ways a family member or friend they can support the participant is simply through their presence. They offer a familiar face and voice. They provide comfort and a sense of safety to help reassure the participant in an unfamiliar environment. They are there to navigate through physical locations and processes that might be intimidating alone.

The experience shared between participant and their family and friends builds strong social connection. As we connect with each member of the group we are helping them to share the experience and so we include everyone present when asking questions, sharing hands-on work, and in the general conversation throughout each session. Family and friends are included as valued members of the larger group. For virtual programs, we even include friends or family members from different addresses to join from their homes and participate together.

That said, including everyone takes time. It means more voices, more ideas, and more waiting for a turn to share with everyone. To be a good facilitator, you have to keep track of who is speaking and who is waiting to ensure sustained engagement for all. It is a balancing act throughout each session.

This is where group size can affect the degree to which family and friends are called upon and included. As we prioritize participants, we call on them first, we call on them more often, and we focus our instructions on them. If we feel that a family member or friend is taking over the conversation, we gently redirect the focus by asking the participants to share their thoughts about the conversation. The larger your group and the more family and friends you have in a group, the more they have to sit back and allow the participant to shine.

A Helpful Presence

In addition to sharing a meaningful experience, family and friends can significantly enhance a participant's experience by assisting with participation as needed. While some participants may not require support initially, facilitators can model and encourage supportive strategies as abilities change. Family and friends can:

- **Clarify communication:** Repeat, rephrase, or remind participants of familiar concepts to aid understanding.
- **Build connections:** Add personal details to conversations.
- **Model participation:** Demonstrate responses and actions during activities.
- **Support hands-on activities:** Repeat steps, demonstrate techniques, or offer targeted assistance.
- **Language support:** Bilingual companions can translate or offer prompts for participants speaking another language.

Be careful that supporting does not change into taking over and "doing for" or "answering for" the person. Even though well-intentioned, family and friends can sometimes benefit from redirection, modeling of supportive actions, or gentle reminders of the program goal—engagement.

Managing Expectations

It is important to understand, and in some cases, manage the expectations and comfort of the family member or friend. They remember what the participant was like at an earlier stage in their life. They will know how much their abilities have changed and may carry a variety of feelings about those changes, even when the participant may not be bothered by or aware of the changes.

Here we refer back to the idea of stigma that was covered in Part I. Stigma is not just about carrying negative attitudes about people who have been diagnosed with dementia, it is also present in the feelings that others may have for the people with dementia in their lives. For some, these feelings are very present and, for others, they can be unconscious. They may include embarrassment, worry or fear, frustration, uncertainty, or a strong need to "help." Stigma can sometimes lead to isolation as others may be worried about taking their loved ones to public places or programs.

Museum programs like *Artful Moments* are very beneficial to help everyone see the participant as capable, creative, and welcome. Family members and friends may experience negative feelings because they feel bad about the changes the participant is experiencing. They may also worry about what others think of the person they love and want to compensate or improve their "performance." We have regularly experienced family members who make apologies or express distress over the perceived errors or delays from their participants.

To help the family and friends overcome their discomfort or their overactive need to "help," we must make sure to reinforce the goals of the program. Teach them what success looks like in the context of the program and model supportive and encouraging strategies. For many, observing validation or positive feedback for their loved ones goes a long way toward helping them feel relieved or proud.

What This Means in Practice

As facilitators, to truly support the experience of the participant we must consistently model and reinforce our purpose, helping the family members and friends to embrace and take part in the philosophy and approach that we use. This means:

- Remembering the goals and philosophy of the program.
- Defining and understanding what success looks like.
- Reinforcing that engagement and pleasure are in the process not the result.
- Taking pleasure in the experience and the sharing of it with a loved one.

WHEN FAMILY AND FRIENDS ARE TOO INVOLVED

To restate our philosophy, our programs provide meaningful, individualized, and engaging activities that encourage participants to be creative, to express themselves, and to connect with others through shared experiences. Our focus is on enhancing the strengths and abilities of the participant regardless of their abilities, state of health, or social circumstances. We focus on the process and the experience rather than a final product or demonstration of learning.

- The primary objectives are engagement and social connection—we are here to have fun together and to share an enjoyable experience.
- We work to enhance strengths and use strategies to enhance.
- The focus is on enjoying the experience, not what the outcome that is created looks like or the words that are spoken. It is about the process, not the product. There is no single, correct way to participate, no best answer, and no "'doing it right" when being creative.

We have found that sometimes family and friends are so eager for the participant to "'do well" that they worry when they think they are not performing. They sometimes have unrealistic or unnecessary expectations that put pressure on themselves and the participants. You may observe this when they answer for the participant, correct their answers or hands-on efforts. They may even take over an activity. We work to adjust our approach for family and friends to suit their needs as well, aiming to support their experiences in spending time together in what may be a completely new activity. For some this is easy and for some, it is not.

Stories from the Museum: Steven and Adele

What we saw: Steven had experienced significant changes in his abilities that were particularly evident during hands-on activities. He had been a painter earlier in his life with a great deal of skill in creating representational works. During the program, he was able to use a paintbrush with gentle prompting but his work consisted of simple shapes and areas of color in sections of his paper. On numerous occasions, we observed that his partner was having difficulty with his abilities "in the moment." At times she would take the brush from him to choose the colors and would sometimes paint for him. She was concerned that he was taking too long and that he "wasn't doing it right" or keeping up with the demonstration. She seemed embarrassed or sad about the changes her husband was experiencing and apologized for him to the facilitator on several occasions.

What we did: Steven was content to paint himself or to let his partner paint for him. If she tried to help him he would let her take over the work and watch. We hoped to increase his engagement in the activities by encouraging him to paint himself. We also hoped to help Adele see (and celebrate) positive engagement rather than feel embarrassed or that her partner was "not good enough." Our challenge was to support Adele in understanding the goal of the program and in feeling comfortable with the process and results in whatever form they took. We used four strategies—validation, modeling, individual reassurance, and redirection.

Validation: We provide regular, personalized, and authentic comments to the participants about their successes. This could be as simple as commenting on the colors that Steven chose or that we liked some aspect of his work. We invited Adele into the validation by saying things like, "Steven, I really enjoy the colors you have used here. Adele, isn't this an interesting arrangement?" Validating each participant's actions and contributions helps both the participant and their family or friends feel better about their experiences. We aim to put everyone at ease.

Modeling: We consistently model positive feedback and supportive techniques to help family and friends assist their loved ones in a way that maintains independence and choice for the participants as they work. This could be simple prompts, questions, or gentle assistance. We also showed them how to demonstrate off to the side rather than on the participant's work.

Individual Reassurance: While the above two strategies are often helpful in making an uncomfortable family member or friend feel better, there are times when we need to be more direct. At the end of the program, the facilitator chatted privately with Adele about her feelings and offered suggestions. These conversations included reminders about the program goals, highlighting the successes that we saw—that Steven was making independent choices and taking pleasure in his work and suggesting other ways she could help rather than doing the work for him. We also left space for her to share her feelings and concerns and reassured her that the participation we saw from her partner was good and that we saw success.

Redirection: One way to reinforce the shared experience between participants and family and friends is to encourage both to participate fully. In this case, this meant giving Adele a canvas and paints and encouraging her to make an artwork of her own, rather than supervising Steven's work. Having her own work to complete refocused her attention, kept her busy, and by default switched her approach to demonstrating her work rather than inadvertently taking over his. They shared the experience and she had a positive result for herself too.

PARTNERED PARTICIPATION STYLES

Throughout the program, family and friends can be a great support, offering comfort, reassurance, and assistance by repeating and clarifying information and completing tasks that may be too difficult for the participant on their own. During each session, we offer both conversations about museum objects and hands-on activities, and we aim to have each person participate as fully as possible. Depending on the participant's abilities, there are several different ways for them to participate with a family member or friend.

Parallel Engagement

When little assistance is needed, the participant and their family member or friend participate individually, answering questions, contributing to conversations, and creating hands-on responses. Each person is called upon separately, has their own materials, and follows the demonstration by the educator. Often, we see the pair conversing, sharing ideas and comments on the other's work. It is a shared experience. Where the participant has difficulties, their family member or friend can help, by repeating instructions, offering prompts to continue working, or demonstrating what to do on the side. The facilitator can also support this process as they move around the room using similar techniques.

Co-creation and Collaboration

Where more support is needed both people can work together. Questions may be asked individually, using the family member or friend to model answers and encourage the participant. For hands-on work, each performs certain tasks with a discussion about who does what. Often the family member or friend will complete the more difficult tasks at the direction of the participant but both have a hand in the work. For some, this is a helpful step where a participant's abilities have changed but, for others, it is just a fun way to work.

Directed Creation

Where abilities have changed and the participant cannot complete certain activities, the family member or friend typically does most or all of the actual hands-on work, but the participant tells or shows them what to do. In conversations, we still try to use other supportive strategies to empower the participants to answer and participate for themselves. During the hands-on activity the participant will choose the colors, shapes, or materials and then point out where they should go. This is a good way to draw out a participant who may have withdrawn from the activity or whose abilities have been more affected by their dementia.

Engaged Observer

While we try to encourage participants to be as involved and self-directed as possible, for some this just is not possible due to interest, mood, or abilities. For participants like this, simply being part of a group, listening to a conversation, or seeing their family member or friend create a hands-on activity is enjoyable, as is the conversation or interaction that can happen while the family member or friend works. In some cases, watching may lead to more participation later but, for others, even this level of engagement offers many benefits. In our work with participants in the later stages of dementia, being an engaged observer was a demonstration of success and engagement "in the moment."

STRATEGIES TO SUPPORT PARTICIPATION.

Having just discussed the different ways that participants can engage in activities, we now focus on four specific strategies or techniques to support that participation. From participants and their family and friends who are unsure about what they should do to those who have difficulties acting, you will find that these strategies can be useful to support meaningful and enjoyable participation.

Modeling

We have talked about modeling throughout this section as an effective and gentle way to guide and improve participation, whether that be ways of communicating or acting, word choices, or strategies to support participants. Modeling is demonstrating through your own actions, words, and methods, the preferred actions, words, and methods that you want your participants and their family member or friend to follow.

This strategy should be front of mind in everything you do. Seeing a facilitator in action is a great cue for others to follow, learn, and help. We aim to lead by example and offer additional subtle interventions to continue positive engagement.

Pair Questions

This strategy is useful for participants who have difficulty understanding or expressing their ideas or as a way to build social connections in pairs. Essentially, you ask a question to both people at once. To use this strategy in a subtle and considerate way, address a question to both members of the pair and ask them together to share their ideas or ask the participant to tell their partner. Family and friends know the participant well and can quietly rephrase, explain, or translate to another language what is being asked and then support answering in the same way.

For example, you could ask, "Nico and Manuel, this table is set for a fancy dinner. Is this the kind of table you would set at home?" In this case, both people could answer together by nodding or shaking their heads. Nico might then answer first, as the family member, saying something like, "Actually, at our house, we have a much smaller table for just the two of us." The facilitator or Nico could then ask Manuel about the small table at home. Both have been engaged together initially, and Nico offered a response to model how to answer. As family and friends become accustomed to the flow of questions they will often jump in with follow-up questions to the participant themselves.

This strategy requires a careful touch so that the family member or friend is supporting and encouraging the participant to participate rather than simply speaking for them. If it does not work this way at first, try again until you get it right. If need be, find a moment to chat with the family member or friend to explain what you are trying to accomplish so that they can act more purposefully.

Directing and Pointing

This strategy can be used in both the conversation and the activity part of the program. Where a participant has difficulty answering questions, the facilitator or the family member or friend can offer two or more choices in the form of words, pictures, or other relevant manipulatives and the participant points to their choice. The facilitator can then share this choice with the group. In hands-on activities, as described earlier, participants can point out their choices of materials and then point out where they want their family member or friend to put them.

Hand-Over-Hand/Hand-Under-Hand

This strategy can be used to support a participant in hands-on activities but should be used sparingly by a facilitator, as it requires close contact and physically moving the participant's hands for them. It is a great strategy to model for the family member or friend, where this close proximity is more comfortable. Essentially, this strategy allows the participant to use materials—to draw or paint, for example, with assistance.

Hand-over-Hand: is when the participant holds a pencil or tool and the partner gently places their hand over top and moves the participant's hand around, effectively guiding or leading the mark-making. It is a collaborative action that results in some kind of artwork or activity. Hand-over-hand is often used as a way to demonstrate something or to get the participant started, shifting to the participant working on their own when they are ready. To be effective, the participant must be able to hold the tool and be willing to be helped. Figure 9.1 illustrates how this approach can be used effectively.

Hand-under-Hand: is when the partner holds the tool and the participant's hand is on top leading the movement. This strategy is effective for participants who may have difficulties holding tools but are still interested in doing the activity. They are more in charge of what happens in this version.

Figure 9.1 Hand-Over-Hand Support. For some participants, having hand-over-hand guidance to participate in an activity is helpful. This may be enough to start some participants working independently. For others it is the difference between acting or not. Source: istock.com/Edwin tan.

EMPATHY AND EMOTIONS

We are mindful that families and friends carry a great deal of emotions with them as they watch their loved one progress through the stages of dementia. Always remember to be gentle with them, aware that they are managing many demands, and often navigating complex circumstances. They are doing the best that they can. In addition, they may also be a source and/or a victim of stigma as well. Despite all that they are going through, they are "there," in the moment, participating with their loved one, even when they may not feel confident or at ease themselves. Our role is to support the best that we can, model strategies, and demonstrate an engaging, inclusive experience.

Try to model best practices throughout your program—how to communicate, how to participate, how to support. There is a lot to be learned through participation and observation.

- Find regular opportunities to talk about program goals—to enjoy time together, to share ideas, and to have fun in the process of looking, talking, and participating in hands-on activities. This is helpful when validating the contributions of participants and during conversations and activities.
- Acknowledge that they may be trying something for the first time and emphasize the importance of having fun and that there are no wrong answers.
- Where needed take opportunities to engage with a participant and their family member or friend to suggest ways that they can work together.
- Where necessary, find a private moment to speak to the family member or friend to offer individualized guidance, reassurance, and suggestions. This can be at the end of a session, or by a follow-up phone call.

10

Staffing and Communication

The secret to a great program lies with the team. The best programs combine clear communication, trust, and an understanding of the museum's collection. It is essential to have team members who are flexible, organized, and know how to help participants successfully engage. With *Artful Moments* we are very fortunate to have built an amazing team that includes program staff and volunteers who bring a diversity of experiences, knowledge, and facilitation styles. They have knowledge of learning pedagogy, art and art-making strategies, and clinical experience in working with people living with dementia, and each contributes to the overall philosophy, development, and delivery of our programs.

BUILDING YOUR TEAM

As a museum beginning this work, you may not have all of the expertise on staff. We encourage you to reach out to others in your community. Many community organizations can support you in knowledge acquisition, training, consulting, and more.

Facilitators and supporting staff or volunteers must be properly trained. They need to have knowledge of the participants. This means understanding dementia, its effects, and the strategies that can be used to support the changing abilities. Your team must also have knowledge of the museum site and its holdings.

Ideally, a program team should consist of two to four people whose roles are clear and are identified to the participants:

- The facilitator leads the conversations about art or objects. They draw the participants into the experience.
- Where appropriate, an additional facilitator leads the hands-on activities though one person can cover both of these roles.
- A support staff or volunteer is very helpful in building engagement—they can watch participants to see who is participating, who is not, and offer prompts to try to re-engage them. The support person can also help by being a kind of "plant" in the audience whom the facilitator can call upon when conversation stalls or to help model participation.
- For virtual and phone-based programs, a support person is very helpful to manage the technology side of things—monitoring chats, making calls, having sidebar conversations.
- For programs that include research or evaluation, consider having a support person dedicated to recording observations.
- Where possible, we also highly recommend having someone with knowledge and experience with dementia join your team even in a short-term capacity. This person can offer coaching as a program develops. There are many service providers who may be able to help.

- The program team should be consistent throughout the program. Comfort and relationship building are important aspects of social connection and the trust that forms allows for much richer participation.

With a team of people working together, be sure that everyone knows what is expected of them and when and where to participate. Some of our support volunteers participate by engaging participants in questions or conversation while others remain in the background. Be cautious—a small number of staff participants can build camaraderie but too many can be overwhelming for everyone.

When preparing to build a program team, think about your current staff, contract facilitators, volunteers, and community partners along with each person's skills and interests. At the same time consider the program you plan to present and the capacity of your existing team to take on one or multiple roles. Identify gaps in knowledge and experience and consider how you will address these needs. This will help you to plan new staff and volunteer needs, as well as their training.

Reflection, Sharing, and Learning

One of the most valuable learning experiences for us when we first started was the opportunity for a ten- to fifteen-minute debrief at the end of each session once the participants had left. This provided the Gallery team with an opportunity to pose questions or problems we had experienced during the session for immediate feedback about the session. The hospital team we were working with had a deep knowledge about dementia and about the specific participants in the program so their observations and advice were very valuable.

The experience was so powerful that we have continued this habit through all of our programs. If you are co-facilitating with others or if you work with community partners, a short debrief can be a wonderful learning opportunity. It is a great time to share observations and discuss challenges and new strategies to try the next time. It is hard to see everything when you are leading a program and becoming aware of things you may not have noticed can help further your development. Sharing your experiences with someone else immediately is a great way to identify success, troubleshoot issues, and grow.

We also recommend a few moments of individual reflection for each facilitator following a session. Many of our facilitators keep a journal of reflections, observations, and ideas for "next time." We add to each session or activity plan by recording the questions we asked and how they were answered, how we felt about the interactions and any interesting or unusual experiences during the session. As a team, we also keep a shared journal of notes and observations made by one of the support volunteers. This record is useful for immediate improvement and for later when you are planning new programs or reporting on programs. A reflective practice is a successful practice.

COMMUNICATION AND LOGISTICS

An important part of the program preparations and delivery is the communication related to the logistics of the program—things like registration, handouts, phone calls, and program materials. In all cases, ensure that your methods of communicating reflect your knowledge of dementia. Ensure that your communication is simply stated, uses large fonts and pictures if possible, and offers the information in multiple ways (written, verbal, etc.). This will help everyone feel welcome and prepared to participate.

Using more than one method of communication (such as a phone call and a written follow-up) can help support the range of abilities you may see in a group and allow you to further customize as needed. Prioritize communication with the participant wherever possible but connect with a family member or friend as needed, with the participant's consent. When you are together, always speak to the person, not to someone else about them. Your communication should reinforce the dignity and independence of each participant. In general:

- Keep language clear and concise.
- Simplify instructions while still maintaining an adult tone.
- Pause or leave space between sentences to allow processing time.
- Reduce distractions—especially sound and visual clutter.
- Where there are multiple facilitators or support staff, prioritize one person to be the lead to avoid switching back and forth, as this can be confusing for participants to follow.
- Avoid extraneous information.

Be thoughtful in your approach in all formats to ensure that all communications are made in a way that supports the participant's abilities. This includes reading and printed material, speaking on the phone, and virtual communication.

Strategies to Help with Reading

Most programs will include text-based materials. Consider everything from the program advertising, the registration process, email communications, and even handouts used during a program. Many participants will appreciate and rely on these materials to help them keep track of information and to prepare for programs—these materials are a lasting record of information and one that can be read and revisited as needed.

- Space out information to make it easier to read and understand—divide into sections or leave blank lines between chunks of information.
- Avoid abbreviations or jargon that require interpretation.
- Use plain fonts such as Arial or Calibri with at least 14-point font size.
- Use **bold** text or bullet points to highlight specific information.
- Use contrast between text and background color such as black writing on white paper.
- Use pictures strategically to help understanding and ensure the picture is clear and realistic.
- Where images are used, make them as large as possible.

Enhancing Communication over the Phone

Phone communication can be more difficult as there are no visual cues to help understanding or expression. Be sure to have a clear message and take your time.

- Introduce yourself and explain the reason for your call even if you have spoken on the phone before.
- Break the conversation down into short pieces of information and check for understanding.
- Speak with an adult rate of speech, but one that is a bit slower. Give the participants extra time to process and to reply.
- Encourage the person to write information down (if they are able) to help with remembering it.
- Send a follow-up email/text/letter to provide important details for reference later.

When delivering programs over the phone, organization and preparation are very important. Ensure the participant has weekly outlines of their preparation and setup, of the activities for the week, and how to use their materials. Also, include information about how to access the program.

- Provide organized reference materials to help communication and clear instructions.
- Aim to be the one to initiate phone calls rather than asking the participant to call you.

- During the program, introduce social norms to let everyone know what to expect and how to act.
- Ensure there is no background noise in your location.
- Speak a bit more slowly and clearly and check for hearing and understanding.
- Include page numbers on all reference materials and refer to pages by number each time.
- Allow time for participants to find the correct page before you start. Describe, the image in detail to ensure everyone is looking at the right page.
- Address participants by name before asking them a question.
- Allow an option for people to "pass" if they do not wish to speak.

When a participant has trouble understanding, take the time to support them. Use reference materials to ensure that they are on the correct page and that they understand what they are looking at, and what they are being asked. Verify details as you go and try to include others as well to make the person feel less centered out. Apply the communication strategies we have already discussed and use the reference materials to help.

When a participant is experiencing difficulty with hands-on activities, again, slow down and describe the process step-by-step, ensuring that they understand and that they try it before you go to the next step. If you have included images of each step in your reference materials, direct them to that page for clarification.

Enhancing Virtual Communication

For online virtual communications, the same strategies of clarity, simplicity, and organization apply. Using online platforms offers some access to visual cues so be sure to watch everyone as you go to get a sense of each person's comfort.

Virtual programs require a great deal of planning and organization in advance to be successful. For your approach in virtual programs, be sure that your participants have clear, printed instructions to use as a reference, including how to access the program, how to prepare or set up for a program, and other support materials as needed. For online programs, weekly emails with this information are very helpful including sending the link to the program prior to the start of the session. We have found it beneficial to send that email on the day of the program so that it is at the top of the participant's email inbox.

- Eliminate background noise and distractions.
- Sit close to your screen so that participants can see you clearly and eliminate visual distractions.
- Ensure that participants can see and hear you—use headphones and a high-quality microphone.
- Speak with an adult rate, though a bit slower. Speak clearly and verify hearing and understanding.
- When you begin, assist participants in using their mic and mute options and in adjusting their cameras.
- Watch your screen closely to observe for signs of engagement, confusion, frustration, etc.

When a participant has trouble understanding, refer back to your visuals. Use your mouse arrow or the drawing tools to point out, circle, or highlight things that will help participants see what you are talking about. Ask questions to confirm that they can see what you are talking about and verify small bits of information one step at a time. Apply the communication strategies to help.

When a participant has trouble with a hands-on activity, use your camera to show them the materials and the steps, one at a time. When you begin, show an image with the supplies needed to help everyone prepare. Talk through the steps one at a time while also demonstrating with your camera.

APPLYING "APPROACH" TO OTHER MUSEUM ENCOUNTERS

Much of the content of this book focuses on program design for people living with dementia—a facilitated experience between participants and the program team in a specific kind of experience. While the types of activities you will plan in a program are specific, the recommended strategies are broadly applicable. By empowering staff and volunteers across the whole museum to better understand and communicate with people living with dementia, you will take important steps toward becoming an inclusive, accessible space. Some of the key points of communication we have discussed that are important for other areas of the museum include:

Enforcing and Enacting Principles of Accessibility

Your communication, like all aspects of your work, should promote respect, dignity, independence, and choice. People living with dementia should feel valued and respected as the people they are. The way we treat others can support or reduce their sense of dignity. We can make choices in our communication style, the words we choose, and the nonverbal cues we model to promote strengths:

- Speak to the person rather than about them to someone else.
- Observe how a person responds to what you are saying and check for understanding sensitively if you notice any uncertainty.
- Avoid making assumptions or asking overly personal questions.
- Repeat and rephrase what you are saying if necessary.
- Slow down, leave time for processing, but maintain an adult tone and vocabulary.
- Try other forms of communication—gestures, writing things down to help the person understand and speak for themselves.
- Ask how you can help and respect their answer.

Use Patience, Flexibility, and Commitment

Good communication takes time and is not always easy. If your approach does not work, try something else. You will have encounters that are a challenge but learn from them rather than giving up. Reflect on your experiences and seek out more knowledge if you need it.

- Monitor your own stress level and remain calm and curious
- Give the person your full attention. If others need assistance, ask them politely to wait or have another colleague help... or ask the person to wait for a moment as you deal with the distractions.
- If the environment is noisy or busy find a quieter place to speak.
- If your approach or communication is not working take a moment to reflect, plan, and try another way—rephrase instructions, ask questions.
- Offer choices one at a time to help clarify needs.

Offer Multimodal Options

Think back to Part III, where you considered the environment in the museum. Wayfinding, entry processes, social norms, and expectations are important parts of everyone's experience of the museum. Ensure that communication is available in different, accessible formats.

- Ensure clear and concise signage for important places like entry and exits, washrooms, reception areas, coat checks.
- Use large print, simple fonts, and high contrast for ease of reading.
- Use standard icons or pictograms, as well as words.

- Have staff or volunteers available to help orient visitors.
- Have accessible maps and other printed resources available to help.

Reframe Perspectives

The perceptions and attitudes of frontline staff will affect how visitors feel in the museum. Remember the ways that stigma occurs and the impact it has on people. If a person feels that they belong and are welcome in your museum, they will be more able to engage.

- Promote a culture that sees and welcomes the strengths of people whose abilities may be different or have changed—one that sees the person first.
- Educate all staff, volunteers, and security to understand dementia and strategies they can use to communicate with people living with dementia.
- Educate staff on how to recognize bias and negative attitudes, and offer opportunities for them to learn about the many different audiences who will visit.

Amplify Lived Experience

Always remember—"never about us without us." Take opportunities to invite people with the lived experience of dementia to participate, share, lead, advise, and advocate. Ask questions and share what you have learned. Celebrate the important roles that people living with dementia along with their family and friends can play within the museum.

- Consult with people in the community about programs, exhibitions, and experiences of visiting the museum.
- Develop advisory groups and a process of consultation. Ensure that the process meets the needs and interests of the participants. Some may enjoy social committees while others prefer private conversations.
- Ask for feedback and use that feedback to adapt.
- Find opportunities for people with lived experience to contribute to the museum—through talks, exhibitions, program delivery, and more.

Message for Success

Approach Matters

Making meaningful connections with others is powerful. Every participant that you encounter brings with them interests, opinions, ideas, creativity, and a deep need to connect with others. With a thoughtful and individualized approach by a skilled facilitator, participants will have an engaging, positive experience.

"Approach" is an essential aspect of your program—if you cannot communicate in a way that is effective for your participants or support them in their communication and participation your program cannot be successful no matter how well you plan.

"Approach" is a skill to practice and build using the knowledge of the participant and careful observation. As these skills develop you will see positive engagement blossom. At the AGH, *Artful Moments* is one of the most meaningful projects we have created. We see the impact the program makes on participants and their family and friends but also on the team. Together we have learned, we have taught each other, and the experience has pushed our skills to new levels.

Facilitators will find their hard work very rewarding. They will see trust and friendships develop with program participants and their families. They will see their subject matter in new ways and this will in turn benefit other programs too.

Always remember missteps are temporary (and inevitable). If something does not work, reflect, debrief, and try something else. Your approach can be immensely flexible—do not be afraid to change or abandon plans "on the fly." Participation and communication go both ways—let the participants lead and follow them where they go. Embrace connection over content and process over product. Celebrate every success and enjoy the experience.

Part V
Activity

Shared Experiences

Museum activities are about creating connections. The activities enable participants to explore museum objects and exhibitions in a way that is meaningful to them. This section is where you will put your learning and planning into action, tailoring your activities to suit the audience. There is no one-size-fits-all approach here—the best activities will be unique to your museum.

Programs like *Artful Moments* are often about adapting many of the activities you already offer to suit your audience—in this case, people living with dementia. In many instances, we don't really change *the activities* we offer but rather *how* we plan and deliver them. Being person-centered means we share the same experiences and opportunities with many different audiences but we adapt the way that we work to suit each person's strengths. Throughout this section, we will present examples and let you know what has worked well for us. We encourage you to reflect on our experiences and be creative in how you apply them to your work.

As we work through the *Model for Successful Engagement*, we come to "activity." This refers to the activities that we do with the participants, and like all other components, this is directed by our knowledge of dementia. This section can be used to make existing museum activities more dementia-friendly, and can also guide the creation of new ones. We will show you how to incorporate your knowledge to adapt conversations about objects and hands-on experiences to be interesting and relevant for people living with dementia. This way, your programs will connect with your participants while still aligning with your museum's overall vision and mission.

11

Museum Activities

Program "activities" are the experiences we present for our participants and what some people may previously have thought of as the program in its entirety. Each museum will favor certain types of activities over others—art galleries will include art-making in their programs, gardens may engage in potting or floral arranging, and some museums may offer creative writing, photography, and more. Each of these will likely offer some version of a tour, talk, or dialogue. The pairing of a looking/listening/discussing component with some hands-on activity is a common format for educational or recreational programming, and the combination of the two offers a full cycle of experiential learning. One of the exciting parts of our collaboration with other museums is learning about the range of creative ideas that our colleagues have. In program planning, people may sometimes interchange the terms "activities" and "content" but for our purposes, we will make a distinction between the two:

> **Content**—encompasses the objects, ideas, and information contained within a program session or experience. Program content is the starting point and forms the building blocks of our activities but it is not until we animate content with a methodology, an approach, and a plan for engagement that it becomes an activity.

> **Activities**—are built around the content but encompass much more. When we expand our thinking to the activity, we consider not only the object and the information but also how we use it. The content becomes an activity when we are doing something with it. A good activity is always person-centered, meaningful, and engaging for participants.

Best practice, demonstrated by research into many museum programs for people living with dementia, suggests several key factors for success including having:

- Participatory activities that are meaningful and of high quality that do not require preexisting knowledge or skill from the participants.
- Experienced facilitators who are knowledgeable about their content but also skillful in participatory, responsive approaches.
- A balance between inspiring creativity and the risk of overwhelming participants with too much complexity.
- Stimulating discussion while not relying on memory or other abilities that may have changed.
- Some underlying structure while also leaving room for individual expression.[1]

Are you a museum that offers guided tours, art-making activities, object-handling sessions, or opportunities to cook, plant seeds, or interact with animals? Each of these things can be modified to become an effective activity that engages a participant's strengths and interests.

DEMENTIA AND CREATIVITY

While the changes in the brain caused by dementia can affect a person's ability to initiate complex ideas or actions, we know that people living with dementia continue to be interested in creative activities. For some, as they become less self conscious, they embrace new enjoyment of art, music, and other creative arts. Studies have also shown that engaging in creative activities relieve stress and improve creativity and resilience. This suggests a link between social and creative activities and the preservation of cognitive functions. Creative activities are not only enjoyable to the person engaging in them, but they are also social activities that strengthen social ties among participants.

Creative activities can be empowering and enjoyable for people living with dementia. Benefits include offering opportunities for self-expression, the joy of partaking in meaningful activities like discussing art and historical objects and creating work of their own in response to what they have seen.

THE IMPORTANCE OF INTERACTIVITY

For many years, museums were storehouses of art and artifacts, places meant for preserving and displaying collected objects and specimens. They offered 'one-directional' interpretation as the site and voice of authority. Museums told audiences what to value and what to think of the treasures held within. Their programs were not interactive, with limited, if any, room for knowledge sharing.

More recently across the museum field, there has been an ongoing shift in understanding about the position and the voice that institutions can and should hold. Coupled with that is a shift in education pedagogy where we move from being a voice of authority to a more collaborative process of interpretation, and even toward a model where the visitor is the initiator and leader of their own experience.

Another important direction in museum work is in how we understand the role and purpose of the objects we hold. Where once museum programs were object-centered—where communicating the correct and important facts and context to every visitor was the focus—many museums are now thinking more about how their objects can support a more important role—the visitor experience. John T. Murphey, a former instructor at the Worcester Art Museum, stresses the importance of engagement and the type of experiences offered. He states that "the primary concern of a museum is not really objects themselves, but with the experiences they cause us," and he calls on museum educators, through their work to use their objects and collections to be a "catalyst to experience."[2]

For the museum, the delivery of interactive programs is a way of inviting the participant into the experience, providing opportunities to explore their connection to the objects on display. Museum educators and interpreters act as a bridge between the object and the visitor, providing information and experiences that are relevant, meaningful, and engaging.

Interactivity for Visitors

Being invited into the process of engagement shifts the responsibility and the leadership in interesting ways, especially for adult participants. Many adults are quite comfortable with lecture-style programs where they hear interesting information from an accepted "expert," but, unless highly motivated, they will not recall most of what is heard or find any real personal connections or meaning in what they have been told. When an experience becomes interactive, participants have to think and process information as they go and build (and share) meaningful connections to move the experience forward. It is harder but also more rewarding. Interactivity can lead to surprise revelations and new perspectives for all involved—including the facilitator. Having led interactive conversations in art galleries for many years, we are continually struck by the insights we hear from participants of all ages and abilities and we learn so much from visitors about the objects we see every day.

Museum educators in every type of museum know that many of our visitors want to engage in their experiences more than simply reading or listening to a litany of facts. As Elliot Kai-Kee from the J. Paul Getty Museum states, "museum educators have intuitively understood that visitors feel a need to actually *do* things in a museum."[3] In the recent publication, *Activity-Based Teaching in the Museum*, Kai-Kee, and his fellow authors explore the many multimodal activities that they use in their programming, all of which speak to the need for a participant-centered, interactive, and engaging range of activities that sprint past the traditional "museum talk" that many visitors still expect.

"Shared experiences" is a recurring theme in this book and in our work. When we consider interactivity, in many programs it refers most often to interaction between the facilitator and individuals in the group. In more dynamic examples, participants will begin to interact with each other but often superficially by acknowledging another's ideas or sharing further ideas. In programs like *Artful Moments*, interactivity has the potential to be much deeper. In addition to the broader audience connections described already, programs that welcome participants and a family member or friend together play an important role in supporting and developing bonds between individuals. For some, using museum objects "to give voice to experiences for which one had no previous language, creates meaning. The ability to communicate that meaning to others can contribute to a sense of belonging to a caring community."[4] Shared activity is a building block for close relationships. Museums provide the opportunity to support sharing, conversation, and empathy-building through responses to objects on display, often with very little prompting.

The experience of interactivity and of prioritizing the voices of visitors in a participatory experience is also very important for those participants whose voices and perspectives have traditionally been left out of the narratives. By contributing (and hearing) other ideas, participants feel welcome, valued, respected, and engaged.

Interactivity for People Living with Dementia

Coming to a museum can be both an exciting and an intimidating experience for anyone. For the person with dementia who is beginning to feel uncertain about their abilities or for the family member who may be nervous about what might happen with their loved one in a public setting, the barriers to cultural participation accumulate rapidly. The experience of unfamiliar places with potentially unknown rules and unexpected conditions is sometimes a deterrent for people living with dementia and their family and friends, as is the worry about places that are not supportive or knowledgeable about dementia. A program like *Artful Moments* can be an invitation for participants to come back to a place where they had pleasant experiences earlier in their lives or to take part in a new experience, knowing that they will be welcomed and supported.

In John Falk's research into visitor motivations, he reminds us that "to be perceived as truly fundamental to their communities, museums will need to rewrite their mission and impact statements to more directly align with the identity-related visit motivations of their visitors."[5] We need to take seriously the commitment to becoming person-centered and strengths-focused in our work. As has been stated previously, we acknowledge that most of the guidance provided in this book is geared toward specialized program design. Many of the strategies and foundational ideas can, and should, be applied across the whole of the museum. We recall these ideas from previous chapters where we consider the social environment of museums but it begs repetition here when we think of interactivity and inclusion of multiple perspectives.

Artful Moments is an interactive, inclusive program for individuals with dementia. We ask questions and support participants in understanding and expressing themselves. We present art and objects in a way that is meaningful and engaging. We provide opportunities to make something and do something in a way that capitalizes on strengths and supports abilities. We encourage you to reflect on your museum's activities and be inspired about how they can be adapted to enable participants to contribute, to be engaged, and to feel welcomed and valued.

Interactivity in Museum Tours and Conversations

Take a moment to think about your current approach to tours and programs.

Who does most of the talking – you or the participants? Who leads the direction of conversation? Is your focus on sharing all of the information you have planned or is it on engaging participants through their interest? Rate your facilitation style, using a scale of 1 to 10.

(1) (2) (3) (4) (5) (6) (7) (8) (9) (10)

1: lecture, no interaction 10: interactive, participant-led conversation

What scares you about embracing a more interactive style? What excites you? What changes can you make now to become more interactive, and move your personal rating a few points higher?

Figure 11.1 Measuring Interactivity in Your Facilitation. Understanding your current approach is an important step in building an interactive practice. Participants' contributions should be valued and prioritized. *Source*: Art Gallery of Hamilton.

A Person-Centered Philosophy in Action

"Person-centered" means more than just interactive. Without intentional methods to center the experience and contribution of participants, a facilitator can slip into a performative version of interactivity where they ask questions just to break up their monologue and get participants to do or say something. If those questions elicit answers and actions that don't have the opportunity to alter or extend the activity, they are not person-centered.

A core part of program planning is the belief that every aspect of design and implementation should be centered on the strengths, interests, and needs of the participants. This is true when we adjust our environment and our approach to respond to each person we encounter. The application of that philosophy also carries forward into our activities. We prioritize individual experience over content and we emphasize the enjoyment of the process, not the final product. We focus on facilitating social connection and engagement rather than formal achievement or traditional learning. We work hard to build an openness in the direction and content of each session—this is where we stress adaptation and responding to the participants "in the moment." Now, we will build on that in key ideas for activities.

Activities Are Meaningful and with a Purpose

The participants are adults with rich histories and abilities that remain well past their diagnosis of dementia. We must always treat them as such. Our choice and style of activities reflect that understanding.

- Activities should use adult language, content, and tone. They should never be childlike and should never be "busywork."
- Content, whether the objects you look at or the hands-on activities you do, should be stimulating, offer an appropriate level of challenge, and encourage participants to relate them to themselves somehow.
- The activities should draw out individual ideas and responses, not formulaic, empty, or prescriptive actions and words.

Activities Allow for Self-expression and Creativity

Studies have shown that creativity is an ability that remains into the later stages of dementia. Find ways to encourage it.

- Encourage unique, personalized responses and work through your choices of questions and hands-on activities.
- Encourage participants to work in their own way and with their own experiences and preferences.
- Value and validate contribution, not correctness. Find ways to encourage participants in whatever form of engagement works for them
- Celebrate a variety of ideas and actions and include everyone.

Activities Are Enjoyable

Participation is about the experience that must be engaging and fun for the participants, regardless of their abilities. As you plan, think about activities that are open-ended with no single right answer or way to do things. This can apply to the questions you ask on a tour or the types of hands-on activities you do. Always remember, the final product is not the main purpose of this program—it's about time spent together and the emotions tied to the experience.

- Activities should welcome numerous answers to any question and many different ways to create hands-on responses, rather than focusing on specific products. This is not a test!
- Activities need to be tailored to match the abilities of the person which means within a range of challenges that is manageable but not too simple.
- Activities must be safe.

Activities Value Process over Product

These programs are not driven by the acquisition of new knowledge or skills. They are not focused on facts, technical ability, or expectations of specific, predefined production. They do not aim to elicit a "correct answer" or a specific finished product.

We focus on the *process* and the *experience* rather than a final product or demonstration of learning. We use museum objects as tools to spark conversation, inspire social sharing, and provide enjoyable activities that allow each participant to express themselves in whatever manner they are able. We focus on enjoying the process—of looking, of sharing, and of making something inspired by the day's experiences. The activities are a vehicle for engagement. Whether or not a participant interprets an object in the way we expect or learns when and where it came from is less important than how much they enjoyed talking to others about it. Whether they followed the steps in a hands-on activity correctly or just moved the paint around on a paper is irrelevant if they had fun doing it.

Take a moment to think about a conversation in your museum that you really enjoyed.

What did you talk about? What did you say and hear? Likely it was a lot about ideas and feelings and not about sharing large amounts of facts, and very likely both parties shared equally in the conversation. How can you apply this to your more formal programs?

Activities Aim to Be Open-Ended

Coupled with a focus on the experience rather than the output is the willingness to go where participants lead in a program without the objective-driven direction determining the content and conclusions of a session. The way a facilitator thinks about the purpose of an activity, whether that be a museum conversation or a hands-on workshop, will influence the way they plan and guide that activity. This in turn will affect how open they are to the interests of participants. A good illustration of this is a comparison of closed and open-ended activities. When we are content-driven, a facilitator may lead a program in predetermined directions. When we are participant-centered, we allow participants' experiences "in the moment" to lead and leave space for all kinds of interesting things to happen.

- **Closed Activities:** have specific outcomes that may fit more into our ideas of a traditional lesson plan—we want people to learn or do *this,* and so as facilitators we must do *this* and *this* to get there.

Facilitators may use this approach for school programs, with a predetermined plan for each conversation and question. In an interactive program, we may follow some tangents to see where a student's ideas may take them but we still return to the overall plan. In closed activities, we measure our success, at least in part, by whether or not they learned the right things or created the expected product.

- **Open-Ended Activities:** will have some structure to hold it all together and to relate all of the parts but beyond that, conversations are allowed to go in interesting and unexpected directions. Sometimes we share the story or details of an object and sometimes we do not. Sometimes our hands-on activities show clear inspiration from works seen in the galleries and sometimes they take shape on their own. Remember, it is all okay! We follow the interests and support a participant-led experience.

Can an Activity Be Too Open-Ended?

Yes, it can. There is an important balance to be found. If an activity is too closed—if it requires specific outcomes to be deemed a 'success', the participant will experience frustration if they make a mistake or "can't do it." Alternatively, they may feel bored or stifled by the lack of options. If an activity is too open, participants may not know what to do or how to start. For people living with dementia, we must provide structure and support, but allow for a range of responses. Differences in initiation, problem-solving, and processing of information are some of the factors that can affect a person's ability to engage. Your facilitation will require carefully balancing between offering clear and specific instructions, modeling responses and supporting expression, and leaving space for individuality and different levels of ability.

APPLYING THE "JUST RIGHT CHALLENGE" TO ACTIVITIES

The concept of "just right" activities originates from occupational therapy and essentially means creating an activity that is not too hard so that it causes frustration, but also not too easy so it feels trivial or meaningless. This concept can be widely applied to many settings and is a great way to think of activities in the program you will develop.[6]

We have previously talked about "meaningful activities"—creating programs that encourage engagement while supporting any difficulties. Be cautious and thoughtful when you begin to adapt activities—you may accidentally take away the meaning or power of that activity while planning to make it "easier." Remember the participant's words in Chapter 4: "People assume that learning new stuff would be very difficult for me. . . . Too many professionals try to take too many things away too quickly. Not asking or testing me for my ability."[7]

Participants *should* feel challenged since being challenged acknowledges and validates their abilities and experience. They should feel that they are contributing important ideas and actions to a program. This will not happen if the activity is too easy. It may feel "childish" or even condescending.

However, modifications must be made to suit the changes in abilities that the participant may experience. For example, language that is too complex or presented too quickly can be frustrating if it does not allow for an adequate processing time. A task with too many steps can be difficult to remember and can cause engagement to fail.

The *Model for Successful Engagement* is used to scaffold facilitation skills toward a fully integrated program that considers each of the pillars in the model to present a well-planned and delivered experience. The "just-right challenge" helps us to understand how an activity paired with our approach can validate and support a participant's sense of achievement.

So how do you find the right level?

Finding "just the right challenge" level takes a mix of knowledge, flexibility, experimentation, and practice. Keep in mind that what is "just right" for one participant may be different for another. Where the "just right" is unknown, begin with your baseline.

In Part IV, we talked about adjusting questions from a baseline to be either more or less complex based on individual needs. The baseline is an open question like, "What do you see?" If the response tells you that the participant will be able to navigate a more complicated discussion, your next question can be more complex, such as "What do you see that makes you say that?" or "Have you ever traveled to a place that looks like this before?" If the first answer is more literal or concrete, perhaps a follow-up to allow for additional concrete comments such as: "Yes, the dog is my favorite too. Do you see any other animals?" Finally, if the participant appears to have some difficulty with an open question, try to rephrase in a more accessible way, "Do you see any animals in this painting?" If this still does not work, try a "yes" or "no" question and model different options to answer like using thumbs up or "Did you notice the dog in the corner?"

You can do the same with hands-on activities. For example, starting with a baseline activity, you may offer more complex options to add detail or expand on the action for those who wish to do more. Conversely, you could simplify the activity by demonstrating specific steps that can be followed or copied. You could also offer a template, and precut materials, or ask the person to show you what they would like to do.

With a baseline activity and some preparation ahead of time, you will be able to navigate each participant through your activity at a level of challenge that is appropriate and effective for them. This helps to ensure that everyone feels included, supported, and accomplished.

PROGRAM FORMAT

Environment. Approach. Activity. Together, the three pillars of the *Model for Successful Engagement* inform every aspect of our program design. The first part of this chapter has explored the philosophy we apply to activity design more broadly while the next two chapters will explore the types of activities we offer. Between these two discussions, we take a moment to focus on the logistics of programs—the way we format our sessions.

Figure 11.2   Making Activities "Just Right." Keeping activities, whether conversations or hands-on, at the right level of ease is important in maintaining engagement. Even if measuring ingredients is too complex for someone, being involved in the process is enjoyable—in this case kneading soft dough is a wonderful experience. *Source*: istock.com/Patrick Daxenbichler.

Conversations and Hands-On Activities in Every Session

Our success in fostering engagement in all of our participants has come from a combination of two kinds of activities: conversations and hands-on activities. We have seen how the combination of the two types of activity complements and supports each other and offers participants a more fully considered experience. In every program at the AGH, whether in-person, virtual, or over the phone, we offer both conversations and hands-on activities every session. This format is reflective of both the Gallery's overall education strategies, and the positive experiences of our participants.

Our goal is to actively engage participants in the creative process. By engaging in both types of activity, each session moves through the complete cycle of looking, reflecting, discussing, and responding or applying. The combination offers many opportunities for activities to be accessible for people with a range of abilities as it accommodates a variety of preferred communication and participation styles.

We find that shifting from conversations into hands-on activities transitions the participant from a more formal structure into a more active and casual type of activity that allows for chatting, experimenting, and play. In a group, some participants will prefer one type of activity over the other but the combination encourages them all to share and to try something new. Moreover, we know that it is often the activities themselves that stimulate social engagement as they are the subject of conversation and offer opportunities to offer opportunities for positive connections to the other in the group.[8]

Activities are inspired by an appreciation of an object's subject, style, or techniques and can lead to the creative exploration of familiar materials. In some cases, hands-on activities that relate to specific objects or processes might seem simplistic or childlike without context. By starting with conversations, the context for the activity is explored first. This process then validates activities and inspires participants to explore further.

Program Length

When gathering in-person for on-site programs we run a two-hour program, evenly split between the conversation and hands-on activities. We allow time for casual talk and greetings at the beginning and a short break in the middle. We often offer tea and a small snack. Where needed, we sometimes cut about ten minutes off the hands-on activity to allow more social time although in the more casual workshop space socializing takes place throughout the hands-on activity time.

For virtual and phone programs, we offer a ninety-minute program, although sessions may continue for up to two hours when participants are engaged. We were initially concerned about "screen exhaustion" or too much time on the phone but have not found it to be a problem for most participants. Virtual conversations last 45–60 minutes with about 30 minutes for hands-on activities. We sometimes make phone programs a bit shorter and always welcome participants to stay only as long as they wish. We always leave the last few minutes to share hands-on work. Many participants are happy to share their work, to laugh about successes and challenges, and to complement their fellow participants. It is also important to respect those who prefer not to share.

In earlier programs, we tried offering the hands-on first, when the participants had the most energy and focus but ultimately decided to keep it at the end. We found that the preference seemed to be for the more formal and concentrated activity to be first, allowing for more flexibility in attention, focus, and energy afterward. Also, time in the exhibition provided inspiration and context for the activity that follows. The best advice for establishing the balance for your program is to listen to your group. Start with an even split and adjust as you go until you find a good fit for everyone.

In any case, by sharing experiences of looking, talking, and making, participants, and their family members or friends can have an enjoyable experience together. They celebrate each other's successes, learn more about each other and laugh, share interests, show pride, and build their self-esteem.

Multi-session Programs versus Drop-In

The decision of how many sessions to offer, the frequency, and the number of sessions a participant is asked to commit to is directly linked to your museum's capacity and goals for the program. The format of your program will affect the kinds of activities that you offer and potentially the depth of relationships that form between participants and staff. When making this decision, consider these factors:

- Staff and site capacity.
- Demands on activity spaces from other programs and visitors.
- The location and accessibility of your museum.
- The size of your exhibition spaces and the frequency of exhibition changes.
- The interest and number of participants.
- Your goals for the experience—from welcoming many participants to building deep social connections with a smaller group of regular attendees.
- Connections with community organizations.

In a scan of museum programs offered for people living with dementia in several countries, there were a variety of program formats, including combinations of:

- Drop-in programs offered on a monthly or weekly basis.
- Multi-session programs offered at regular intervals either weekly, biweekly, or monthly.
- Individually booked single visits for care facilities, community service providers, and clubs.
- In-person programs presented at the museum.
- In-person programs presented in care facilities and community hubs.
- Virtual programs offered either online or by phone.

Recommendations

When planning programs, we recall the program goals and philosophy—to build engagement and social connection. Social connection and comfortable participation are most successful when trust and familiarity have been established. We have found that there are many benefits to the multi-week format:

- It enables establishing trust and familiarity among staff and participants.
- Participants benefit from familiarity with the program space and activities.
- Staff get to know participants, their stories, preferences, communication style, and abilities.
- Planning extends over six to eight weeks—we develop the program as we learn from each other— we can adapt and anticipate program activities and needs over time.
- Participants grow in comfort and typically gradually increase their interactions as the weeks progress
- For virtual and phone-based programs, we provide supplies and resource kits to participants in advance of the program. These kits allow us to plan activities with supplies we know everyone will have and they allow participants to continue working in between sessions. This would not be possible for drop-in programs.
- On the administrative side, having returning participants and stronger relationships is advantageous in reducing workload and the associated costs.
- We now see at least half of our participants returning each season, and that strengthens the building of relationships even further.

While we had recognized the connective experience that happened among participants right from the beginning, it was really made clear during the programs in 2020 and 2021 when the Gallery closed its doors and shifted to virtual programs during the pandemic. At a time when people were forced to stay home and avoid contact with others, social isolation became a serious concern, particularly among seniors and those whose connections with others were already reduced. Over our multi-week sessions, people who had never met in-person formed meaningful friendships. Conversations offered social connections that had been sorely missed.

A challenge that exists with ongoing programming, whether pre-registered or drop-in, is in creating new content each time. Depending on the size of your museum and the frequency of exhibition change, you will need to think about ways to divide your exhibitions into a series of smaller thematic groupings. For larger institutions, this should not be too difficult, but if you are a small museum, you will have to be creative in how you plan a series.

Activities Must Be Safe

Safety is always an important consideration in museum programs. For participants in specialized programs, there are considerations beyond what you might anticipate for other programs.

Many safety issues related to the environment have already been addressed. This includes site-related concerns like accessibility, visibility in walkways, potential for slips and falls, lighting, and appropriate seating. For the conversation activities, this will cover most of your safety-related concerns. Safety is especially important in using tools and materials during hands-on activities and you must keep in mind the range of abilities of your participants.

For participants in the later stages of dementia, you must consider the safety of tools and materials more carefully and adapt your activity to suit their abilities. For example, where using scissors is more difficult you could have items precut. Toxic materials like acrylic paint or clay could be substituted for safer food-based modeling or colored materials. One of our most common considerations is with paint water—avoid using old mugs or cups for activity materials. Instead, use containers that are less likely to be mistaken for drinks. Be cautious with heat or sharp tools. Have a first aid kit, an emergency contact, and a safety management plan in place that is accessible and familiar to all facilitators.

Finally, consider the safety of your participants, especially those who attend on their own or are dropped off and picked up at the end of a program. Ensure that you know how they will arrive and depart and have contact numbers on hand. We have had experiences with participants who wish to leave before their ride has arrived, and this may not be safe. Sometimes one of our volunteers will sit with them or have a cup of tea together while they wait. It is important to ensure that each participant gets to the right place and person.

Applying Knowledge of Dementia to Activities

When planning activities, remember to consider the five areas of abilities so that you can anticipate where potential areas of difficulty may occur:

1. Cognition
2. Language
3. Perception
4. Mood and Emotions
5. Physical abilities

Think about the words you say, how fast you say them, and how much time you are accustomed to leaving between questions and answers. Consider the familiarity and ease of use of the materials and techniques you choose and the emotional or triggering potential of objects. Consider whether participants may feel proud or frustrated with their skills and whether they are physically able to hold pencils, use scissors, or manipulate hard or heavy materials. Always remember to:

- Follow a consistent routine during the activity to help participants know what to expect.
- Use familiar activities to draw upon the person's long-term memory.
- Carefully consider the overall complexity of the activity to ensure that it does not become too complicated and cause frustration.
- Break tasks down into concrete one-step actions so that the person only has to process one step at a time.
- Offer multimodal options to support participants during activities—say each question or instruction out loud, demonstrate, and consider having a large poster with steps listed or an individual handout for each participant.
- Simplify activities—limit them to four to six main steps.
- Think about physical considerations—walking, standing, holding tools, vision, and hearing and adapt to suit the needs.

Remember, that to "modify" does not mean to "dumb it down" but rather to clearly understand the purpose and goals of an activity and to plan for smaller steps and scaffolding within an activity to help participants move successfully through the important steps. Simplify. Eliminate the parts that are not necessary for engagement.

PLAN WELL BUT BE FLEXIBLE

Activities should be flexible, responsive, and well-planned. Be well prepared with supporting resources and all of the environmental needs met—such as additional seating, reducing or eliminating distractions, and accommodating limited movement around a large space. Know what you are going to talk about and what you are going to do for your hands-on activity and have everything set up in advance. Have questions planned and the stories you will share organized. This will save you from feeling rushed and reduce distractions.

Plan for Everything BUT Be Prepared for Anything

In a group, the mood, abilities, and state of mind can change dramatically from week to week and even during a session. There are many factors outside of your control, or that you may be unaware of, that can have an impact. Your participants may be experiencing fatigue, stress carried over from earlier in the day, pain, hunger, medication, side effects, and more. Even participants you know well can experience changes. With this in mind, try to prepare yourself with an array of solutions to choose from. These "back pocket" tricks can make it easier for you when the unexpected happens:

- Do not be too attached to your plan. If you need to make an activity shorter or change it altogether to improve engagement—DO IT!
- Activities should be flexible so they can be modified up or down to match the participants' abilities that day and encourage maximum engagement. This applies to questions, but also to the steps used in a hands-on activity.
- Know your content well so that you are comfortable shifting gears.
- Get to know your audience—as you spend more time together you will get to know how people work and what they like.
- Be observant—look for signs of engagement and signs of distress. Watch for people who are withdrawn and not participating. Check-in with people often and by name to keep them connected.

- Get others to help you—a volunteer or second staff member who attends the program can watch participants and interject a prompt or question to re-engage someone that you may not have noticed could use additional support.

If you have a good plan and a lot of back-up preparation in place you will be ready for (nearly) anything. A colleague once phrased it well, saying that "being open and flexible when facilitating these types of programs will achieve the greatest results, but even the best-planned programs may work well one day and fail the next."[9] We all learn and grow from our experiences and over time you will gain confidence and comfort with knowing when and how to adjust your program.

NOTES

1. Gill Windle, Andrew Newman, Vanessa Burholt, Bob Woods, Dave O'Brien, Michael Barber, Barry Hounsome, Clive Parkinson, and Victoria Tischlet, "Dementia and Imagination: A Mixed-methods Protocol for Arts and Science Research," *BMJ Open* 6 (2016): 3, https://doi.org/10.1136/bmjopen-2016-011634.
2. Elliott Kai-Kee, Lissa Latina, and Lilit Sadoyan, *Activity-Based Teaching in the Museum* (Los Angeles: J. Paul Getty Museum, 2020), 30.
3. Elliott Kai-Kee, *Activity-Based Teaching*, 32.
4. Patrice Rancour and Terry Barrett, "Art Interpretation as a Clinical Intervention Toward Healing," *Journal of Holistic Nursing American Holistic Nursing Association* 29, no. 1 (2011): 69, https://doi.org/10.1177/089801019358768.
5. John H. Falk, *Identity and the Museum Visitor Experience* (Walnut Creek: Left Coast Press, 2009), 239.
6. Optimum Health Solutions, "Just Right Challenge," *The Occupational Therapist*, 2020, https://opt.net.au/optimum-life/occupational-therapists-just-right-challenge/.
7. Dementia in a New Light, "Stigma Stereotypes," accessed April 2024, https://dementiainnewlight.com/content/stigma/stereotypes.
8. Candice D. Reel, Rebecca S. Allen, Bailey Lanai, M. Caroline Yuk, and Daniel C. Potts, "Bringing Art to Life: Social and Activity Engagement Through Art in Persons Living with Dementia," *Clinical Gerontologist* 45, no. 2 (2021): 332, https://doi.org/10.1080/07317115.2021.1936737.
9. Reflection of an *Artful Moments* facilitator, 2013.

12

Planning Conversations

For many museums, tours are one of the key methods used for facilitating connections between visitors and the objects on display. Tours may take many forms from in-person to virtual and with a range of dialogical and interactive or multimodal techniques. In the pages that follow, we will explore tips and strategies that we have found most effective when working with people living with dementia as a guide to how you might do this at your museum. We will look at some examples from our programs and will also consider how to apply these techniques to other kinds of collections.

The kind of program that we describe works in a variety of presentation formats—in-person, online, and over the phone. While each of these formats requires some specific ways of working and communicating the general strategies used apply to all of them.

A participant-centered focus, combined with careful, detailed planning is the key to success. A well-planned and well-prepared program allows you to adapt as needed "on the fly," and by having the setup and organization done beforehand, you will reduce stress for yourself and distraction or confusion for your group.

WHY "CONVERSATIONS"?

There are countless ways to approach a tour audience with different kinds of information presented and different levels of interactivity. Some tours are planned in detail and others run "off the cuff," with content chosen "in the moment." You will make many of these decisions based on your goals and your role at the museum. Most importantly your plan should reflect your audience.

Wording is important and over the years our team has considered a variety of terms, including "art appreciation" and "tours." We have settled on "conversations" as the most accurate and encompassing way to signify the kind of experiences participants can expect when they visit us.

"Conversations" suggests a sharing of ideas, a back-and-forth approach, and a pleasurable exchange. We do not set out to impart large amounts of information to our visitors as suggested by the term "art interpretation," though we do tell stories about the art and artists we view. The experiences we offer have a slower-paced and more expansive exploration of the work. We do not use scripts and as with any good conversation the participants' ideas may take us in a variety of directions both conversationally and in the exhibition spaces. There is no fast-paced highlights tour in our program, and we do not rush through the exhibitions to see as much as possible or even to ensure we see everything in our plan for the day.

Dr. Terry Barrett, who has written extensively about art interpretation, expressed it well when he stated: "Through art, people can express ideas and feelings that they cannot express otherwise." He believes that to miss taking time to consider what we see means that we miss out on the opportunity to know the art, ourselves, and others. He later writes: "When we choose to interpret out loud to others who want to hear us, we become active participants in public life rather than passive observers."[1]

Figure 12.1 Museum Conversations and Engagement. Giving participants meaningful opportunities to express their ideas and experiences is empowering, especially for people who may feel they have less to contribute. Participants and their family and friends can all benefit. *Source*: Art Gallery of Hamilton

In this, we favor a constructivist approach to museum education where meaning and connection are made through an interaction between the participant, the object, and the facilitator. Researchers have used this approach to effectively engage people living with dementia in conversation as a way to reduce the pressure for recall of previously learned information or past experiences with museum objects. While the initial impetus draws heavily on an understanding of dementia, this combination results in an activity that is far more meaningful than simply a "fun time out." It enables an experience in which participants can engage on many levels—cognitively, socially, and physically.[2]

SELECTING OBJECTS FOR CONVERSATION

The objects on display and those that are accessible in your collection in other formats will form the basis for your conversations. You will likely already have some favorites that you know well to make the planning process easier. Apply your knowledge of dementia to your considerations, including the five areas of ability affected by dementia—cognition, language, perception, mood and emotions, and physical abilities. In the following pages, we will consider the possible impacts of:

- Object choices, in subject, appearance, and interpretive potential as well as how visually complex or confusing they may be.
- Where the objects are displayed, remembering accessibility, the amount of walking distance and movement in between objects, and how easy they are to see based on position, size, lighting, and clutter.
- The number of objects selected for each session. Likely, it is fewer than you expect.

Subject Matter and Appearance

Museum objects can often stir up memories from the past, thereby encouraging participants to recall things from their own lives to make personal connections. This allows them to tap into long-term memory. In addition, storytelling inspired by objects is a valuable tool to create interest and engagement, as well as strengthen social connections and close relationships. We design first with a social and meaningful experience in mind, not a learning goal—the stories and personal moments are what make programs special.

Images and objects that are familiar are a great way to start conversations. In art, something that is representational will be easier to understand than something abstract or conceptual. Other objects such as domestic items, memorabilia, or tools are a great way to connect with memories.

Consider objects that are less visually complicated. In art, this means images that are simpler rather than those that are full of many small details or disorganized elements. For other objects, this means a single object rather than a collection of many or something with lots of parts.

When we first began this work, we followed these two recommendations quite closely through-out a session. Even now, we usually follow them in the first week or two of each new program and in our choice for the first object of every session. A comfortable starting point allows participants to settle in, to understand how to participate, and begin to develop rapport with the group.

That said, we do not follow the rules strictly. Once we get a better sense of the group and their abilities, we can start to introduce more challenging objects, where we feel it is appropriate for participants. We use more familiar works earlier in a session to scaffold participants into knowing what to look for and guide them gently into more complex artworks. We also include supporting resources to help—photographs or other helpful images as comparisons, printed handouts to allow for a closer look, and lots of prompting to identify what to look at.

In our first virtual program, we started with paintings of Hamilton—something very familiar, representational, and comfortable for our group but by the final week, we looked at five abstract art-works—three paintings, a sculpture, and a neon lightbox. Had we started with abstraction in the first week it would not have worked at all but by the end, the group enjoyed the new ideas and our facilita-tors had learned the strategies needed to engage and scaffold participants through conversations. As you become more comfortable with your approach and participants, you will feel more comfortable trying new or less conventional things.

Our choices are also influenced by the appearance of the overall display that contains each object, its proximity to other objects, and its location, as described in Part III. We favor displays that contain single objects or a small number with a lot of space around them, objects that require limited travel to get to, and the display height, visibility, and absence of glare. Depending on your collections, the examples we have used may be very relatable to your planning. However, museums with different collections may need to adapt the guidelines to better suit their specific holdings.

Get a sense of what works for your group, and guide their looking and thinking with your first selec-tions. Later, try adding more complex objects. Use your knowledge of dementia and what you have learned about approach strategies to help you. Observe the results and continue to adapt as you go.

Sensitivity and Triggers

It is important to be careful with sensitive or emotionally charged content. If possible, learn whether participants have any triggering subjects in their history. Earlier memories are preserved longer than more recent ones, so for someone whose orientation to time and place may have changed, those memories can feel very present. If they are unpleasant they can be upsetting. An example is someone who was a residential school survivor and found images of churches and clergy to be triggering. In another example, we opted not to use a painting of a young woman dressed in black and holding an infant's clothing because of the potentially upsetting subject matter of child loss.

It can be difficult to know about triggers or potentially difficult subjects. In some cases, we have asked whether there are any sensitive subjects that participants would like us to know. On occasion, a family member or friend has shared something for us to keep in mind. Otherwise, we recommend taking a moment to think about the emotional weight of an object before selecting it, as well as your comfort in talking about it. Stirring pleasant memories and associations encourages a warm and enjoyable experience.

Abilities May Affect Selections

When choosing objects for your conversations take a careful look at each one from the participant's perspective, including consideration of vision and perception. Without that frame of mind, you may take for granted that objects will be interesting to talk about without noticing aspects that could cause difficulties for some participants. The examples that follow highlight some of these concerns:

Vision changes: In part II we talked about changes that occur to a person's sight as part of aging. These include greater difficulty seeing things that are very small, very detailed, or have low contrast. Glare, as on shiny objects or things under glass, can also make objects difficult to see. Other eye conditions such as cataracts and macular degeneration can also affect a participant's ability to see the objects. Be sure to look at your selections from your participants' point of view—sit on a chair in your exhibition and look at the object to see how well you can see it.

Depth perception and spatial understanding: A person living with dementia may experience changes in how they interpret space and distance. This can affect their understanding of things that are close or far away from them and can cause misreading of some elements. They may perceive large dark areas as holes. Objects with a lot of complexity or artworks that are more busy or abstract can cause confusion. Conditions such as agnosia (where familiar objects become unrecognizable) can also affect some people.

We pay attention to glare in the exhibition spaces and will avoid an object where the glare from lights or highly reflective glass are present. These are all vision-related guidelines for success and we follow these guidelines pretty closely.

Based on this, the general recommendation is to avoid objects and artworks that are very small, that are under glass, and that are very busy or full of detail. Complex abstract compositions are more challenging as well. As a best practice, we avoid small, dark, or highly detailed work.

Some museums will choose to display single objects with a lot of space around them. These are ideal selections as there is very little to distract from the object. In other cases, objects are displayed as part of a larger display—a salon-style installation of paintings hung closely together, a large display case where similar objects are grouped, or a visually dense style of exhibition with many didactic panels, infographics, and diagrams. For some participants, these displays can be overwhelming and they may have difficulty focusing on the item being discussed. Plan carefully and consider extra supports to help participants see and focus in these settings. One strategy is to provide a printed reproduction for each person to hold and refer to as needed—be sure to check for glare from shiny printed surfaces as well.

Location of Objects

Where your chosen objects are located is as important as the objects themselves. "Where" could even be your first step in planning an activity. As we consider the impact of the display location of objects, keep in mind that there are many environmental factors to consider. The area should be free from distractions such as sound and other people if possible. The objects should be easy to see—well-lit, displayed at eye level if possible, and be of sufficient size.

You will have many objects to choose from, potentially spread over multiple rooms or outdoor locations. In a public tour, you may be used to traversing these spaces to see a broad selection of items to suit your tour plan. In our Gallery, a public or school tour can cover many rooms over two floors, depending on the audience. This is not the case for an *Artful Moments* program. We are conscious of the need to limit travel as much as possible. Fatigue and accessibility can be a factor for many participants but so can the disorientation and difficulty with transitions that participants can experience with a lot of movement and the resulting changes in surroundings. We recommend:

- Choosing objects that are all on display in the same room or in close proximity to reduce the need for walking and the stress of transitions from place to place.
- Ensuring that the chosen locations are all accessible for participants who use mobility devices or for whom stairs and other barriers would limit their participation.
- Ensuring that there is seating at EVERY stop—this means setting up seating in each location ahead of time.
- Organizing your conversation so that you move in one continuous direction—reduce the need to change direction or turn.
- Ensuring that the objects you have selected are clearly visible, well-lit, and ideally in an area with little clutter or distraction. Objects at seated eye level and larger objects will be the easiest to see. If the objects are small make sure that participants can get close enough to see them. As you are considering your selections and assessing visibility, be sure to sit down yourself and view the piece from the vantage point of a participant.

When planning our programs, we often start by choosing the room we will use for that day and then look at the works on display there and if needed in one adjoining room. From there we chose four to six works to focus on. Because we work with six- or eight-week programs, we have opportunities to discuss other important artworks in another location in subsequent sessions.

THEMES AND CONNECTIONS

To create an effective and engaging conversation, we use a thematic approach each week, with the selection of works sharing something in common to help frame the conversation. Think about what thematic links you can make among the objects you select—themes should be relevant to the four or five objects you select but may not reflect curatorial exhibition concepts. Simple is better. Familiar and meaningful to the participants is best.

Once you have found a number of suitable objects in a good location, coming up with a theme or idea to connect them helps participants follow the conversation. Themes can be as simple as "portraits," "mediterranean plants," or "cooking." For some participants, this will help them compare different objects they have seen that day while for others, recalling something seen earlier in a session may be more difficult. Be sure to observe carefully to determine the kind of connections or comparisons each group member makes.

Providing handouts for each session with images of all the objects discussed can be a great support for participants as it allows them to reference the objects discussed earlier. In some cases, the theme will be most helpful to you in guiding the experience. While making comparisons is useful, be sure you do not plan a conversation that is dependent on recall. Each object should offer its own enjoyable conversation points.

For in-person programs, the themes may already be present as you navigate a curated space. The objects will be all around the participants and ready for conversation. Planning by choosing specific works is still important in allowing you to prepare questions and information, AND it will allow you to prepare printed materials to support participants.

For virtual programs, you may have a much wider selection of digital images readily available. Themes will help you to make interesting choices that complement each other well. Themes do not need to connect or follow a specific trajectory from week to week but you may choose to start with more familiar and accessible themes and progress to ideas that are more complex in later sessions. For example, our first session is always something familiar like "Hamilton in Painting" which comprises five paintings and photographs of the city over 100 years. Participants see familiar street scenes and may remember times that they spent there. In the weeks that follow, we will use a variety of themes that include people in settings, landscape, or domestic scenes, and by the last week, we may try abstraction.

When deciding on the objects and the order of your conversation try to build interesting connections between objects. Your theme will provide the guiding idea for the conversation and you can use each new object to build upon the last. Your connection is how you link the two objects together—how they relate. This may be continuing an idea or it may be a contrast. Thoughtful connections help to move your conversation along and build on ideas that have been shared. They also allow you to repeat or return to your main ideas, supporting the participant's understanding and enjoyment. We also recommend that for in-person programs you try to move in one direction if possible, rather than back and forth which can become disorienting. Balancing thematic direction and physical direction will require careful planning.

How Many Things to Choose

Ultimately, your exhibitions and approach will determine the ideal number of content points for a program. Based on our experience the ideal number of objects is usually less than you think. Our focus is to have a rich, conversational experience where all participants have opportunities to contribute in a way that is comfortable for them and not rushed.

For most on-site programs, we choose five objects to focus the conversation. However, being surrounded by exhibitions we can always add additional works to support ideas or offer contrasting perspectives. We watch to see if participants seem interested in other things in the room and try to accommodate what has captured their attention. In-person programs tend to be the most fluid for this reason.

If you are working in another kind of exhibition space, you will need to consider your content focal points in a similar way. For example, in a historic house museum, your session could be one room. In initial conversations, you could talk about the room as a whole using observation and interest, and then select three or four objects within that room to examine more closely.

For virtual online programs, we plan for a conversation that lasts 45–60 minutes and use four or five objects. There are occasionally one or two supplemental images to support a point. Phone programs are usually a bit shorter so we use four. If you are unsure, you can always include an extra object in your slide show just in case, although we have found that if an object appears in the printed materials participants don't like to skip it.

Depending on your own space and approach, you may experiment with a few more or less than what we have suggested, but we would advise you to opt for less movement and transition in favor of more conversation about each object.

PLANNING CONVERSATIONS

Once you have selections made for each session, it is time to plan. We have purposely avoided using terms like "lesson planning" or "scripting" as we feel that these terms are contrary to our goals, but you may find similarities in how you plan other programs.

To begin, make a detailed outline. When you take the time to plan the main ideas, questions, and explanatory statements it provides an opportunity to closely examine your word choices, the length of your statements, and the amount of information you can share. For the person living with dementia, being clear and concise is beneficial to their experience. As you plan, you can find ways to streamline what you say and select only the most important or interesting pieces of information to share. One facilitator describes their planning like this:

> I make sure that I know as much about the object as I can and that I have spent a lot of time looking at it myself. Then I store it all away, only to be used if someone asks me. It seems like a

lot of work but knowing more makes me more comfortable. Then I can just sit back and enjoy the experience. Sometimes I get to share the things I know and other times I learn to see the art in a new way, a way that I had never considered. Our participants are very thoughtful and each person brings a unique viewpoint. I love the process of it.[3]

The Order of Objects

With your selections made, decide on the order for the session. For in-person programs, think first about movement around the space. Try to limit movement and flow in one direction as much as possible rather than weaving back and forth around a room. After considering the movement around the space or for virtual programs where movement is not an issue, consider starting from the most familiar or recognizable and moving into more complex works later. Think about ways that conversation about one object can lead naturally into the next.

What to Talk About

Take some time to look at your chosen objects with fresh eyes. What catches *your* attention first? What do you want to know more about and what seems like the most interesting or intriguing thing about your objects? Remember, this is a conversation, not a history, botany, or art lesson. First impressions are a great starting point, as are observations—"What do you see?" "What is the object made of?" "What do you think it was used for?" "Does it make you think of anything else?"

Have a bit of interpretive information about your object at hand but do not make this the focus. A few key points are all you need to fill in some of the questions your participants might have. Use this information sparingly and, as needed, to prompt or continue the conversation. We sometimes save two or three interesting tidbits for the end to confirm or summarize what has already been said. Information should be used to guide and add interest not to correct.

We have worked with many facilitators who favor a teaching-style presentation. They begin with a short introduction of ideas—what the object is, details of its making or provenance, how it fits into a larger social or historical context or anecdotes that can add some personal relevance. They then proceed to ask questions—guiding the exploration of participants, checking for understanding, and helping to fix the object into a larger narrative. Many visitors are quite familiar with this style of tour or presentation. In short, this style is "teach first" and interact second.

For many participants with dementia, this approach is not effective. Changes in a person's abilities mean that maintaining attention without specific engagement can be difficult. By front-loading the experience with information, you are asking the participant to remember what they have heard and to process a lot of information quickly. Your follow-up questions are more of a test than an invitation to contribute.

In contrast, in our programs, we ask first and share information second. By starting with carefully planned questions we engage each person right away. We address them by name, rephrase questions (and responses) for each person, and have direct contact with each participant frequently. Participants are supported in maintaining attention and initiating participation and the need to recall information is eliminated. When we do share other ideas and facts it is always in response to a participant's idea or question ensuring it is relevant and meaningful "in the moment." As one researcher reminds us, "asking questions that are designed to elicit personal responses . . . compels [participants] to actively participate in making meaning."[4]

Creating Support Materials

As you plan, think about supplementary materials or images that might be useful to help understanding. This could be a tactile object or a picture to add to the story. Make notes in your planning document about what supplemental materials you might use but be sure they are *really* important and use them sparingly. Too many extras become distracting.

Once your plan is complete, create a handout for each of your participants. For in-person programs, this may be a page with the objects that are being discussed at that session and key information like titles, artists, and dates. For virtual programs, this is part of the program package.

Planning all the weeks of a multi-session program is essential for virtual programs so that you can send the participants a complete program kit before the program starts. For in-person programs you may also find this helpful and can provide a full program package for participants to keep on the first day—though think about the added burden of bringing it with them each week. If you want the flexibility to adapt an in-person program based on the participants' interests each week, you may also opt to provide day-of handouts if necessary for an in-person session.

Day-Of Preparations

The day of a session is all about organization and eliminating distractions. Have your handouts printed if you are providing them, your supplemental materials at hand, and seating arranged in the exhibition spaces ahead of time. If you are in multiple locations during your session, have multiple sets of seating in place rather than moving seats around. Review your information plan and you plan for questions. Be sure to take a moment for yourself to breathe and set aside your business. Then, have fun!

Preparing for Virtual Conversations

For both online and phone-based programs, you can plan activities in a very similar manner as for in-person sessions. While your techniques to support participants may be more difficult, relying more on verbal instructions and descriptions, these programs are also very engaging and rewarding.

The biggest factor in your success is organization. Planning a six- or eight-week program of conversations and hands-on activities can be time-consuming, but effective organization makes everything run smoothly. The bonus is that you are not limited to what is currently on display at your museum. If you have a collection of digital images you can mine them for interesting themes and connections. The first step, just as with an in-person program, is to choose a theme and images. For our programs, we select four or five objects for an hour-long conversation.

Participants must be able to see what you are discussing. For online programs, this means high-resolution slides, ideally images that you can zoom in on as needed. Familiarize yourself with the zoom, pointer, and drawing tools to help direct viewers and add close-ups or supporting images as slides if they are helpful (remember not too many!). For phone-based programs, create a binder of full-page images takes the place of the screen. Use page numbers for easy access and with each new page, start with a short description to ensure everyone is on the correct page.

A program kit should include a conversation summary page for each session with color pictures of all the day's objects and large text labels with information like labels, artist name, identification of the plant, animal, object etc. The pages that follow the summary page are the larger format images of each object—one per page for discussion.

APPLYING APPROACH TO CONVERSATIONS

With a solid plan in place, all of the supplemental resources in hand, and your participants in front of you, it is time to get started. The chapters in Part IV contain a great deal of what you need to remember about program delivery. Remember particularly what you have learned about dementia, and keep in mind the strategies for your approach.

To Support Understanding

Position yourself in front of your group and ensure the object for discussion is easily visible to everyone. Pause and make sure you have everyone's attention before speaking. Be prepared to explain to the participants what they are going to be doing and how they can participate each time you focus on a new object. Do not assume that standing in the space will be enough of a cue for them to understand what you would like them to do. Use additional cues such as pointing at the object and demonstrating possible replies like a show of hands or thumbs up. You can use these cues throughout the conversation as well by pairing your words and nonverbal actions. Give everyone a few moments to just look at the object in front of them. Share your opening comments and questions slowly and one at a time and give everyone a moment to process.

Keep your questions and statements short and straightforward and avoid jargon or overly complex terminology. Shorter sentences are easier to follow. Always ask one question at a time. Be prepared to answer your own question especially if adjusting your questions does not alleviate difficulties that a participant might experience. Sometimes sharing what you think is enough to help others get started too.

To Support Initiation

In a lot of programs, we ask a question and wait to see who indicates that they would like to respond—with a raised hand, a nod, or eye contact. For participants with dementia, sometimes having to take the step of raising a hand or interjecting an answer to a question can be hard. Some may feel self-conscious about answering. Watch your participants carefully to see who appears keen to share but also draw out others who may not raise their hand. Say their name first and repeat the question. Ensure you offer opportunities for sharing to everyone in the group and offer options for verbal and nonverbal interaction. Be patient, positive, and encouraging, and be sure to leave time for processing.

To Support Expression

Remember to model multiple ways of answering questions. Some participants will answer when called upon but others may need additional support. If one person has just answered and you call on another, repeat the question. For a participant who has difficulties answering or one who you already know benefits from more support, ask the question in another way and consider suggesting choices to answer. Demonstrate nonverbal options like thumbs up and thumbs down as you talk. Keep your tone light, and encourage people to have fun with their ideas so no one feels pressure to be "right."

As your conversation continues, paraphrase participants' answers to ensure others have heard especially if the answer was long. Use what has been said to suggest the next question and build upon what has been said. Refer back to the object to connect comments that are made. Bridging people who have gone off-topic back to the conversation—can be accomplished by rephrasing questions and comments to refer back to the object or the general theme.

Keep track of your timing—conversations can take some time and rushing through a final work will cause anxiety or annoyance, as may skipping something on your list of works.

Part of your role as facilitator is to play the "host" and to read the room. Start with a moment to socialize and check-in with everyone to see how they are feeling. Get everyone comfortable and start with an introduction of the day's theme. This helps everyone orient themselves and gives them clues about what to look for and how to respond to questions.

As you guide the conversation, keep an eye on each participant to see how each of them is managing the content and the pace. Gently draw out those who are not participating and give extra support to make them feel comfortable and valued. Be a good listener and offer moments to check-in with everyone. Pay attention to their energy levels and the amount of enjoyment, frustration, and/or disengagement you see. Leading a conversation is a balancing act but it can be a lot of fun too. Never forget to laugh along with the group and enjoy the process yourself.

Giving everyone a chance to contribute is important so try to keep track of who you have called on. In an in-person program, this can be more fluid and you will be able to read facial expressions and body language to understand whether people are feeling connected. In virtual programs, we have found that having a class list handy and discreetly checking off each time a participant is called upon is helpful to keep things balanced especially with a larger group.

A nice way to summarize and conclude a conversation is to briefly review the key ideas and the works that you have talked about in an overview. Participants can refer back to their printed summary sheets (if they have them) to remind them of what they have seen and for virtual programs you can even put all of the objects you have discussed on one screen.

We often like to spend a moment sharing favorites to wrap up a session. What started as a passing comment about a painting going home with someone because they loved it so much has actually turned into a routine. Participants even remind us if we forget. After the summary, we ask each person, in turn, which of the objects discussed they like most or would like to see in their home. There is often a lot of sharing about why they chose that particular piece and some have even thought about which room it would go into at home. One of our regulars has a whole (imaginary) collection of artwork spread across all of the rooms of her home—there is a reason for the location of each.

Having now spent up to an hour with this first activity, participants are often ready for a short break. This will relieve the fatigue that may be caused by the conversation and they may also need a moment to help transition from one activity to another. During in-person programs, we gather in the workspace and have a short snack and social break before starting into the hands-on activity. Virtually, we take five minutes to stretch, make a cup of tea, and arrange supplies for the hands-on activity. In either case, as you wrap up the first part, be sure to help people transition into the next activity by telling them exactly what they are going to do next.

HOW TO TALK ABOUT MUSEUM OBJECTS

Educational and museological pedagogy gives us many different ways to approach an object in a museum. We may consider its purpose, social and historical context, subject, technique, and material, along with a slew of other interpretive strategies. Some educators use carefully planned narratives, and engage in storytelling and questioning strategies; some use thinking routines and strategies for looking, while others simply go with the flow of the group.

Whatever your current approach, there are ways to adapt it to better support participants living with dementia. Your role is to enhance their ability to communicate, to better understand, and to express themselves through adjustments to your pace and level of language, the amount of time you spend talking to your group, and your goals for the experience.

As you consider making adaptations, remember to apply the philosophy and goals of your program and your knowledge of the participants in all decisions you make. A lecture-style, scripted tour does not fit within this framework nor does the requirement for participants to acquire content knowledge. When collecting information to share, ask yourself how it will add to the experience, if it will be meaningful to the participant, and how engaging it really is. Be selective.

This program is about an engaging and supportive experience, the enjoyment "in the moment" of a cultural setting and collection. It is an opportunity to look and share ideas and opinions, to contribute to a conversation, and to enjoy the company of others.

As a facilitator, your conversations are an opportunity to share some of the things you have observed, to model how to participate, to move the conversation along, and to build rapport with your group. This sharing is what makes your experience a conversation rather than a lecture and takes the pressure off you to be the "expert." There is ample opportunity for you to share information and stories, but it must be carefully and thoughtfully included as part of the experience, not the entirety of it. Focus on drawing out the ideas of your group and add a few "gems" of information when and if they add to the conversation. Also, be sure to leave space for participants to share their knowledge and experience—they have a lot to share and appreciate opportunities to contribute.

- Don't worry if you don't know something.
- Don't be afraid to say you don't know.
- Embrace the knowledge and experience of your participants.
- Ask what they think and work it out together.

Storytelling and Conversations

A good story can capture the attention and imagination of a group in many programs. Often, facilitators are accustomed to adult groups who visit museums and want to be led through their experience, with a chance to ask questions at the end. A presentation style like this is not dementia-friendly. It relies on memory of what was said, processing speed to interpret and understand information at a rapid pace, and the ability to maintain attention to be successful. It does not promote interaction, or opportunities for social connections, and is less engaging. It is also possible that there will be too much information for the participants to process and enjoy.

Good Approach: How to Adapt a Storytelling-Style Program

- Focus on the two or three most important ideas, especially those directly related to the object.
- Do not assume (or test!) prior knowledge to make sense of your information
- Keep it short and simple.
- Leave breaks for conversation.
- Find ways to encourage participation, such as raising hands in agreement with a statement or question, interacting with visual, auditory, or tactile objects, or asking and answering questions as you go.
- Remember to take a few moments to have participants *look* before you begin speaking without interrupting them.

Better Approach: Visual Thinking and "Observation" to Spark Conversation

No matter what kinds of objects your exhibitions and collections include, encouraging participants to talk about what they see (and hear) is a sure way to build engagement and interest. Start by giving them a few moments to look and include a simple prompt to help them get started. Then ask them to share what they notice. To support participants in their observations, you can start with simply listing things they see, and then build the story together as you go. Ask things like:

- What colors has the artist used?
- What is this object made of?
- What kinds of furniture do you see in this room?
- What would that plant feel like if you touched it?
- What is the first thing you notice?

With direct questions like this to start, you can move fairly quickly through the group allowing each participant to participate right away and building a list of topics to explore further in the moments that follow. All of these questions can also be stepped up or down, as described in Part IV, to accommodate different levels of ability. "What colors has the artist used?" easily transforms into "Has the artist used warm colors like red and yellow or cool colors like blue and green?" or even "Has the artist used any blue in this painting?"

For long answers, remember to paraphrase what a participant has said to support the understanding of another participant or highlight a single item or thought. If you start with descriptions, you can hold off on the interpretation or meaning of the object until everyone has had a turn. You can then start to probe a bit with questions that build on what has already been said:

- Do those colors change how you feel looking at this painting? What do they tell you about the people or place?
- Do you think this object is old or new? Was it made by hand or a machine? Why do you think that?
- Based on the furniture, what was this room used for? Whose room was this?
- What else do you notice?
- *Or to help with communication*: Did you notice (*something specific*)?

Your conversation may go off-topic or in a direction that you did not expect. That is okay. Participants may be reminded of memories and experiences and this is a great way to connect with loved ones, as well as with other people in the group. You may even choose objects that purposely generate memories from earlier in a participant's life to inspire fond reminiscence. Ask questions to draw out more sharing or to encourage other members of the group to share too.

Use your storytelling skills to insert small bits of information about the object where this information helps continue the conversation or to wrap up the group's ideas at the end. When participants are engaged with the object from their conversation, they will often be interested in learning a little more. You can also use your additions to help transition to the next object in your program linking with your overall theme. Strategic and spare use of information can be very effective as it does not overwhelm the participants or take too long. Save the rest of the facts for another program.

Physical and Sensory Interventions

Much of what we have covered in this section is dialogue-based. Conversations form the basis for how we communicate with participants, and while we have considered verbal and nonverbal communication in this chapter and in Part IV, the focus has been on language. There are many other ways to experience and respond to museum objects that can be included in programs for people with dementia in very effective ways.

In an exhibition setting, including tactile resources to support your conversation can be very meaningful. In our programs, we have used fabric samples to demonstrate what clothing in a painting might feel like, samples of wood or stone to support understanding of a sculpture that cannot be touched, and fragrances to add depth to the visual experience. Figure 12.2 shows an Artful Moments group exploring a portrait bust through touch and conversation.

Body, movement, dance, sound, and more offer both an access point into a museum object and potentially a way to respond to one. Consider the impact of playing a sound to accompany a conversation in an exhibition—the added understanding that the sound an object may once have made can contribute, the atmospheric elements like blowing grass, rushing water or crickets might add to a landscape, or the mood of a piece of music communicated in tones, speed and rhythm. Participants may move their bodies in response to an experience as well. If you are open to a variety of interpretations and expressions, your program opportunities are nearly endless.

GETTING STARTED: BUILD A PROGRAM PLAN

To begin, walk through your exhibitions. Based on what you have just learned, create groupings of four or five objects to make up a single session conversation. Think about what connections you can make between them. Remember to keep travel, visibility, and other environmental factors in mind.

List of Objects—Write the details of your chosen objects (for example artist, title, date, media) in the order you plan to discuss them for each session.

Theme & Opening Statements—Think about what connections you can draw between each of your selections. The best conversations are those that have a good overall theme and that introduce objects as a way of continuing the conversation.

Figure 12.2 Sensory Experiences. While not always possible, tactile experiences can be very powerful for participants. Museum collection objects that can be touched, selections from teaching collections or other tactile materials can allow participants to access strengths and activate interest and engagement. *Source*: Art Gallery of Hamilton.

Write a short explanation of your theme—the reason your chosen objects make sense together. Then using that outline to guide you, write an opening sentence or two—what you will actually say to your group—to begin the conversation. Remember to keep it short, clear, and engaging. Planning this introduction ahead of time allows you to edit your words into a meaningful but concise form.

Planning Questions—Next, think about how to engage your group in an actual conversation. The questions you ask will encourage participants to look carefully and think about the object in front of them and will invite everyone to participate in a way that is meaningful and comfortable for them. Having planned a few key questions in advance will help you structure your plan enough to be cohesive and well executed. By having possible modified options in mind, you will also be able to adapt seamlessly without stumbling.

Write two or three questions for each object. Keep your theme and the interesting information you wrote earlier in mind and use your questions to guide your participants to see the connections you have already made. Try creating some modifications to each question to simplify or add complexity.

NOTES

1. Patrice Rancour and Terry Barrett, "Art Interpretation as a Clinical Intervention Toward Healing," *Journal of Holistic Nursing American Holistic Nursing Association* 29, no. 1 (2011): 68, https://doi.org/10.1177/089801019358768.
2. Paul M. Camic, Victoira Tischler, and Chantal Helen Pearman, "Viewing and Making art Together: A Multi-session Art-gallery-based Intervention for People with Dementia and Their Carers," *Aging & Mental Health* 18, no. 2 (2014): 166, https://doi.org/10.1080/13607863.2013.818101.
3. Reflection of an *Artful Moments* facilitator, 2023.
4. Rancour and Barrett, "Art Interpretation," 69.

13

Making Things Together

Museum facilitators know the magic of hands-on activities. They are the finishing touch in the learning experience, creating something inspired by what was seen and discussed.

There are other benefits as well. With two different types of activity, most participants will find ways to participate in a way that they enjoy. Some may be less interested in talking but will really enjoy tactile "making" or "doing" experiences. A shift from exhibitions and conversations that can be more formal and focused, into the hands-on workshop provides an atmosphere that is casual, social, and flexible. There is time for personal dialogue among participants, their family members, and friends. The shared experience can be very intimate and meaningful.

That said, be aware that some participants may find the hands-on activities intimidating or frustrating—finding that they cannot do things as they could before. For these participants, it is essential to have a variety of supports in place—from encouraging words and space for processing complex emotions to adaptive tools, materials, and steps in an activity.

Doing an activity together is also a great relationship builder. Participants who attend with a family member or friend will share their experience and can work together in a variety of ways depending on the participant's abilities. They can laugh together, remember earlier times, and take pleasure in their work. The hands-on activity also offers bonding between participants who are all trying something together. We include a moment to share our work at the end of each session. While no one is required to share what they have done, participants admire each other's creations.

WHAT MAKES A GOOD HANDS-ON ACTIVITY?

A good activity may be one you are already doing. Activities for people living with dementia do not require inventing or reproducing a specific kind of activity but rather adapting your existing activities to suit the specific needs and abilities of your participants. We have had wonderful success with art-making at the AGH, but as an art gallery, this makes sense. Your activities are your own. Are you an historic site with a working kitchen? Making bread can be adapted for this audience and the textures and smells can be very powerful. Plus, there will be lots of connections to memories of time spent making food. Are you a conservation site or garden? Planting seeds in pots will have a similar effect.

Hands-on activities also work in a variety of presentation formats—in-person, online, and over the phone. The types of activities you can do may vary from one format to another but with some creative thinking, many will translate to virtual online programs and phone programs. While each of these formats requires some specific ways of working and communicating, the general strategies used for these activities apply to all.

Selecting Hands-On Activities

Most activities that are offered in other museum programs are suitable for the programs described in this book. This includes everything from drawing and painting, baking, planting, music-making, and more. With careful planning, an understanding of the participants, and a thoughtful application of knowledge of dementia you can adapt hands-on activities for great results.

Hands-on activities are most effective when they link to the theme presented in your conversation. Conversations can provide inspiration or context for the activity and the activity can in turn build more understanding about the objects discussed. Imagine the impact of trying out a material or process seen in an artist's work or working with kitchen tools and ingredients from long ago. Remember:

- Participants will work at different levels—some will perform all steps independently or with some assistance, while others will indicate placement, colors, or instructions for their family member or friend to complete for them.
- Results do not have to match what was planned. Be prepared with plans to adapt or accommodate an activity to suit a variety of abilities.
- Encourage and validate all forms of participation. Remember, in this program, the experience is about the process not the finished product.
- Most importantly, you should always use meaningful activities and allow opportunities for individual creativity. Avoid prescriptive activities or busywork.

To choose the best hands-on activities, think about what you already offer for other audiences. We have found that our school programs are often one place to look. We cannot stress enough that while suggesting activities that we do with children we never think of our participants as childlike. Rather, the benefit of some school programs is that they are already designed to be more dynamic and process-oriented than more formal adult classes. We apply a similar strategy to many other adult and corporate programs where our focus is exploration and process rather than acquiring specific technical skills. Another benefit of these activities is that they are already tied to our exhibitions and collections in some way taking their inspiration from the art on our walls.

Make Activities Matter

We aim to provide hands-on activities that foster creativity, individual expression, and personality. They should never be prescriptive tasks that result in specific, identical results. The joy in these programs is in expressing each person's unique ideas and interests. To achieve this, hands-on activities should be:

Meaningful: An activity is considered "meaningful" when it has a clear purpose that resonates with the participant. It is not just about filling time, but about actively engaging in the process. Consider the difference between coloring a pre-made picture and creating your own artwork inspired by a museum exhibit. While both involve an art activity, the first is passive, while the second allows for creativity and personal expression.

Meaningful activities go beyond the final product. Whether painting, baking, or gardening, the focus is on the experience itself. Participants can learn about the materials and techniques used, and even imagine themselves as artists or craftspeople. This deeper understanding fosters a richer connection to the museum's collection.

Flexible: Activities must offer participants different ways to respond. For example, this could mean choosing the subject matter, colors, or placement of items in art activities, or making choices of different kinds of plants or containers in a garden project. In other programs, an open-ended activity gives participants the most freedom. However, in *Artful Moments*, providing some direction is typically

Figure 13.1   Make Activities Matter. Hands-on activities can take many forms, depending on the museum and the exhibitions that inspire them. The key to an engaging activity is that it means something to the participant, offers them space for creativity and self-expression. *Source*: istock.com /CasarsaGuru.

needed, as initiating or inventing something from scratch can be difficult. There should be clear steps, presented one at a time.

Led by Process not by "Talent": Many participants may join a program with no prior experience. Many are worried about how they will do. They may say things like "I just can't draw well," or think they are not "good" at doing things. By choosing activities that do not rely on a preexisting skill and by stressing the importance of process, participants can relax and explore. By adding careful step-by-step guidance, the activity becomes much more enjoyable.

Individually Creative: Your goal should always be for each participant to create something that is their own. Never plan for a specific final result where everyone's final work is the same. You will find that some participants will follow your steps and your demonstration very closely but they should also have the freedom to do their own thing. If you demonstrate the technique in the steps, possibly with multiple options, and try not to focus on the appearance, you will allow for this openness.

Familiar: This is a very subjective description, but some activities are easier than others. Most participants will know what to do with a paintbrush while printmaking is less familiar. A garden is sometimes easier to create than an abstract painting. If the activity starts with something familiar participants will feel more comfortable. In a multi-week session, you can scaffold them up to something less familiar by building their confidence.

PLANNING HANDS-ON ACTIVITIES

Once you have selected your hands-on activities, it is time to plan your lesson. The more prepared you are with step-by-step instructions, support materials, and possible individual adaptations the better your program will be. There are myriad possibilities for activities but similar planning steps can be used to ensure an enjoyable experience in each case. Here are just a few ideas:

- Painting a watercolor cityscape
- Making a garden collage
- Planting a tea cup container garden

- Baking bread in a historical home kitchen
- Candle dipping in an historical workshop
- Percussion exploration in response to beat, sound, emotion

Try a run-through on your own: Work, step-by-step through the entire activity yourself making note of each major step, any potential areas for difficulty, and any materials or tools that are necessary. If you plan to use this as a virtual activity or printed lesson plan, take photos of each step. Try to limit your activity to four or five main steps, and keep note of your time. For an hour-long activity, you should be able to complete the activity yourself in about ten to fifteen minutes. If there are more steps or time required, simplify the activity.

Consider the safety and ease of use of your materials and tools: A jumble of options spread on a worktable can be confusing and intimidating. Rather than inspiring creativity for many participants too much is a barrier to engaging. Limiting tools and materials will make your activity easier to follow. This means things like having only two paintbrushes, a limited palette of paint colors, or using one bowl or spoon or premeasured materials. Use adult-appropriate materials to maintain dignity and link materials and techniques to the objects previously discussed to provide context for simpler approaches. These guidelines are meant to keep the activity comfortable for each participant's level of ability. This does not mean that you should prepare so much that your activity is a "cookie cutter" craft where each person's work looks the same. It is important to allow for individual choices and creativity but by streamlining the materials you make these individual actions easier.

Consider the dexterity and physical abilities of participants: Some accommodations can be a standard part of your setup while others should be on an individual basis, recognizing that each participant will have different areas where support may be beneficial. Have options for support handy so that you can offer them if needed.

- Add special grips to items like pencils, brushes, and spoons, or have some larger tools available.
- A weighted tool may help a participant who has a hand tremor.
- Having bowls with an anti-slip silicone bottom or taping down a paint palette will help too.
- Scissors may be difficult for some participants, so have precut options available for those who need them.
- Think carefully about materials like clay that can be hard to work with if it is not soft enough to manipulate easily.

Prepare support materials: After your test run, you will be all set to prepare the materials for the program.

- Have a finished sample of the activity. This gives participants an idea of what they will be making. You may even keep different versions or examples at different steps to help explain the process.
- Gather any reproductions or other reference resources that are needed.
- Finalize your list of tools and materials. Organize for each step of your activity.
- Write a simple lesson plan for each step for reference later. Prepare a very simple written list of steps. Reduce to just a few words and just a few steps. During the lesson, display it in very large print on large paper for reference or use it as a handout for each participant to have their own copy . . . OR do both.
- In advance of your program, prepare any precut materials, or other assistive materials.

Plan for Safety

When planning hands-on activities, think carefully about safety, keeping participants' range of abilities in mind. Remembering changes in abilities and age-related changes to physical ability and vision, you may adjust your use of sharp tools or heat but materials like paint or clay will likely be safe for participants in earlier stages of dementia.

For participants in the later stages, consider the safety of tools and materials more carefully. Tools may be used inappropriately or unsafely if the person no longer recognizes the tool or is unable to plan how to use it.

Sharps: Tools like scissors, stationary knives, or kitchen knives bear careful consideration. Scissors are safe for many participants but conditions like arthritis or hands that are unsteady can make cutting more difficult. Other sharp tools should be considered only based on your knowledge of each participant's abilities. Having materials precut is a good alternative. If you are providing precut items, be sure to offer a selection so that the participant can make individual choices. Your substitutions and modifications are about removing difficulties, not creativity.

Accidental ingestion: Always use water containers that do not resemble food containers (such as mugs or drinking cups). For many participants in the earlier stages, accidental ingestion will be less of a concern. If you are using paint or similar materials, be sure to have cloths or cleaning wipes for cleaning hands handy and avoid having food or drinks in the workspace. For participants in the later stages of dementia, be more cautious about your choices. For programs in outdoor spaces, be aware of plants or materials that may be toxic and identify them to participants or find safer alternatives. For participants who may have difficulty recognizing unsafe materials or recognizing that their hands are messy, keep an eye on substances that may be harmful if swallowed or make different choices.

We often work with acrylic paints, modeling clay, and printmaking ink in our programs, which means that you can still use a wide range of materials and tools in your hands-on activities. Be sure to take precautions and ask family members, friends, or staff, to pay careful attention to any potential risks. If you keep safety in mind, you can make most activities work.

Burns and other hazards: If you present activities in a location with a working kitchen, open fire, or other hazards plan carefully to avoid burns. Some participants may not recognize hot surfaces or be able to distinguish high temperatures quickly. Consider the roles of participants and facilitators as it pertains to taking things in and out of ovens, near flames, or other situations.

Plan for Adaptations

In a group, participants will have different abilities and will work at different speeds. Your lesson plan will form a baseline for the activity that many participants can complete with limited support. From this plan, develop an adapted plan with greater support, and if your group has a wide range of abilities you can even consider a third plan with the highest level of support, alternative materials, steps, and even the final product.

If your baseline lesson asks a participant to follow along, completing each step independently with guidance, then your first step of modification would include supports like some pre-prepared materials—precut shapes or templates, premeasured ingredients, or other assistance. This is where a participant's family member or friend can also step in to assist or co-create. Your next step of modification would be having adapted or substituted materials or processes, as well as offering more direct assistance in each step. Add a list of additional materials or supporting steps to your lesson plan.

An example we have used is a cut-paper collage inspired by Henri Matisse's later work. Our baseline is to provide colored paper, scissors, and glue for participants to cut shapes and arrange them into a finished work. The first level of adaptation is to provide precut shapes, either in combination with blank paper for cutting, or instead. Participants may still glue the shapes or have their family member or friend help. The alternative plan includes precut felt shapes and a felt board for participants to arrange designs easily, or precut paper shapes and a sticky surface for arrangements.

Preparing for Virtual Hands-On Activities

For online- and phone-based programs, activity planning is very similar to in-person activities. Supportive techniques may be more difficult, relying more on verbal instructions and assistance from others at the home but it can all be done with great results. Activities and materials should be simplified to suit at-home work.

- A Program Kit with supplies needed for each activity is provided after registration. We have considered adding labels for unfamiliar items.
- An activity page with clear instructions, a list of materials, and images of the activity steps/process is included in the Kit.
- Weekly communication helps participants prepare. For online programs, we send program links and a list of supplies needed each week.
- When we begin online, we show each material required on-screen and describe it to make sure everyone has what they need. For phone programs, we include a photo of supplies needed each week and refer to it in the introduction.
- Being organized and well set up for your demonstration is essential. Have an organized workspace with only what you need for the activity in view.
- For online programs, we recommend having a second camera pointing at your workspace. Ensure your demonstration is oriented correctly for their screens, and that they can see the whole work area. Spotlight your screen for full coverage. Go slowly, describing and demonstrating the activity one step at a time, allowing time for participants to work along with you—repeat with a second example when needed.
- For phone-based programs, include written instructions and photographs of each step for reference that they can use as you talk.

Setting Up for a Hands-On Activity

On the day of the program, have everything ready to go before your group arrives. Moving around to hand out supplies can be distracting for participants and will add to your sense of rush. If everyone can simply come in and sit, your program will feel calm and focused. Ensure your demonstration is set up, that your sample projects and instructions are displayed where everyone can see them, and that all pre-prepared materials and handouts are on the tables or close at hand.

Much of this preparation goes back to what you learned about the environment in Part III. Ensure everyone can hear and see you and your "demonstration area" clearly. A U-shaped table configuration is much better for sharing and community-building than a classroom setup with rows facing the front, but this will depend on your space. Do not crowd participants—a participant and their family member or friend, or two participants at each table is ideal. If a participant sees or hears better on one side, make sure their partner sits on their "good side." Give participants time to settle in comfortably and to adjust to the space—both related to the changing light or temperature and in the transition to a different room. A few moments for them to adjust will make participants more comfortable and will allow for socializing. Before you begin, do a quick check-in to make sure everyone is comfortable, and be sure to let them know where the washrooms are located.

To set up supplies, ensure that only the items that are necessary for the activity are placed on the table. Remove any clutter. You can deliver extra tools or materials as they are needed. Keep the workspace as organized as possible and use trays or containers to hold anything that might roll away. Use a contrasting surface where possible to make materials easy to see—for example, a white paper on a light-colored table may be difficult for some participants to see. Keep everything within the participants' sight lines on the tabletop. All of this will support participants to participate independently.

For virtual programs, give everyone time to gather their supplies and settle in. Use your desktop camera to show what the supplies look like to make it easier for participants to set up. Have your materials ready to go and ensure your demonstration space is easy to see, with a contrasting color tabletop and paper.

APPLYING APPROACH TO HANDS-ON ACTIVITIES

By this point in your program, you have finished a conversation, taken a short break, and are ready to shift to a hands-on activity. For some participants, this is the most exciting part of the program while others approach it with a bit more hesitation. Your workspace is set up for each participant, your own supplies and demonstration space are ready to go, and your sample project and simple instructions are on display.

Having done the work to plan your lessons, gathering support materials, appropriate tools, and supplies and having your participants ready to work, it is time to get started. Again, most of what you need to remember during the program delivery is covered in Part IV, so do keep in mind the strategies you learned there.

To begin, briefly describe the activity and how it relates to the conversation you have just finished. If you are responding to a specific object from your conversation, have a reproduction available for each participant so they do not have to rely on recall. Your explanation can be done in just a few words and sets the tone for the activity. Your connection may be subject matter, materials, and technique, or a more broadly thematic link.

To Support Understanding

- While speaking, use visual examples and point them out as you go. This includes your sample activity, printed instructions, materials, and tools. Ensure everyone can see your examples well and use printed pictures and text on every table when needed.
- When you begin, demonstrate one step, give instructions, and leave time for participants to work before moving on to the next step. While a full demonstration from start to finish may be your standard practice for other programs, it is not effective in this case—it relies too much on maintaining attention, avoiding distraction, and having to remember several steps in order. With programs that rely on a full demonstration, the next phase is often a period of working time where participants are left to work on their own—for similar reasons, this is not a supportive experience either.
- Observe participants for understanding and engagement. Offer individual support for any participants who seem to be having difficulties. Repeat or clarify instructions to participants one-on-one, demonstrate what they should be doing off to the side of their work (never on their work).
- Ask individual participants questions or reframe instructions to allow them to express their feelings about activities.
- Give family members or friends in attendance tips on how to help and encourage them in assistive strategies. Ensure that you are always addressing the participant or both people, not talking about or over someone.
- Keep instructions short and language simple
- Leave time for participants to process your instructions and act.
- Be encouraging and positive, and allow space for participants to share their progress.

To Support Initiation

If, after your demonstration, you see a participant who has not started to work, there are a few ways to help. Approach them individually to check-in. Ask if they would like you to help them get started.

- Provide instructions in a simpler way—and one step at a time. Demonstrate what you would like them to do so that they can follow. Be sure to use an adult tone and normal volume but speak slowly enough that they can follow.
- Give them time to process what you are saying and demonstrating. If the participant has joined the program with a family member or friend, show them as well.
- If this does not help enough, try again with fewer words and ask them to follow along with you. Try handing them a tool—like a pencil or paintbrush—as the familiar tool might be enough of a cue to get started.
- As a next step, ask if you can help them get started. Work with the participant's family member or friend to try some of the facilitation techniques outlined in Part IV—techniques like hand-over-hand, or having the participant direct you or their partner by pointing to things.
- Try asking participants to show you what they would like to try—pointing to a tool or material. Pick it up, and ask them a follow-up question, perhaps if they can point to where they'd like you to place it.

Some participants will benefit from additional support with materials and processes. For example, a participant who has difficulty loading paint onto a brush themselves will benefit from assistance doing this. Once they have the paint, they can move it around their painting. Family and friends can be helpful with this kind of assistance. A participant who cannot fill a container with soil may still enjoy arranging plants into a pre-filled container or helping to pack the soil.

Be sure to give participants lots of time and remember to stay calm and patient. If these steps do not help, you can also ask if they would like to watch for a moment and try again in a little while. Remember, participation is not just actively making things, it can also be in enjoying watching others work.

To Support Expression

In this case, expression is synonymous with the production of an activity. We may also use the term "creation" or "action." Offering the assistance just described to ensure understanding is also a part of encouraging expression—the act of making something and participating in hands-on activities. In the next section, we will describe ways to help support specific situations. Using communication strategies can also help—offering verbal and nonverbal cues to answer questions, or having them point at things can help clarify their feelings.

To Support Changes in Physical Ability

Observe participants' progress through the activities. If you notice someone having difficulties with their fine motor skills, dexterity, or other skills, step in and ask if they would like some help. You or their family member or friend can cut out shapes, fold heavy paper, stir thick mixtures, or perform other simple tasks that are difficult without taking over their work. You can also have pre-made options on hand if needed. Be sure to facilitate their involvement and decision-making wherever possible—think of yourself as a spare set of hands only which ensures the activity is theirs.

For Participants Who Are Frustrated

Some participants may become quite frustrated when they are not able to complete an activity as they wish. There are many possible reasons for this and you may not be able to address all of them. Provide reassurance and offer support by saying, for example, "You are doing well, but this part is tricky. Would you like me to help with this part?" Be curious and ask the person to tell you more about what they are trying to do and then ask how you can help. Remember to stay calm and patient.

It may be that they are unsure of what to do next or have forgotten the steps. Notice where they are in the process, offer encouragement for the work they have accomplished and explain and demonstrate the next step. You can use your own curiosity to explore the process with them or offer suggestions of what you would do next.

It may be that the task is too difficult, which means you can take time individually to work through modified steps with words and demonstration or offer pre-prepared materials to help. This is where having an activity plan with two or three different levels of complexity can come in handy—you will be prepared with an alternative if and when you need it. You can also offer assistance by asking where they would like something placed or what color they would like to use next.

There may be other factors at play that you cannot know. Encouraging words and support can help or offering another option to help them to participate. You can ask if they would like to see you try. Demonstrate a simple version of the activity for them to watch. Once they feel better, they may want to step back in or they may simply enjoy watching the work.

If the family member or friend is showing signs of distress, offer reassurance to them as well. They may not know how to help or may be upset by the participant's frustration. They may carry insecurities about their abilities in the activity. They may be struggling with the changes they see in their loved one. They may be concerned with the participant working too slowly or not following instructions. Try to engage the family member or friend in your demonstration and ask lighthearted questions to lighten the mood.

Doing Their Own Thing

Many participants will work through the activity with ease, following the steps and enjoying the process. Many results will be typical to the activity but, in some cases, a participant will create something completely different, out of differences in ability or interest. This is absolutely fine. If a participant is happy with their work, it is a good opportunity to find something to compliment and validate. Your goal for participants is to enjoy the activity not to create a specific result.

Sometimes family members or friends need help to understand this. We have seen family members who are concerned that their loved one is not "doing it right" or is not keeping up. They may be carrying a lot of worry or feelings of loss on behalf of their loved one or they may feel badly about their changes in ability. They may carry their own insecurities about their ability to complete the activity too. In these cases, it is a great opportunity to help them see past their feelings and to appreciate their participant's enjoyment. This is a chance to redirect the unconscious stigma that many people carry. Our strategies to help a family member or friend embrace the process of our program are to model validation and encouragement, to demonstrate appropriate ways to offer assistance, and when necessary offer a distraction or outlet by providing them with their own materials to work side by side.

In an early program, we planned painting activities for several sessions. One was a simple landscape and one was a paint and collage garden. One participant spent every session happily painting stripes on his paper. He embraced the process of mark-making and playing with color and created a finished painting of which he was visibly proud. For him, each session was a success. With coaching, his family member came to appreciate his enjoyment and engagement.

Sharing and Celebrating

A nice way to wrap up a hands-on program is to give people a chance to share their work. In person, this can be through casual mingling or virtually this can be holding up their work to the camera. Offering positive feedback and congratulations makes participants feel accomplished and included and makes a great point of social connection. As a facilitator, model positive comments and ensure your feedback is meaningful—find something specific and positive to comment on. This ensures that your input feels authentic and not patronizing.

Some participants may not feel like sharing each session, and that is okay too. In some sessions, especially virtually, participants may enjoy watching the work of others and will return to the activities on their own later.

If you can shift your program to a more casual, social moment at the end, participants will have the opportunity to connect and slowly transition to the next stage of leaving the program to go home. They will feel good about their time with you and about themselves. Many will continue to talk about their experience with their family member friend, or others after the program.

STAFFING FOR ACTIVITIES

We have invested a lot of care and time in developing our team. Our success is due to the combination of knowledge and experience of each team member and the spirit of shared learning and responsiveness that forms the basis of our program. We understand that a good program is a team effort and rely strongly on each of these roles for our success. A program could be presented entirely with a single facilitator, but if you can work with a small team, your experience will be much more fruitful.

While it is a good idea for all facilitators and support staff or volunteers to have a strong understanding of dementia and activity-related knowledge, the best team combines people with expertise in several different fields.

Content-expertise: Knowledge about your collections and exhibitions will drive your activities. This knowledge will begin with the museum staff and volunteers and also includes knowledge of educational strategies and hands-on skills.

Participant-expertise: An in-depth understanding of dementia and best practices for communication and care is the foundation and the success of *Artful Moments*. This expertise can originate from a variety of community partners, and their ongoing support can offer great value and opportunity to your programs. We strongly recommend that the museum team who will lead the activities invest in learning to understand dementia and seek out and welcome support from outside experts.

The combination of the two is powerful. One of the strengths of our program is the sharing of knowledge between facilitators and other team members. We maintain a nonclinical approach to programming but we have learned from and continue to be supported by practitioners in a variety of care fields. All team members are trained to understand all aspects of the program knowledge and to apply it in their roles.

Program-expertise: This is the shared learning and experience built with the *Model for Successful Engagement* framework. Using content- and participant-knowledge to inform the understanding of Environment, Approach, and Activity, all team members gain knowledge and experience in program presentation.

Staff Roles

Our program relies on five distinct roles but, in many cases, there is overlap—one person may perform multiple roles simultaneously. Use this list to think about how to structure your team as you are starting out and over time. Many museums offer wonderful programs with a single facilitator.

Conversation facilitator: This is the person who leads the conversation activities in a program. They research the collection and exhibitions, select objects for discussion, prepare program outlines and support materials, and lead the activity. This role may be led by the museum education staff, tour guide, or a contract facilitator, so long as they are well acquainted with the approach for this program and have received education on working with people living with dementia.

Hands-on facilitator: This person leads the hands-on activities. They use the conversation theme to inspire their work, incorporate knowledge of the objects under discussion, and plan an activity that builds on some aspect of the theme. They create a lesson plan, source and prepare materials and tools, and set up the workshop space. They lead the activity demonstration and guide participants through the activity. This role may be led by the museum education staff or a contract facilitator who is also well acquainted with the program approach and knowledge of dementia. In many cases, the conversation and hands-on facilitator are the same person.

Support volunteers: These team members can help to support a program in a variety of ways. During conversations, they can offer small interjections where discussion lags and they can call on or engage a participant that they notice has not participated. They can record observations of the session for research and evaluation and they can offer feedback and insight that a facilitator may have missed. During hands-on activities, they can circulate among the group, offering individual assistance as needed as well as ongoing observation, or they can sit with a participant who has come on their own as support and company. This role can be led by a variety of people—tour guides from the museum, volunteers with health care or other related backgrounds, or people with a keen interest in this program. Even though they do not perform a frontline part of program delivery, their training in both content- and participant-knowledge will aid in their success.

Community partners: Community partners are a great way to build and reinforce the knowledge of the participant. They can offer training, assessment, and resources to help your program. If you work with a community program, retirement home, or care facility, these partners will often connect with their own groups and attend with them. They can be a valuable source of feedback and growth. Community organizations can offer support to your programs. In addition, many college and university programs are looking for opportunities for students. You may find students studying occupational therapy, nursing, gerontology, or other fields interested in volunteering or even doing a field placement with your program.

Researchers: These team members can be staff, volunteers, or community partners depending on your capacity. Program evaluation is an important, though often overlooked, part of program delivery. The next section will talk more about some of the tools that have been used in evaluating our program. Research projects are a wonderful opportunity to learn more about the impact your program has on participants and to contribute knowledge to the field of museum programming. Clinical partners, universities, and graduate students may all be interested in connecting with your program, and the shared learning that results from interdisciplinary collaborations is truly exciting.

Reflections and Debriefs

Having completed a session, it is a great idea to take a few minutes to reflect and make notes about the successes and difficulties. This will be very valuable to help with your development and can provide an important piece in program evaluation.

From one session to the next, you will have great successes and moments that did not go as well as expected. A past facilitator shared wise advice: "Being open and flexible when facilitating these types of programs will achieve the greatest results. Even the best-planned and organized programs may work well one day and fail the next." Do not get discouraged. Remember the goal is engagement—not a checklist of facts or a completed project. Many factors can affect a program and while you can plan for many, some may be out of your control. Thoughtful reflection can help you identify and understand both.

Your reflections about the objects you chose for a session, the observations and discussion of participants, as well as their engagement and results from the hands-on activities will inform your development as a facilitator and your future selections for programs. Writing about any surprises or new insights is a great way to store the positive experience you have after each session and provide anecdotes to use later in proposals, reports, and presentations—many of the stories shared in this book come from the authors' notes and reflections.

If you can share program delivery with others—another staff member, volunteer supporters, or community partners—their observations will be equally valuable. They will notice different things than you did particularly if your attention has been focused on facilitating the session. Having community partners with expertise in working with people living with dementia is a great opportunity for coaching and ongoing development. We strongly recommend setting up a plan to collect and store their observations and recommendations as well.

· During our early programs, we found one of the most valuable learning experiences in our program and facilitation development was in the ten or fifteen minutes immediately following a session. The clinical staff offered their observations about participants and each facilitator's successes and challenges. They offered suggestions for growth and improvement. They pointed out successes and we were able to ask questions and discuss our ideas. This process evolved organically but we quickly saw that these moments proved to be invaluable. Even now, we still make time to talk together at the end of every session and program, in-person and virtual.

One of our authors developed a routine following program delivery that has given her a very personally driven experience. The debriefing conversation happened at the end of the session after the participants left but before the team disbanded. Later that day she made time for a personal reflection—recording a list of the objects discussed, including small pictures where possible. She noted the main points of the conversation and the questions she asked as well as some of the responses. Where she had already created a session plan, she was able to add to it and update the plan for future use. She reflected on how she felt during the session and areas that felt incomplete. She added notes about the team debrief as well. She was fortunate to have a volunteer join her for most sessions to record observations throughout the session that captured important moments that she had not noticed. With all the parts together, she had a complete record. All of this information becomes a key ingredient in program evaluation later.

If you have the opportunity to hold team debriefs and personal reflections, we highly recommend it.

Message for Success

Museum Experiences Are Fun!

No matter what kind of museum you are, your space is filled with incredible treasures. These objects can spark exciting experiences filled with conversation, creativity, and engagement. By designing activities around them, you can create enjoyable and meaningful experiences that everyone can enjoy, regardless of their background or abilities.

Our programs are built around understanding participants, the museum environment, and how we approach activities. But without activities inspired by the museum's treasures, both the famous and the quirky, hidden gems, the experience isn't complete. Use these objects to create activities that bring them to life.

Remember, the activities you choose for people with dementia don't have to be brand new. We encourage you to adapt existing activities based on what you have learned about dementia and how to create a dementia-friendly environment. Focus on interaction and responding to participants' needs to make them feel comfortable and engaged. Sharing and being heard is important for everyone, including people with dementia.

Some activities will be hits, some might not. That's okay! Reflect and learn from each day's successes and challenges, and build on that experience. Your unique collections, exhibitions, and team will shape your activities, making your program special. By using our recommendations and tips, you will achieve a welcoming and enjoyable experience for everyone.

Part VI

Engagement and Well-Being

The Process and the Outcome

Throughout previous chapters we have covered the knowledge and steps needed to build a dementia-friendly program, focusing on understanding the participants, making adaptations, and using helpful techniques. Now we will discuss measuring success and the positive impact your program can have.

The framework of the *Model for Successful Engagement* directs our program and guides this curriculum. Its structure shows how each part of the framework is essential to achieving the outcome and reinforces the importance and interconnection of all of the work you have done in this learning program.

The *Museum*—YOUR museum—forms the foundation of the model, including the collections, exhibitions, staff and expertise, and site. Knowing your work well is an essential first step.

Knowledge of the *Participant* is the center. Here is where we focus on an understanding of dementia while also keeping in mind the person themselves. Being person-centered means seeing the participants, not their diagnoses, and applying the knowledge you have to fully empower their abilities and support changes.

Three pillars—*Environment*, *Approach*, and *Activity*—support this work. How you set up your space and your social environment, the way you communicate and facilitate, and the adaptations made to activities all determine how well your program will run.

Engagement occurs when all elements of the framework have been addressed successfully for program delivery. It is the process by which outcomes are achieved—improved well-being, with all that entails. Engagement (or lack thereof) will show you if everything is in place. If you do not see engagement, it is time to go back to the pillars and the knowledge of the participant to figure out what modifications are needed to improve it.

Our work and research show that by engaging in a well-designed program, participants will feel an enhanced sense of well-being. These programs create positive experiences that touch on different aspects of the meaning of "being well."

14

Understanding Engagement

The term "engagement" means capturing the attention or interest of a participant. It is about connections with the social and physical environment including active participation in an activity. In this context, we must always look for engagement through observable actions—things that you can actually see a participant doing (or not doing), rather than impressions about what we may think participants feel.[1]

When working with people living with dementia, prioritize a person-centered approach, where your aim is to provide experiences for participants that have relevance and importance to them. Experiences are not about "filling time" or busywork.

Meaningful Engagement comes from connecting with the participants as equals and allowing them to contribute, be seen, and be heard for who they are. This idea may be less measurable than the simple definition above, but when we discuss the "signs" of engagement, it will help you to identify and value indications of meaningful engagement. To ensure meaningful engagement, we must:

- Encourage participants to communicate for themselves in a manner that is comfortable for them.
- Listen actively and use strategies to support understanding and expression.
- Create an environment that supports and reinforces strength and encourages sharing without fear of being judged or dismissed.
- Ensure that participants are able to direct what happens during an experience and make decisions that matter (such as what ideas are discussed during a conversation or the way they interpret a hands-on activity).
- Recognize and appreciate participants' skills and abilities.

In our early work, we focused strictly on engagement ("in the moment") for people living with dementia as a measure of our program's success. We felt that if we were able to capture participants' attention and encourage them to participate in activities, it would demonstrate that the program "worked." Many research tools have been designed to capture signs of engagement and in the research that was conducted, we were able to demonstrate that our programs met this goal with participants at various stages of dementia. The findings of this study are summarized below.[2]

To evaluate engagement in participants in the mid- to late-stages of dementia, direct observations were made using the "Apparent Affect Rating Scale (AARS)."[3] This scale measures interest, pleasure, sadness, anxiety, and anger through observations of certain behaviors displayed by the program participants. A questionnaire was completed by family members who attended the program to gather their perspectives.

Through this first research study, we concluded that the program offered activities and a structure that promoted a person-centered approach and created activities that family members or friends could share with participants. Participating in activities seemed to help family members and friends shift their focus to the more positive aspects of caregiving such as the satisfaction in seeing their loved one find renewed interest and joy in an activity.[4]

Observing and evaluating engagement is an effective measure of how well you are connecting with your participants. It is also a good starting point for further development and evaluation of your program.

LIVING "IN THE MOMENT"

When working with people living with dementia you will hear terms like "engagement in the moment" used frequently. Focusing on the present moment helps participants by reducing the need to remember things. This makes it easier for them to participate and enjoy the activity. For some participants, each session is a singular experience, and so, your program should not depend on recalling activities or information from previous sessions.

We are reminded that, "When we meet a person who is living with a chronic, progressive disease like dementia and focus on where they are in the moment instead of harkening back to who they used to be, we see a capable individual."[5]

Effective programs focus on participants' strengths. This involves fostering connections with people and objects, encouraging communication in preferred styles, and facilitating the sharing of experiences. This participant-centered approach maintains a sense of self-worth and dignity by focusing on current abilities and fostering positive social interaction. There is no expectation of past recall or new learning; instead, the program celebrates the unique strengths and connections each participant brings.

As a facilitator, this means planning, acting, and reflecting on experiences in real time, moment to moment. By focusing on the present moment, you empower participants, show respect, and validate their experiences.

What Engagement "In the Moment" Means

- An experience designed for self-expression, creativity, imagination, social connection, and feeling valued rather than strictly to convey information.
- Activities that are not dependent on previous learning so that memories of earlier experiences are not required for success. Keep in mind that many participants may recall previous experiences, so also allow participants to build on previous visits through their own connections and insights.
- Reframing ideas of "success" to match the program philosophy and helping participants and their family and friends do the same.
- Focusing on facilitating positive experiences as they happen. Be flexible and responsive. Follow where your group leads and have fun as you go!
- Reflecting on and identifying your expectations to define what is "success" for this program and embrace the moment.

Reading the Room

As museum educators and facilitators, many of you will be very familiar with the idea of "reading your audience" during a program. As you speak or demonstrate, you look around your group for signs that you are doing well—that you are connecting with participants, holding their interest, and maintaining their understanding of your content. Based on what you see, you adjust what you are doing. To begin you look for the obvious signs of engagement but as you become more experienced or as you get to know your participants more, you notice more subtle signs too.

What Does Engagement Look Like?

- Participants raising their hands, asking and answering questions, or adding to the conversation.
- Participants laughing at jokes and nodding agreement or appreciation of what is said.

Figure 14.1   Reading the Room. To get a good sense of how a program is going, we pay careful attention to the nonverbal cues we see in participants. In an engaged program, participants may look at other members in the group who are talking, lean in to participate in conversations and show many subtle signs beyond just raising their hand or speaking. *Source*: Art Gallery of Hamilton.

- Participants taking action in hands-on activities to follow instructions or explore creatively in their own way.
- Participants pointing things out to each other or quietly exchanging thoughts about the object being discussed. (Note that this is different from pairs who chat quietly to each other about unrelated topics—*that* is a sign of disengagement.)

These are great indicators of engagement in its most active form. But, there are other signs that participants are connecting with you, each other, and the objects and space where you are gathered. As you look around your group pay attention to:

- **Eye contact**—Where is the participant looking? At the facilitator or at the object being discussed? At the other participants, or their family member or friend?
- **Facial expression**—Is the participant smiling or frowning? Do you see signs of interest?
- **Body language**—Is the participant comfortable and alert? Are they facing their body toward the conversation or activity? Do they lean forward when looking at objects (a sign of interest that we see in visitors of all ages)? Do they lean in to be closer to their friend or loved one, or other participants (this shows heightened social connection)?
- **Actions**—Are they participating physically? Do they raise their hands, nod their head, give "thumbs up"? Do they lean in to look more closely or to connect with their family member or friend? Do they participate in the activity?
- **Mood**—Does the participant seem happy or content? Are they generally interested?
- **Communications**—Does the participant offer comments or questions about the object or to participate in the conversation in other ways? Do they communicate nonverbally that they are engaged?

Seeing the positive indications of engagement is a great indicator that you are connecting. However, the participant may be engaged even in the absence of these observations. As a person with dementia begins to experience changes in their abilities, their actions and communication may change too. The timing of these changes differs between individuals but generally, they increase as dementia progresses. For example:

- In the later stages of dementia, a person's expression of emotions may be more flat. They may laugh less and smile less often. This does not always mean they are not enjoying their experience.
- Some participants may have a harder time initiating participation—raising their hands or beginning to work on an activity. This does not mean they do not want to participate, they may just need some support to get started.
- As abilities related to communication change, participants may offer comments that are less related to the conversation or their words may become more difficult to understand. When they share things, use strategies to help with understanding and expression or simply appreciate and validate their participation

Signs of Disengagement

Just as it is important to recognize signs of engagement in your participants, pay attention for signs that your connection or their attention has begun to wane. The more familiar you are with participants and their typical ways of engaging, the easier it will be to recognize when they are starting to disengage. There are signs to look for that will help you notice shifts in engagement that may happen over a session or program.

The first clues that a participant might be getting tired or overwhelmed are usually in a change in their behavior. They might stop looking at you, the object, or other participants. Their prior pleasant mood might change, and their body language may seem less comfortable, or they may start to fidget, or to wander away. They might also start talking about something unrelated or show signs of distress.

In one program, we noticed that a participant's level of engagement fluctuated. By observing and learning how he usually interacted we became more efficient at noticing these changes and understanding why they might happen. This awareness helped the facilitator reconnect with the participant when needed.

Henry participates with his daughter each week while his wife takes time to rest. He enjoys coming to the program because he feels good when everyone remembers his name and listens to the things he tells us about his life. We have noticed in the past that he stays connected and active when we make sure to call on him regularly, though he does not often contribute to the conversation unprompted. On this particular day, he spoke a lot during the conversation even adding a story from his past. He was content and involved. When we switched to the hands-on activity he chatted with others at first, but then we noticed that he suddenly started worrying about his wife at home and asking his daughter about her several times. This was a sign of becoming disengaged from a program that had held his attention well to this point. At the same time, we saw that he was having trouble keeping up with the steps in the activity. He was feeling confused and at that moment he disconnected.

We saw Henry's disengagement through the shift of his attention away from the activity, instead focusing on his worry for his wife. He stopped painting and was no longer watching the facilitator or her demonstration. He began speaking to his daughter, asking about phoning home, and acting like he wanted to leave.

The best clue that a participant has disengaged is a visible change in their mood, appearance, or actions. Here are some things to look for:

- **Eye contact**—The participant stops looking at the facilitator, objects, or other participants. They may look around the room, or off in the distance.

- *Facial expression*—Participants who were once smiling are not, participants may look unhappy, sad, or confused. Remember that some people may not show expressions of mood as strongly as others—you are looking for a *change* from their usual presentation.
- *Body language*—Does the participant seem uncomfortable, or in pain? Do they lean away from the facilitator or others (showing discomfort)? Are they fidgeting or wandering away?
- *Mood*—Participants will arrive at the program with different moods, often related to external factors. They may also sometimes show a range of moods throughout the session or program. Is their mood different from their usual presentation? Remember that some participants, particularly those in the later stages of dementia, may show emotions that are less expected and may be unrelated to the program. Often it is the *change* in their mood that tells you more than the mood itself.
- *Actions*—Participants do not engage with objects or activities. They may fidget, walk around the room, or wander away. They may leave or ask to leave.
- *Communications*—Participants do not add comments or answer questions. They may ask questions, talk about unrelated things (like worries about home), or complain (to the group, facilitator, or their family member or friend).

Reengaging Participants

When Henry found the instructions difficult to follow, his engagement was lost, and he shifted to his worry about something outside of the program—his wife at home. To re-engage with Henry the facilitator took a moment to connect with him individually. She acknowledged where he was "in the moment" and validated his worry. When he mentioned his wife aloud, the facilitator replied, by saying: "Henry, you speak so fondly of your wife. I know you are worried about her, and I know that you care for her very much. You will be able to take this home to show her. Let's do a bit of this together." Then she showed him the steps one at a time, slowly, checking for understanding at each step and allowing him to complete each step before moving to the next. With his focus, "in the moment," on his wife, it would have been hard to shift his attention back without acknowledging his concern, "in that moment."

This thoughtful and validating attention helped him reconnect, just as we had seen in the past during conversations when his attention was sparked each time we called on him. Alternatively, Henry's daughter could offer him support for the activity as well. However, ideally, this would happen after the facilitator connects with him first and as an additional layer of support rather than the only one.

When working with a group, a facilitator might find it hard to stop in the middle of a demonstration to attend to one person, but with a group of participants with dementia, it is a good idea to take steps one at a time, pausing to make sure everyone understands and has completed that step before moving on. While participants work on their activity, the facilitator can connect individually with those who need extra support before moving the whole group onto the next step together. This is also where having a second facilitator or volunteer participate can be helpful as they can offer individual attention as needed while the group keeps working.

When you notice that a participant has disengaged, either during your program or as part of your post-program reflection, your first step is to think through the pillars (environment, approach, activity) to determine where changes or support are needed. In Henry's example from our reflections, support was needed for the activity. We realized that the instructions for how to complete the activity were either too complex or were delivered too quickly without giving time to process and work.

Think about the moment you first noticed the disconnect and what was happening at the time. Or, if your experience was that many participants in the group did not fully engage, reflect on the session to try to pinpoint areas of challenge. For example:

Environment

- Were there distractions in the room (sound, movement, other people, difficult lighting)?
- Was the object hard to see?
- Was the facilitator hard to hear?
- Was the workspace too cluttered or were tools hard to choose?
- Was the experience of getting into the program stressful?

Approach

- Did you use strategies to support expression and understanding?
- Did you connect with each participant individually and respond to their specific needs for support?
- Did you allow time for the participant to process what was said and enough time to act?

Activity

- Was the activity at the "just right challenge" level?
- Did you include lots of opportunities for participants to share their ideas?
- Did the activity promote independence and creativity?
- Did you allow for enough time and support for participants to feel successful?

Learning and Growing as a Facilitator

The above examples highlight some ways to recognize levels of engagement. When faced with challenges, revisit previous chapters to refresh yourself with the recommendations and your knowledge of dementia. It might feel overwhelming at first, but with awareness and practice, identifying and responding to changing engagement levels becomes more intuitive.

When reflecting on your sessions, note what worked well and moments where you felt connected to the group. This positive self-reflection will boost your confidence and help you grow as a facilitator.

ENGAGEMENT WITH MUSEUM OBJECTS

Engagement with museums can have significant benefits for people living with dementia. This is true whether the experience involves looking at and discussing objects or creating hands-on expressions of their ideas and interests. Museum objects can be a vehicle for meaningful self-expression. Indeed, engagement with these objects, through close looking, discussion, and hands-on response offers a person with dementia the chance to:

- Explore and exchange ideas about art, objects, artists, periods of history, and natural history.
- Make meaningful contributions in group experiences, supporting a desire to be seen and heard as a whole person.
- Experience intellectual stimulation and the enjoyment of learning activities, regardless of whether that learning will be retained later.
- Make connections between personal stories and the world at large.
- Access personal experiences and long-term memories.
- Participate in a meaningful activity that fosters personal growth.

In addition, there are positive benefits for family members or friends who accompany the participant. They experience the participant engaging, expressing themselves, and enjoying experiences in a safe, comfortable environment. They see them as a whole person with lived experiences, creativity, talent, and ideas. Their relationship that may be centered on offering care and support can shift, at least for a short time, to an equal partnership. As well, they can experience and appreciate the experience themselves and socialize with others.

A growing body of research is confirming the anecdotal evidence that the arts can improve quality of life, reduce stress, and allow people to better connect to the world.[6] By offering programs like *Artful Moments*, your museum can be part of this experience.

OUR WORK WITH ENGAGEMENT

Key concepts to appreciate for helping individuals with dementia engage fully:

Each person's abilities are unique and individualized. It is vital to promote their continued abilities, rather than focus on what has changed because of their dementia. A facilitator should look to pull out whatever strengths they see in each participant to encourage their participation. By providing opportunities to use these retained abilities, we provide the conditions for feelings of success and contribution.

Individuals' strengths remain across all areas of the brain including cognition, language, perception, mood, and physical abilities. Participants may have more skills available to them in different areas and at different times in the program as abilities may fluctuate with time of day, medication changes, amount of sleep, and progression of the disease. Typically, participants in the earlier stages will retain more strengths than those in the middle to late stages.

With an understanding of dementia and its impact, facilitators will learn to recognize the participant's strengths and abilities. Over time, the facilitators may be attuned to experiences in which the individual may do well and anticipate where difficulties may occur.

Based on this awareness, the facilitator can offer each participant the "just right challenge"[7] and recognize when and how to adjust and facilitate the participant's engagement. Our experience and previous research[8] have shown that a program works to create meaningful engagement for people living with dementia across the disease trajectory including participants in the later stage of the disease.

NOTES

1. Jiska Cohen Mansfield, Maha Dakheel-Ali, and Marcia S. Marx, "Engagement in Persons with Dementia: The Concept and its Measurement," *American Journal of Geriatric Psychiatry* 17, no. 4 (2009): 300, 304.
2. More information about this research project may be found in two articles: Afeez Abiola Hazzan, Janis Humphrey, Laurie Kilgour-Walsh, Kathy Moros, Katherine, Carmen Murray, Shannon Stanners, Maureen Montemuro, Aidan Giangregorio, and Alexandra Papaioannou, "Impact of the 'Artful Moments' Intervention on Persons with Dementia and Their Care Partners: A Pilot Study," *Canadian Geriatrics Journal* 19, no. 2 (2016): 58–65. Janis Humphrey, Maureen Montemuro, Esther Coker, Laurie Kilgour-Walsh, Kathy Moros, Carmen Murray, and Shannon Stanners. "'Artful Moments': A Framework for Successful Engagement in an Arts-based Programme for Persons in the Middle to Late Stages of Dementia," *Dementia* 18, no. 6 (2017): 2340–60.
3. The "Apparent Affect Rating Scale (AARS)" is presented in the article: M. Powell Lawton, Kimberly Van Haitsma, Margaret A. Perkinson, and Katy Ruckdeschel, "Observed Affect and Quality of life in Dementia: Further Affirmations and Problems," *Aging Mental Health* 5 (1999): 69–81.
4. Humphrey et al., "'Artful Moments,'" 2340–60.
5. "Living with Dementia Means Living in the Moment," *Crisis Prevention Institute,* accessed January 2024, https://www.crisisprevention.com/en-CA/Blog/living-with-dementia-means-living-in-the-moment.
6. Two examples of this research are: Gail Kenning and Mandy Visser, "Evaluating Quality of Life and Well-being at the Intersection of Dementia Care and Creative Engagement," *Dementia* 20, no. 7 (2021): 2441–61. Carolyn Todd, Paul Camic, Bridget Lockyer, Linda J. Thomson, and Helen J. Chatterjee, "Museum-based Programs for Socially Isolated Older Adults: Understanding What Works," *Health & Place* 48 (2017): 47–55.

7. The "Just Right Challenge" is explored more in Chapter 11. For a full description of the concept visit: Optimum Health Solutions, "Just Right Challenge," *The Occupational Therapist*, 2020, https://opt.net .au/optimum-life/occupational-therapists-just-right-challenge/.
8. More information about this research project may be found in two articles: Hazzan et al., "Impact of "Artful Moments'," 58–65. Humphrey, ""Artful Moments,'" 2340–60.

15

Moving toward Well-Being

The word "well-being" is prevalent in discussions of health and happiness across all fields including museums. Experts generally see it as a positive state that encompasses a variety of factors, such as physical health, happiness, feeling connected to others, and having a sense of purpose. Well-being is not limited to a single factor, nor is it a fixed or permanent state. Well-being is about achieving balance in multiple dimensions simultaneously and it fluctuates with what is happening in one's life. For this reason, we talk about enhancing or improving well-being—that is affecting a positive shift in a person's state rather than simply achieving well-being as an end state.[1] As with our approach to engagement, to identify and measure improved well-being as a result of our work, we must clearly describe the dimensions that we use to define it and have measurable outcomes.

As described previously, our initial work focused on demonstrating engagement—capturing the participant's attention and action in arts-based activities and encouraging them to participate in conversations and hands-on experiences ("conversations" denotes communication that is both verbal and nonverbal). Participants in our first two studies were living with mid- to late-stage dementia and were experiencing significant changes in their abilities. We thought that if we could provide engagement "in the moment" it would meaningfully impact their lives. We invited family members to participate in the program so that they would be able to offer assistance to their loved ones.

In subsequent work, it became clear that engagement, while an essential component of the experience, did not fully capture the impact we were seeing and hearing about from participants. While they enjoyed the activities and experiences they had "in the moment," their feedback told a much larger story.

We learned that by being engaged, participants were experiencing an improvement in their mood, their self-image, and their relationships. For some, that improvement happened within the timeframe of the program itself but anecdotally we heard from many participants and their loved ones that the effects lasted much longer, even after the memory of the program itself began to fade.

When she first started attending the program, Soraya looked forward to seeing her "art friends" each week, often chatting with her niece about the other members of her group in between programs. On program days, she wanted to wear something special for her day at the gallery. A year later, while Soraya and her niece were still regular participants, her abilities had changed and her memory of the other participants' names or the gallery itself were more difficult to access. Even so, her niece told us that her mood picked up each time she came and that in the day or two after a program, she would ask, "When can we go back to that place, to see those ladies?"[2]

In each program, we saw engagement—and so much more. Within most of the pairings of participants and their family member or friend, we saw two people who had experienced life and love together reconnecting over shared activities. Program experiences helped family members see their loved ones having positive and meaningful experiences at a point in their lives when those opportunities were harder to find. We discovered that engagement was a process by which we made a larger impact. We realized that we had been seeing improved well-being right from the start and *that* was the real outcome of our program.

Working with people living in the community, we started focusing on the social side of our programs and the power of shared experiences. This became even clearer during periods of social isolation when we connected with participants virtually. The feedback we collected emphasized the importance of these shared experiences.

A decade of experiences and research led us to a key realization: engagement, while crucial for connection, wasn't the whole story. Our programs were actually improving participants' well-being. But what exactly did "well-being" mean in this context? To find out, we consulted experts in museums, psychology, and healthcare.

SELECTED THEORIES OF WELL-BEING

In its 2016 report, the Canadian Index of Wellbeing adopted this definition:

> Community well-being is "the presence of the highest possible quality of life in its full breadth of expression focused on but not necessarily exclusive to: good living standards, robust health, a sustainable environment, vital communities, an educated populace, balanced time use, high levels of democratic participation, and access to and participation in leisure and culture."[3]

While this report focused on the well-being of communities at large rather than the individual, we see that several interrelated dimensions work together to create what we call "wellbeing." It is an effort to move beyond economic definitions of "doing well" to embrace a larger idea of success. While this definition is outside the scope of our specific work, it is a useful starting point.

It is encouraging to note the importance placed on participation in culture as one of the defining factors leading to improved well-being, acknowledging that "as forms of human expression, leisure, and cultural activities help to more fully define our lives, the meaning we derive from them, and ultimately, our well-being. This remains true throughout our lives regardless of age, gender, or social group."[4]

The World Health Organization defines health as "a state of complete physical, mental and social well-being and not merely the absence of disease or infirmity" while describing well-being as "a positive approach to living."[5] The National Wellness Institute adds that wellness is a "conscious, self-directed and evolving process of achieving full potential."[6]

There are countless theories and definitions of well being, from the highly scientific to the more exploratory. Depending on the source, you may discover anywhere from four to twelve or even more "dimensions" or elements that positively or negatively impact an individual's well-being. With a particular focus on both wellness in museum spaces and well-being for people living with dementia, the following theories have the most relevance to our work:

John Falk, Well-being in Museums

Dr. John H. Falk has spent a lifetime researching museum experiences. His work has significantly impacted the way that museum professionals think about the places we work, the types of audiences we serve, the roles we can play in people's lives, and the interests and needs of our visitors. Falk moved us past standard demographic categories and into an understanding of the reasons behind a museum visit and behaviors enacted there. Falk's work is a must-read for all of us. Continuing his visitor investigations, Falk has recently released a book on the subject: *The Value of Museums—Enhancing Societal Well-Being.*[7]

First, Falk's earlier work[8] on visitor motivations denotes five identity/motivation categories that he theorizes describe every museum visitor. Interestingly, an individual can fit into multiple categories, even over the span of a single visit, depending on their individual motivations and the context of their visit. The categories are:

- **Explorer**—wants to see and learn something new, often wanders until they find something of interest.
- **Facilitator**—is interested in supporting the experience of someone else who attends with them.
- **Experience seeker**—wants to see the "attractions" and make memories.
- **Professional/hobbyist**—wants to learn, to see and study specific things related to their interest.
- **Recharger**—wants to relax and restore themselves in a peaceful or inspiring place.

Each of these identities/motivations serves a need or interest for the person "in the moment," and affects what they see, how they connect, and what they take away from their experience.

In more recent work,[9] Falk reconsiders visitor experiences in museums through the lens of well-being. He suggests that well-being is a "biological process that is about achieving balance." He also sees museum visits as a necessary part of that balance. For Falk, well-being is a process of survival.[10]

In his book, he identified four categories of well-being into which a number of related elements are grouped and later added a fifth category that identifies a new, unique concept which he says has only emerged in recent history. These categories are:

- **Personal well-being**—including wonder, interest, identity fostering a sense of belonging, and stronger sense of self.
- **Intellectual well-being**—capturing learning and curiosity, problem-solving, and the ability to gather and apply information.
- **Social well-being**—centered on relationships, connections between loved ones, shared experiences, and coherence with others.
- **Physical well-being**—bringing people to gather together, to interact, explore, learn within a healthy, safe, anxiety-free, and restorative environment.
- **Global well-being**—occurring when a person feels they are contributing to the greater good, the just and equitable treatment of humanity.[11]

The overlap between visitor motivations and well-being categories is fascinating. It highlights the importance of museums designing experiences that match what visitors are looking for (motivations) and helping the visitor achieve a greater sense of well-being (outcome).

Martin Seligman, Positive Psychology

Historically, psychology often focused on problems and how to fix them. In contrast, psychologist Martin Seligman had a different idea. He thought it was important to focus on the good things in life and find ways to make them even better. Seligman called this new approach "Positive Psychology."[12]

Seligman originally proposed that the ultimate goal of "Positive Psychology" was the attainment of happiness and life satisfaction. He believed that happiness could be analyzed into three measurable elements: positive emotion, engagement, and meaning, and later expanded his study to well-being. With the consideration that individuals have experiences that, while important, may not fit with the idea of "happiness," he reframed the goal of "Positive Psychology" as "flourishing" rather than being happy. To "flourish" is to have a positive emotional state as well as positive feelings of self-esteem, optimism, resilience, vitality, self-determination, and/or positive relationships.[13] Seligman's PERMA Theory of well-being comprises five measurable elements:

- **Positive Emotion**—includes happiness and life satisfaction, along with a number of others like comfort, pleasure, and warmth.

- **Engagement**—is about "flow," the feeling of being completely absorbed in an activity or experience. Engagement, for Seligman, also includes the notion of using a person's highest strengths and talents.
- **Relationships**—more specifically positive relationships, understanding that social connections drive and impact nearly everything we do.
- **Meaning**—defined as "belonging to and serving something that . . . is bigger than the self." This is distinguished from a more personal interpretation of something meaningful *to an individual*, which would be categorized as "positive emotion."
- **Achievement**—connected to the ideas of success, winning, accomplishment, and mastery for its own sake.

Falk sees well-being as a balancing act between different aspects of life, and one that is constantly changing. Seligman focuses on each aspect individually, like separate puzzle pieces, that can be measured independently. Both theories contribute to a better understanding of well-being.

Clarke et al.: Measuring Well-Being in People with Dementia

Living a life filled with rich and meaningful experiences is essential to achieve a sense of well-being. For people living with dementia, this is no different. According to researchers,[14] well-being has often been used interchangeably with other concepts like health or quality of life. The authors contend that understanding the differences is important when it comes to encouraging and supporting people with living dementia in the pursuit of their own well-being. As part of their research in lived experiences, they identified six descriptive themes that they later grouped into four categories:

- **Emotional well-being:**
  - *Feeling positive*—feelings of hopefulness, humor, positive attitudes, acceptance, optimism.
- **Psychological well-being:**
  - *Going beyond*—strengths, personal growth, making meaning, transcending challenges of dementia.
  - *Agency and purpose*—keeping going, remaining active, autonomy, resilience.
  - *Positive sense of self*—self-worth, sense of identity, and self-efficacy.
- **Social well-being:**
  - *Connections and belonging*—close relationships, sense of belonging and acceptance, social participation, social engagement.
- **Life satisfaction:**
  - *Valuing life*—general sense of feeling well and being satisfied with life.

It is important to consider this work carefully, as it is based on the experiences and self-reporting of people living with dementia. Listening to and understanding what is meaningful to our participants is essential for the development, delivery, reflection, and analysis of our programs.

Do-Live-Well Framework

In step with the idea of well-being moving beyond biomedical, physical health care models toward a broader, social understanding, the *Do-Live-Well* framework is based on the "fundamental message that what you do everyday matters."[15] This idea stems from the recognition that participation and engagement socially, physically, intellectually, and emotionally in all aspects of life is essential for well-being. "The purpose of the framework is to prompt reflection and discussion about the ways in which everyday activities impact health and wellbeing."[16] The three-part framework outlines eight dimensions or types of experience that lead to health and well-being outcomes, including:

- Activating your body, mind, and senses.
- Connecting with others.
- Contributing to community and society.
- Taking care of yourself.
- Building security/prosperity.
- Developing and expressing identity.
- Developing capabilities and potential.
- Experiencing pleasure and joy.

Five activity patterns are identified as influencing factors on the dimensions of experience. These patterns prompt consideration of "not only the nature of what people do, but how they engage" in chosen occupations or activities.[17] These include:

- Engagement
- Meaning
- Balance
- Control/choice
- Routine

The Do-Live-Well framework highlights a key connection: the dimensions of experience and activity patterns influence each other and ultimately impact health and well-being outcomes. Importantly, the framework recognizes that external factors, like personal circumstances and social influences, can affect any part of this model.

Our review of the *Do-Live-Well* framework showed strong overlaps with other theories we have discussed. Specifically, the *Do-Live-Well* dimensions of experience and activity patterns closely align with the kind of experiences we strive to create (and have demonstrably achieved) through our museum programs.

For example, *Do-Live-Well's* "activating, connecting, and contributing," "identity," and "capabilities" connect directly to Falk's framework of personal, intellectual, social, physical, and global well-being. Similarly, we see connections to the emotional, psychological, and social well-being, and life satisfaction highlighted by Clarke, et al.'s research, as well as to Seligman's emphasis on achievement and meaning.

Museums offer a rich sensory and intellectual experience. They can activate both body and mind, creating a visit that feels personally relevant while also connecting you to the wider world.

Throughout this book, we have advocated for the value of shared experiences and the social connections that are fostered in well-designed, interactive encounters with museum objects. By participating in these experiences, participants are receiving the benefit of social connection, personal validation, and shared learning simultaneously offering these same benefits for others in the group.

In the *Do-Live-Well* framework, our team is particularly interested in the sixth and seventh dimensions as they relate to museum experiences: the development and expression of identity, and the development of capabilities and potential. Identity is the sense we have of ourselves as unique individuals. According to the research conducted by the *Do-Live-Well* team, "engagement in activities is fundamental to the evolution of an identity."[18] And further, "interests, preferences, values, personal strengths, and other characteristics of identity fuel engagement in preferred activities" leading to "a sense of meaning and purpose."[19]

Opportunities to challenge oneself and further personal growth through meaningful activities lead to self-actualization. When we ask participants about their ideas and stories, and when we provide opportunities to contribute to group experiences, we are supporting their identity. When we offer opportunities to experience the 'just right' level of challenging activities or to try something new and creative, we build on their capabilities and potential, even if just "in the moment."

As far as activity patterns in the *Do-Live-Well* framework, we have already discussed the first and second patterns of engagement and meaning at length. When we add in the fourth pattern of control and choice, we are reminded of the conditions for empowering individuals and respecting their autonomy in their own lives. By emphasizing the importance of control and choice, we remove the stigma and sense of helplessness that can sometimes be projected on a person whose abilities have changed. For a person living with dementia, these are all powerful experiences.

PARTICIPANTS' INSIGHTS

While in our initial project, we used observations of participant's actions to determine engagement, we later shifted to a model of self-reporting through surveys, research tools, and focus groups in subsequent projects. In our work, we aim to empower and validate the voices and experiences of our participants and this priority also carries into our research. We provide the opportunity for people living with dementia to speak to their own experiences, rather than measuring them through the lens of a researcher's observations.

Feedback from participants and their family or friends is important, beneficial, and inspiring. It is often filled with insight into their experiences and what participation in these programs means to them. We collect feedback and recommendations for improvements, and we adjust our programs accordingly.

When asked about what went well for them, many participants enthusiastically expressed enjoyment of all aspects of the program and talked about how much they enjoyed the outing, the art they saw, and spending time with others. One person told us that "seeing the art and learning about artists was a thrill."

When asked what they achieved, participant responses were varied but often highlighted a sense of pride in contributing to the group and creating their own artwork. They talked about the positive feelings they had and the enjoyment of being in good company. One participant's daughter told us that her experience was so important to her, as "time well spent with my mom—the program has been more than I hoped for . . . very positive and fulfilling. Participating in this program has been a joy."[20]

Other participants reported feeling enthusiastic and "fired up" about their participation. They described being "enlightened" and "satisfied" and agreed that the session provided an enjoyable way to share time. One participant found it eye-opening to see different interpretations and was pleased that she did not find herself wondering, "What am I doing here?" A family member who accompanied her mother said that she liked that the program was not only for "caregiver relief," but about sharing and something that she wants to be part of—"it's like a date with my mom."[21]

For a deeper look at outcomes, we turn to a long-standing participant. In an interview about her experiences in *Artful Moments*, she shared this:

> I saw that it was an art-related thing at the gallery and I'm attracted to those kinds of things. I realized that it would be people like me there, so it was very non-threatening. [I enjoyed] looking and talking about the art. When everybody contributes and you're listening to what they're seeing and thinking, it inspires you into seeing more than you would have seen, and feeling more confident. It was that sharing that really attracted me.
>
> The kinds of questions that were asked prompted me to really think further. To look at the art and know that I can make sense of it, that stays with you so it's not a single afternoon experience which fades away, but there's a real deep participation.

Figure 15.1 Well-being in Museums. Improved well-being comes from a balance of many different areas of life—being active, connecting with others and the world, feeling engaged and refreshed. Museums offer opportunities for all of these. *Source: istock.com/Toa55.*

> *You can feel very comfortable in [talking about] a work without judgment. You can be free to be yourself by the kind of ambience that's created there. It's very collegial. I see people who have gained confidence and more. At one time, they would answer with hesitation but you see how people grow into it. It's got that kind of open acceptance of you. You get to know people, like people, enjoy being together.*[22]

From this powerful feedback, we see themes of social connection, accomplishment and inspiration, shared experiences, and more. Other than subtle references to "people like me" and "being free to be myself," this participant does not talk about having dementia, she focuses on the experiences that she had. This feedback could be about any well-facilitated program for any audience, which is exactly the point. We use our knowledge and methodology to ensure that she has the kind of experience that is meaningful to her, resulting in positive experiences and feeling *well*.

MEASURING WELL-BEING

Our first study focused on engagement. Our purpose was to determine whether *Artful Moments* would facilitate positive engagement "in the moment" for people in the mid- to late-stage of dementia and to collect and understand the perceptions of the family members who shared the experience with their loved ones. Engagement was measured using direct observation tools over a year.[23] The study showed that by delivering a program guided by the *Model for Successful Engagement* we were able to achieve positive engagement for participants.[24]

Since then our work has shifted beyond this initial line of inquiry. We realized that "engagement" was not an end itself, but, rather, it was the process by which we achieved a more significant outcome of "well-being."

In a subsequent study, we explored the impact on participants' feelings of social connection and reduced feelings of isolation using the *Museum Well-Being Measures Toolkit*[25] that was developed to assess the impact of museum/art gallery activities on aspects of health and well-being in those who participated in those activities. The Toolkit was easy for participants to complete themselves and it yielded valuable feedback. By focusing on participant-driven data collection rather than observation, we were able to empower participants to speak for themselves, giving them agency and personhood. Their feedback has since helped to guide our program development, evaluation, and sharing. From this study, we found positive well-being outcomes.[26]

At the end of the study, we gathered feedback through a focus group that revealed: the tool was easy to use, and provided useful and easy-to-analyze data. We did find though that when it was used for each session it became overly repetitive and over time participants' responses were largely the same. Focus groups at the end of each eight-week program yielded the richest data.

Using the _Museum Well-Being Measures Toolkit_ as a framework and with the permission of the developers of this Toolkit, we began to work with a blank tool. We had a focus group with some of our participants to determine the most relevant approach for the final tool. As we move ahead, we consider that a tool that is easy to use and meaningful for participants is the most effective method of measuring well-being.

Exploring New Tools

Well-being is different for everyone and achieving improved well-being should be intentional—taking action to "be well." So, if well-being is personal to the individual the tool should be as well. We need to empower and amplify the voices of participants, and to gain an understanding of their experiences in their own words. The best way to do this? Ask them. Our current method of evaluating our program begins with the question, "What do you hope to get out of the program today?"

After a short preamble about well-being, we offer a few examples, telling participants that their goals or intentions are their own and they may answer as they wish. The tool leaves space for up to six goals or intentions. At the end of the session, they rate their experience on the achievement of the goals that they had at the beginning of the session using a one to five scale.

Our primary research focus is participants, but in a shared experience, it is important to consider the perspectives of others involved in the program. This includes family or friends who attend with their loved one, volunteers and support staff, and even facilitators themselves. We identify which category each respondent fits into to streamline data analysis. As well-being is as unique to each person as are their motivations for attending our programs, it is important to capture individualized, authentic feedback. This is why we encourage participants to generate their own goals for the day.

Why ask for six goals or intentions? When joining a museum program, we anticipate that at least one goal may be specifically tied to the content of the program. That could be something like "to see historical planes" or "to learn to paint." To inspire deeper reflection about other kinds of outcomes, participants are encouraged to consider multiple goals. We have noticed that more reflective, personal goals often emerge after two or three more straightforward ideas have been entered.

When completing the survey, we support different and changing abilities using similar facilitation strategies as the rest of the program—considering the environment, approach, and activity. We offer support through lists of suggestions, printed stickers that can be selected, and assistance from others. Questionnaires and focus groups add to our evaluation process. The use of these less structured approaches provides information to help keep the work relevant and meaningful for the museum and the participant.

EXPLORING WELL-BEING IN _ARTFUL MOMENTS_

Drawing on research from museums, psychology, occupational therapy, and dementia care, alongside our findings, we have begun to develop a working definition of well-being specific to our work with people living with dementia. While researchers used different terms, recurring themes emerged. Considering the outcomes achievable in our museum programs, we narrowed our focus to six key categories of inquiry:

- Connection with pthers
- Being active
- Feeling fulfilled
- Meaningful experiences
- Recharging
- Contributing

These categories, informed by our research findings and responsive to participant feedback and experiences, serve a dual purpose. They guide our understanding of well-being outcomes in participants and provide a standard for evaluating our work through the *Model for Successful Engagement*. Ultimately, this definition reflects both the lived experience of dementia and the impact of our museum programs.

Connection with Others

The impact of social connection in our programs has been demonstrated from the beginning. We have observed and heard from participants how their experiences have positively impacted their lives. Close relationships such as those between family members and friends as well as new relationships with opportunities to share an experience with other participants and program facilitators have an important role to play in a person's well-being.

Museums are uniquely positioned to have a positive impact on social well-being. Each institution houses a treasure trove of objects and collections that can spark connections. People can explore shared memories and interests ignited by these artifacts, while also discovering new things together. Couples connect over artwork, families see each other in new ways through shared experiences, and friendships blossom among participants. By welcoming communities and fostering shared experiences, museums inherently have social connection embedded within their mandates.

Being Active

Being active can encompass physical health and well-being—movement and exercise that is good for body and mind. It can also include a broader idea of being a part of a community—attending public spaces and events. Participating in this way is important for well-being and counteracting feelings of stigma and bias. Being active improves self-esteem and confidence.

Being active in a museum may mean physical engagement by moving through a space or environment, experiencing indoor or outdoor centers, or activating the senses in a range of activities. Museum programming increasingly considers the body, as well as the mind, in many initiatives. Museums also play a role in welcoming and activating their communities through their work—moving people away from circumstances of isolation and neglect toward civic, creative, and social activities.

Feeling Fulfilled

Feeling fulfilled encompasses more than happiness and pleasure. It is a rich blend of positive emotions, a sense of pride and accomplishment, a feeling of purpose, the ability to explore one's identity, and a sense of agency—control over one's behavior and thoughts. There is immense satisfaction for many people when they have intellectually stimulating experiences and discover things about themselves, others, or their environment. For some, this translates to "lifelong learning," exploring curiosity, or the pleasure of acquiring new skills or knowledge.

Museums are uniquely positioned to use their collections, exhibitions, and activities to enact powerful connections with participants' self-image and experiences of validation and accomplishment. Identity is expressed through all of these factors and the resulting communication and sharing further supports identity by sharing it with others. Finding their place in the larger narratives offered by museum experiences affirms personal value. Being invited to participate in experiences is not only enjoyable but offers meaning and accomplishment as well. Museum experiences allow participants to make choices and direct their own experiences. It is a core function of museums to create programs with a framework of support and engagement in mind.

Participating in a program like *Artful Moments* offers opportunities for all of these things by allowing individuals living with dementia to contribute and participate in experiences, offering them the autonomy to do so within their abilities and providing opportunities to succeed.

Meaningful Experiences

Throughout this book, we advocate for the enjoyment of the process and experience rather than the acquisition of new learning. This takes into consideration the changes that a person living with dementia may experience due to disease progression. While traditional measures of learning are less central in this kind of program, it should be understood that participating in learning activities— learning "in the moment"—brings with it engagement, self-esteem, positive feelings, and validation of personhood. It feels good to discover new ideas and talents and this stimulation is a powerful part of well-being.

Museum activities offer opportunities to explore interests and memories of earlier experiences and to connect to personal areas of expertise. They can inspire wonder and curiosity. Museum experiences are rich, complex, and multifaceted, and often unique to each person. Activities such as those we have described in this book are purposeful, important to the participant, and offer many interpretations and results.

Recharging

To take time to refresh, to rejuvenate, or to find peace or inspiration is important for well-being. Time alone or with family and friends in a restorative space can significantly enhance one's health, mood, relationships, and resilience.

Museums are a haven for the exploration of nearly every interest. Art galleries ignite creative inspiration. Gardens, greenhouses, parks, and zoos connect us with nature. Historical exhibits spark a sense of nostalgia. Museums can also offer beautiful music, engaging stories, and even delicious meals. Truly, the possibilities are as endless as the museums themselves.

We borrow this category name from Falk's research, noting that museums offer a unique and purposeful space to experience meaningful restorative moments. People living with dementia may find themselves worn down by their daily routines. The burdens associated with caring for a person with dementia are well-researched and documented. Coming to a museum program can be a way for participants on their own or together with a family member or friend, to step outside of their regular experiences, finding a renewal of their positive feelings. The same can be said for family caregivers who either participate in programs with their loved ones or are able to have some respite from their caregiving duties. Interestingly, in one study of a museum program, researchers found that 45 percent of participant pairs aligned their motivation with the idea of recharging.[27]

Contributing

Several researchers have found that giving to others through acts of kindness, facilitating experiences for others, and offering support can improve one's own well-being.[28] This may be due to the positive feelings and the sense of accomplishment that we have when we contribute and a sense of purpose and connection with others. When you 'give' to a loved one by sharing and supporting a positive experience, the well-being gained may be even higher.

Contributing to a museum experience fosters well-being for everyone involved. While it is easy to see how attending with a participant can be fulfilling, the benefits extend to facilitators as well—after all, well-being is important for everyone! Sharing the experience, acknowledging the enjoyment of the moment, and appreciating contributions by others are all key ingredients in fostering a sense of well-being.

A sense of contribution also comes from sharing knowledge and experience. When a participant sparks a conversation with their unique perspective or offers advice based on their background, it creates a sense of contribution. Museums that focus on participant-led experiences are ideal for fostering this. Through conversations where everyone's contributions are valued, the exploration of a topic is enriched for the entire group.

WHY IS THIS IMPORTANT?

Our exploration of prominent well-being theories revealed a fascinating harmony. The themes echoed across each framework with significant overlap. Social connection and being active were universal. As Falk suggests, finding opportunities to get out, connect with the community, and share experiences is not just enjoyable, it is a fundamental human need.[29] The importance of recharging and contributing was also a recurring theme. While "recharging" focuses on the personal benefits gained from an experience, "contributing" emphasizes giving back to others. Interestingly, even this act of giving is seen as ultimately enhancing the contributor's own well-being.

Another pairing of themes is feeling fulfilled and having meaningful experiences. While these two ideas are closely connected, the difference is related to the focus: Feeling fulfilled is about the person and their intrinsic states such as positive feelings, validation of personhood, and a sense of accomplishment; meaningful experiences however, are focused on the activity, ensuring that each task or experience is important work that is personally significant, and allows for creativity and personal impact for every participant.

These themes guide us in our understanding of what participants experience in our programs, what they value, and what they are looking for. We use this knowledge to design programs that truly promote well-being. With this framework in place, every part of our planning process considers how it can contribute to the overall well-being of participants.

- Is the environment, approach, and activity designed to foster social connection among participants? Can they easily see, hear, and communicate with each other? To connect with others, each part of the *Model for Successful Engagement* plays a part.
- Is the program accessible—whether through physical site access, financial considerations, or a variety of platforms? To be actively involved, barriers to access must be addressed.
- How will a person feel as they participate in your program? Have you built-in opportunities for positive emotions, self-esteem, and validation? Fulfillment is personal but can be achieved with careful, purposeful planning.
- Do the program activities encourage individual and varied responses? Do they draw on each participant's knowledge, interests, and ideas? Are they open-ended, at an adult level, and valuable? These are the ingredients of meaningful experiences.
- What is the mood or tone of the program? Is it warm and open, calm and inspiring, and fun? A sense of recharging can come from many different moods.
- Does your approach to the experience allow opportunities for participants, their families and friends, and the facilitators to contribute? Contributing takes many forms and there are ways to plan to support each one.

Well-being is something that we all strive toward. It is about finding balance in our lives, and continually reflecting and adjusting our focus as we move toward being "well." Many factors can affect our sense of well-being and how we feel in one moment may be different from the way we feel in another.

The experiences we choose to take part in and deliver—specifically museum experiences—can have many positive impacts on the sense of well-being that participants have 'in the moment'. For many participants, these positive impacts extend for some time after their time together.

Programs in museums with cultural, scientific, or historical collections have much to offer for people living with dementia and their family and friends. They can have a powerful impact that touches on social connection and relationships. They provide opportunities to engage in the community and cultural life, and offer meaningful experiences that validate the person, not the diagnosis. When people living with dementia and their family and friends are welcomed and supported in museums, their daily lives expand and move beyond barriers and stigma that may have previously prevented participation. When they are given opportunities to contribute to programs and their communities they are empowered and those communities are richer for the inclusion. Your museum can make a difference too.

NOTES

1. The concept of striving toward improved well-being, rather than it being a fixed state, appears in many sources of study. Two that we have focused on are: Chris Clarke, Bob Woods, Esme Moniz-Cook, Gail Mountain, Laila Øksnebjerg, Rabih Chattat, Ana Diaz, Dianne Gove, Myrra Vernooij-Dassen, and Emma Wolverson, "Measuring the Well-being of People with Dementia: A Conceptual Scoping Review," *Health and Quality of Life Outcomes* 18 (2020): Article 249. John H. Falk, *The Value of Museums, Enhancing Societal Wellbeing* (Lanham: Rowman & Littlefield, 2022).
2. An *Artful Moments* family member recalls her experiences, 2020. Names have been changed for confidentiality.
3. University of Waterloo, *Canadian Index of Wellbeing* (2016), 11, https://uwaterloo.ca.
4. University of Waterloo, *Canadian Index of Wellbeing*, 60.
5. Daisy Fancourt and Saoirse Finn, "What is the Evidence on the Role of the Arts in Improving Health and Well-being? A Scoping Review," Health Evidence Network (HEN) Synthesis Report 67 (Copenhagen: WHO Regional Office for Europe, 2019), 2.
6. "Six Dimensions of Wellness," *National Wellness Institute*, 2023, www.nationalwellness.org.
7. To learn more about Falk's work on well-being, please consult: John H. Falk, *The Value of Museums*.
8. To learn more about Falk's Visitor Motivations, please consult: John H. Falk *Identity and the Museum Visitor Experience* (Walnut Creek: Left Coast Press, 2009).
9. To learn more about Falk's work on well-being, please consult: Falk, *The Value of Museums*.
10. Falk, *The Value of Museums*, 34.
11. To learn more about Falk's additional of global well-being to his work on well-being, please visit: John H. Falk, "Global Well-Being: A 5th Dimension of Value," *Institute for Learning Innovation* blog post, November 8, 2022, https://www.instituteforlearninginnovation.org/global-well-being-a-5th-dimension-of-value/.
12. To learn more about Seligman's work, please consult: Martin E.P. Seligman, *Flourish* (New York: Atria paperbacks, 2011).
13. Seligman, *Flourish*, 238.
14. To learn more about this research, please refer to: https://doi.org/10.1186/s12955-020-01440-x.
15. Sandra E. Moll, Rebecca E. Gewirtz, Terry M. Krupa, Mary C. Law, Nadine Larivière, and Melaine Levasseur, "'Do-Live-Well': A Canadian Framework for Promoting Occupation, Health, and Wellbeing," *Canadian Journal of Occupational Therapy* 82, no. 1 (2015): 11.
16. Moll, "Do Live Well," 17.
17. Moll, "Do Live Well," 15.
18. Moll, "Do Live Well," 14.
19. Moll, "Do Live Well," 14.
20. Artful Moments participant interview, 2021. Names have been changed to respect privacy.
21. Artful Moments participant interview, 2019. Names have been changed to respect privacy.
22. Artful Moments participant interview, 2023. Names have been changed to respect privacy.

23. Observation was conducted using the Affect and Engagement Rating Scale, a modification of the Philadelphia Geriatric Center Affect Rating Scale, which measures interest, pleasure, sadness, anxiety, and anger through observations of certain behaviors. The full study can be found here: M. Powell Lawton, Kimberly Van Haitsma, Margaret A.Perkinson, and Katy Ruckdeschel, "Observed Affect and Quality of Life in Dementia: Further Affirmations and Problems," *Aging Mental Health* 5 (1999): 69–81.

24. To read more about the research conducted in early *Artful* Moments programs, please refer to two articles: Afeez Abiola Hazzan, Janis Humphrey, Laurie Kilgour-Walsh, Kathy Moros, Katherine, Carmen Murray, Shannon Stanners, Maureen Montemuro, Aidan Giangregorio, and Alexandra Papaioannou, "Impact of the 'Artful Moments' Intervention on Persons with Dementia and Their Care Partners: A Pilot Study," *Canadian Geriatrics Journal* 19, no. 2 (2016): 58–65. Janis Humphrey, Maureen Montemuro, Esther Coker, Laurie Kilgour-Walsh, Kathy Moros, Carmen Murray, and Shannon Stanners, "'Artful Moments': A Framework for Successful Engagement in an Arts-based Programme for Persons in the Middle to Late Stages of Dementia," *Dementia* 18, no. 6 (2017): 2340–60.

25. For more about the toolkit please see: Linda J. Thomson and Helen J. Chatterjee, "Assessing Well-being Outcomes for Arts and Heritage Activities; Development of a Museum Well-being Measures Toolkit," *Journal of Applied Arts and Health* 5, no. 2 (2014): 29–50. Linda J. Thomson and Helen J. Chatterjee, "Measuring the Impact of Museum Activities on Well-being: Developing the Museum Well-Being Measures Toolkit," *Museum Management and Curatorship* 30, no. 1 (2015): 44–62. Linda J. Thomson, Bridget Lockyer, Paul Camic, and Helen J. Chatterjee, "Effects of a Museum-based Social Prescription Intervention on Quantitative Measures of Psychological Wellbeing in Older Adults," *Perspectives in Public Health* 138, no. 1 (2018): 28–38.

26. Art Gallery of Hamilton, *Final Report to the Ontario Trillium Foundation from the Art Gallery of Hamilton.* Prepared by Esther Coker, Janis Humphrey, and Maureen Montemuro, 2019.

27. Rafaela Ganga, Gayle Whelan, and Kerry Wilson, *Evaluation of the House of Memories Family Carers Awareness Day* (UK: Institute of Cultural Capital, 2017), 26.

28. New Economics Foundation, *Five Ways to Wellbeing: New Applications, New Ways of Thinking* (2010), https://neweconomics.org.

29. Falk, *The Value of Museums*, 52.

Message for Success: You Can Do This!
Final Thoughts from Laurie Kilgour-Walsh

Thank you so much for joining us in *Artful Moments: Building Museum Experiences for People Living with Dementia*. Creating this publication has been a labor of love for all of us and we are honored that you have spent this time with us.

Every new program begins with an idea. It grows and improves with practice and reflection. It was this way for us—a spark born from a chance meeting. Together, we dove in with lots of enthusiasm and some uncertainty about whether it would work. And it did, more than we could ever have imagined.

Having started *Artful Moments* more than a decade ago ... I can honestly say that my work with this program has been among the most meaningful experiences in my career. What I have learned from my colleagues and participants has changed the way I think about art and museums. In every museum artifact or work of art, I see the potential to change lives. It has also changed the way I lead programs in every aspect of my work. I am honored to share the program that I love with you.

I had a wonderful team to teach me, to work with me, and to encourage creativity and foster openness to new ways of thinking. Some things worked really well and some did not, but every experience allowed me to learn and try again. But, just like you, I started at the beginning with lots to learn.

In your museum and in your work with visitors you have all of the ingredients for a great program at your fingertips. Add the ideas and recommendations that we have shared with you in this book and you will create something wonderful. Take small steps and build on them. Find your own way to create the program that is right for you, your museum, and your participants.

It will be worth it.

References

AGE Advanced Gerontological Education. "Gentle Persuasive Approaches (GPA) in Dementia Care." Accessed January 2022. https://ageinc.ca.

Alzheimer's Association. "Communication and Alzheimers." Accessed March 2024. https://www.alz.org/help-support/caregiving/daily-care/communications.

Alzheimer's Association website. "What is Dementia." Accessed December 2023. https://www.alz.org/alzheimers-dementia/what-is-dementia.

Alzheimer's Disease International. "Dementia Friendly Communities." Accessed January 2024. https://www.alzint.org/what-we-do/policy/dementia-friendly-communities/.

Alzheimer's Disease International. "Dementia Facts and Figures." Accessed March 2024. https://www.alzint.org/about/dementia-facts-figures/.

Alzheimer Society of Brant, Haldimand Norfolk, Hamilton & Halton. "What Is Dementia, Accessed December 2023. https://alzheimer.ca/en/about-dementia/what-dementia.

Alzheimer Society of Canada. "Dementia Friendly Canada." Accessed January 2024. https://alzheimer.ca/en/take-action/become-dementia-friendly/dementia-friendly-canada.

Alzheimer Society of Canada. "Dementia Friendly Communities." Accessed January 2024. https://alzheimer.ca/on/en/take-action/become-dementia-friendly/dementia-friendly-communities-ontario.

Alzheimer Society of Canada. "How Canadians Perceive Dementia." Accessed March 2023. https://alzheimer.ca/en/about-dementia/stigma-against-dementia/how-canadians-perceive-dementia.

Alzheimer Society of Canada. "Dementia Numbers in Canada." Accessed March 2023. https://alzheimer.ca/en/about-dementia/what-dementia/dementia-numbers-canada.

Alzheimer Society of Toronto "Dementia Friendly Communities". Accessed March 2024. https://alz.to/dementia-friendly-communities.

Alzheimer's Society (UK). "Early Stages of Dementia." Accessed December 2023. https://www.alzheimers.org.uk/about-dementia/symptoms-and-diagnosis/how-dementia-progresses/early-stages-dementia#content-start.

Alzheimer's Society (UK). "Late Stages of Dementia." Accessed December 2023. https://www.alzheimers.org.uk/about-dementia/symptoms-and-diagnosis/how-dementia-progresses/later-stages-dementia#content-start.

Alzheimer's Society (UK). "Middle Stages of Dementia." Accessed December 2023. https://www.alzheimers.org.uk/about-dementia/symptoms-and-diagnosis/how-dementia-progresses/middle-stage-dementia#content-start.

Alzheimer's Society (UK). "Turning Up the Volume: Unheard Voices of People with Dementia." May 2017. https://www.alzheimers.org.uk/turning-up-volume.

American Medical Association. "What is Scope of Practice." Accessed May 2022. https://www.ama-assn.org/practice-management/scope-practice/what-scope-practice#:~:text=state%20to%20state.-,Why%20is%20scope%20of%20practice%20important%3F,of%20a%20fully%20trained%20physician.

Art Gallery of Hamilton. *Final Report to the Ontario Trillium Foundation from the Art Gallery of Hamilton.* Prepared by Esther Coker, Janis Humphrey, and Maureen Montemuro, 2019.

Baum, Claire and Andrew Westover. "Values-Engaged Gallery Teaching with Andrew Westover." *Art Engager Podcast* Episode 102, January 25, 2024. https://thinkingmuseum.com/captivate-podcast/values-engaged-gallery-teaching/.

Bell, Virginia and David Troxel. *The Best Friends Approach to Alzheimer's Care.* Baltimore: Health Professions Press, 2001.

Bell, Virginia and David Troxel. *The Best Friends Dementia Bill of Rights.* Baltimore: Health Professions Press Inc., 2013.

Camic, Paul A., Victoria Tischler, and Chantal Helen Pearman. "Viewing and Making Art Together: A Multi-session Art-gallery-based Intervention for People with Dementia and Their Carers." *Aging & Mental Health* 18, no. 2 (2014): 161–8. https://doi.org/10.1080/13607863.2013.818101.

Chatterjee, Helen J. and Linda J. Thomson. "Museums and Social Prescribing." In *The Caring Museum: New Models of Engagement with Ageing,* edited by H. L. Robertson, 304–41. Edinburgh: Museums, 2015.

Clarke, Chris, Bob Woods, Esme Moniz-Cook, Gail Mountain, Laila Øksnebjerg, Rabih Chattat, Ana Diaz, Dianne Gove, Myrra Vernooij-Dassen, and Emma Wolverson. "Measuring the Well-being of People with Dementia: A Conceptual Scoping Review." *Health and Quality of Life Outcomes* 18 (2020): 1–14, Article 249. https://doi.org/10.1186/s12955-020-01440-x.

Clarke-Vivier, Sara, Corie Lyford, and Lynn Thomson. "Strengths and Challenges of Arts-based Programming for Individuals with Alzheimer's and Related Dementias." *LEARNing Landscapes* 10, no. 2 (2017): 97–113. https://doi.org/10.36510/learnland.v10i2.804.

Cohen Mansfield, Jiska, Maha Dakheel-Ali, and Marcia S. Marx. "Engagement in Persons with Dementia: The Concept and its Measurement." *American Journal of Geriatric Psychiatry* 17, no. 4 (2009): 299–307. https://doi.org/10.1097/JGP.0b013e31818f3a52.

Crisis Prevention Institute. *Living with Dementia Means Living in the Moment.* Accessed January 2024. https://www.crisisprevention.com/en-CA/Blog/living-with-dementia-means-living-in-the-moment.

Dawson, Pam, Donna Wells, and Karen Kline. *Enhancing the Abilities of Persons with Alzheimer's and Related Dementias: A Nursing Perspective.* Michigan: Springer Publishing Company Inc., 1993.

Dementia Australia. "About Dementia." Access March 2023. https://www.dementia.org.au/about-dementia.

Dementia in a New Light. "Stigma Stereotypes." Accessed April 2024. https://dementiainnewlight.com/content/stigma/stereotypes.

Ellena, Eric and Berna Huebner. "I Remember Better When I Paint: Treating Alzheimer's Through the Creative Arts." www.irememberbetterwhenipaint.com.

Falk, John H. *Identity and the Museum Visitor Experience.* Walnut Creek: Left Coast Press, 2009.

Falk, John H. *The Value of Museums, Enhancing Societal Wellbeing.* Lanham: Rowman & Littlefield, 2022.

Falk, John H. "Global Well-Being: A 5th Dimension of Value." *Institute for Learning Innovation Blog Post,* November 8, 2022. https://www.instituteforlearninginnovation.org/global-well-being-a-5th-dimension-of-value/.

Fancourt Daisy and Saoirse Finn. "What is the Evidence on the Role of the Arts in Improving Health and Well-being? A Scoping Review." In *Health Evidence Network (HEN) Synthesis Report 67.* Copenhagen: WHO Regional Office for Europe, 2019.

Future Learn. "What Is Interpersonal Communication?" Accessed March 2023. https://www.futurelearn.com/info/blog/what-is-interpersonal-communication#:~:text=Essentially%2C%20it's%20the%20process%20of,online%20or%20over%20the%20phone.

Ganga, Rafaela, Gayle Whelan, and Kerry Wilson. *Evaluation of the House of Memories Family Carers Awareness Day.* UK: Institute of Cultural Capital, 2017.

Golembiewski, Jan and John Zeisel. "Salutogenic Approaches to Dementia Care." *The Handbook of Salutogenesis,* Second edition (2022): 513–32, https://doi.org/10.1007/978-3-030-79515-3_48.

Hamilton Council on Aging, "What We Heard Report: Empowering Dementia-Friendly Communities Project." Hamilton & Haldimand, 2021.

Hazzan, Afeez Abiola, Janis Humphrey, Laurie Kilgour-Walsh, Kathy Moros, Katherine, Carmen Murray, Shannon Stanners, Maureen Montemuro, Aidan Giangregorio, and Alexandra Papaioannou. "Impact of the 'Artful Moments' Intervention on Persons with Dementia and Their Care Partners: A Pilot Study." *Canadian Geriatrics Journal* 19, no. 2 (2016): 58–65. https://cgjonline.ca/index.php/cgj/issue/view/22.

HealthLink BC. "Five Ways to wellbeing." Accessed November 2022. https://www.healthlinkbc.ca/mental-health-substance-use/well-being/five-ways-well-being.

Humphrey, Janis, Maureen Montemuro, Esther Coker, Laurie Kilgour-Walsh, Kathy Moros, Carmen Murray, and Shannon Stanners. "'Artful Moments': A Framework for Successful Engagement in an Arts-based Programme for Persons in the Middle to Late Stages of Dementia." *Dementia* 18, no. 6 (2017): 2340–60. https://doi.org/10.1177/1471301217744025.

Kai-Kee, Elliott, Lissa Latina, and Litit Sadoyan. *Activity-Based Teaching in the Art Museum: Movement, Embodiment, Emotion.* Los Angeles: Getty Publications, 2020.

Kenning, Gail and Mandy Visser. "Evaluating Quality of Life and Well-being at the Intersection of Dementia Care and Creative Engagement." *Dementia* 20, no. 7 (2021): 2441–61. https://doi.org/10.1177/1471301221997309.

Kitwood, Tom. *Dementia Reconsidered. The Person Comes First.* Michigan: Open University Press, 1997.

Kitwood, Tom. "Toward a Theory of Dementia Care: Ethics and Interaction." *Journal of Clinical Ethics* 9, no. 1 (1998): 23–34.

Klug, Kim, Stephen Page, Joanne Connell, and Emma Bould. *Rethinking Heritage: A Guide to Help Make Your Site More Dementia-friendly.* UK: Historic Royal Palaces, 2017. www.hrp.org.uk/about-us/learning/.

Lawton, M. Powell, Kimberly Van Haitsma, Margaret A. Perkinson, and Katy Ruckdeschel. "Observed Affect and Quality of Life in Dementia: Further Affirmations and Problems." *Aging Mental Health* 5 (1999): 69–81.

Leduc, Amanda. *Disfigured: On Fairy Tales, Disability, and Making Space.* Toronto: Coach House Books, 2020.

Livingston, Lucas, Gerri Fiterman Persin, and Deborah Del Signore. "Art in the Moment: Evaluating a Therapeutic Wellness Program for People with Dementia and Their Care Partners." *Journal of Museum Education* 41, no. 2 (2016): 100–9.

London School of Economics and Political Science. "As Many as 84 per cent of People Living with Dementia Report Experiencing Discrimination - New Toolkit Aims to Reduce Stigma." October 7, 2022. https://www.lse.ac.uk/News/Latest-news-from-LSE/2022/j-October-22/As-many-as-84-per-cent-of-people-living-with-dementia-report-experiencing-discrimination-new-toolkit-aims-to-reduce-stigma.

MacPherson, Sarah, Michael Bird, Katrina Anderson, Terri Davis, and Annaliese. Blair. "An Art Gallery Access Programme for People with Dementia: 'You Do it for the Moment'." *Aging & Mental Health* 13, no. 5 (2009): 744–52. https://doi.org/10.1080/13607860902918207.

Marković, Slobodan. "Components of Aesthetic Experience: Aesthetic Fascination, Aesthetic Appraisal, and Aesthetic Emotion." *Iperception* 3, no. 1 (2012): 1–17. https://doi.org/10.1068/i0450aap.

Mayo Clinic. "Aging: What to Expect." Accessed February 2023. https://www.mayoclinic.org/healthy-lifestyle/healthy-aging/in-depth/aging/art-20046070.

McMaster University Health Sciences. "Bringing Clarity to Dementia." Accessed December 2023. https://igericare.healthhq.ca.

Mitchell, Gail J., Christine Jonas-Simpson, Joy Richards, Susan Brown, and Vonna Bitove. "Creating a Relational Arts-based Academy for Persons Living with Dementia (Innovative Practice)." *Dementia* 20, no. 3 (2019): 144–53. https://doi.org/10.1177/1471301219895647.

Moll, Sandra E., Rebecca E. Gewirtz, Terry M. Krupa, Mary C. Law, Nadine Larivière, and Melaine Levasseur. "Do-Live-Well: A Canadian Framework for Promoting Occupation, Health, and Well-being." *Canadian Journal of Occupational Therapy* 82, no. 1 (2015): 9–23. https://doi.org/10.1177/000841741454891.

Museum of Modern Art (MoMA). The MoMA Alzheimer's Project: Making Art Accessible to People with Dementia (A Guide for Museums). Accessed December 2022. https://moma.org/meetme.

National Institute on Aging. "Hearing Loss: A Common Problem for Older Adults." Accessed March 2023. https://www.nia.nih.gov/health/hearing-loss-common-problem-older-adults.

National Library of Medicine. "Hidden Age-Related Hearing Loss and Hearing Disorders." 2018. https://pubmed.ncbi.nlm.nih.gov/30931204/.

National Wellness Institute. "Six Dimensions of Wellness." 2023. https://nationalwellness.org.

New Economics Foundation. Five Ways to Wellbeing: New Applications, New Ways of Thinking. 2010. https://neweconomics.org.

O'Neil, S. and J. Davis. The Muse Guide: A Training Manual for Muse Workshops. Harvard Graduate School of Education. Project Zero. Project MUSE, 1996.

Optimum Health Solutions. The Occupational Therapist's "Just Right Challenge". 2020. https://opt.net.au/optimum-life/occupational-therapists-just-right-challenge/.

Owen, Rebecca, Katherine Berry, and Laura J.E. Brown. "'I Like to Feel Needed, You Know?': A Qualitative Examination of Sense of Purpose in Older Care Home Residents." Aging & Mental Health 27, no. 2 (2023): 236–42. https://doi.org/10.1080/13607863.2021.2017849.

Public Health Agency of Canada. Dementia in Canada, Including Alzheimer's Disease: Highlights from the Canadian Chronic Disease Surveillance System. Public Health Agency of Canada, 2017. https://www.canada.ca/en/public-health/services/publications/diseases-conditions/dementia-highlights-canadian-chronic-disease-surveillance.html#box1.

Rancour, Patrice and Terry Barrett. "Art Interpretation as a Clinical Intervention Toward Healing." Journal of Holistic Nursing American Holistic Nursing Association 29, no. 1 (2011): 68–80. https://doi.org/10.1177/089801019358768.

Reel, Candice D., Rebecca S. Allen, Bailey Lanai, M. Caroline Yuk, and Daniel C. Potts. "Bringing Art to Life: Social and Activity Engagement through Art in Persons Living with Dementia." Clinical Gerontologist 45, no. 2 (2021): 327–37. https://doi.org/10.1080/07317115.2021.1936737.

Rewerska-Juśko, Magdalena and Konrad Rejdak. "Social Stigma of People with Dementia." Journal of Alzheimer's Disease 78, no. 4 (December 2020): 1339–43. https://doi.org/10.3233/JAD-201004.

Rosenberg, Francesca. "The MoMA Alzheimer's Project: Programming and Resources for Making Art Accessibility to People with Alzheimer's Disease and Their Caregivers." Art & Health 2, no. 1 (2009): 93–7.

Sauer, A. "5 Reasons Why Music Boosts Brain Activity." Accessed March 2023. https://alzheimers.net/why-music-boosts-brain-activity-in-dementia-patients.

Sauer, Philip E., Joan Fopma-Loy, Jennifer M. Kinney, and Elizabeth Lokon. "'It Makes me Feel Like Myself': Person-centered Versus Traditional Visual Arts Activities for People with Dementia." Dementia 15, no. 5 (2016): 895–912. https://doi.org/10.1177/1471301214543958.

Seligman, Martin E.P. Flourish. New York: Atria paperbacks, 2011.

Silverman, Lois H. The Social Work of Museums. New York: Routledge, 2010.

Stallings, Jessica Woolhiser. "Collage as a Therapeutic Modality for Reminiscence in Patients with Dementia. Art Therapy." Journal of the American Art Therapy Association 27, no. 3 (2010): 136–40.

Stride. "Don't Forget I'm Human: Stopping Dementia Stigma." Accessed April 2024. https://stridedementia.turtl.co/story/anti-stigma-toolkit/page/2/2.

Thomson, Linda J. and Helen J. Chatterjee. "Assessing Well-being Outcomes for Arts and Heritage Activities; Development of a Museum Well-being Measures Toolkit." Journal of Applied Arts and Health 5, no. 2 (2014): 29–50. https://doi.org/10.1386/jaah.5.1.29_1.

Thomson, Linda J. and Helen J. Chatterjee. "Measuring the Impact of Museum Activities on Well-being: Developing the Museum Well-Being Measures Toolkit." Museum Management and Curatorship 30, no. 1 (2015): 44–62. https://doi.org/10.1080/09647775.2015.1008390.

Thomson, Linda J., Bridget Lockyer, Paul Camic, and Helen J. Chatterjee. "Effects of a Museum-based Social Prescription Intervention on Quantitative Measures of Psychological Wellbeing in Older Adults." *Perspectives in Public Health* 138, no. 1 (2018): 28–38. https://doi.org/10.1177/1757913917737563.

Todd, Carolyn, Paul Camic, Bridget Lockyer, Linda J. Thomson, and Helen J. Chatterjee. "Museum-based Programs for Socially Isolated Older Adults: Understanding What Works." *Health & Place* 48 (2017): 47–55. https://doi.org/10.1016/j.healthplace.2017.08.005.

University of Waterloo. *Canadian Index of Wellbeing.* 2016. https://uwaterloo.ca.

WebMD. "Age-Related Vision Problems." Accessed February 2023. https://webmd.com/eye-health/age-related-vision.

Windle, Gill, Andrew Newman, Vanessa Burholt, Bob Woods, Dave O'Brien, Michael Barber, Barry Hounsome, Clive Parkinson, and Victoria Tischler. "Dementia and Imagination: A Mixed-methods Protocol for Arts and Science Research." *BMJ Open* (2016): 6. http://dx.doi:10.1136/bmjopen-2016-011634.

World Health Organization. "Dementia." Revised March 2023. https://www.who.int/news-room/fact-sheets/detail/dementia.

World Health Organization. *Social Isolation and loneliness Among Older People: Advocacy Brief.* Geneva, 2021.

Zeilig, Hannah, John Killick, and Chris Fox. "The Participative Arts for People Living with a Dementia: A Critical Review." *International Journal of Ageing and Later Life* 9, no. 1 (2014): 7–34. https://doi.org/10.3384/ijal.1652-8670.14238.

Index

abilities, 27-30; and activities, 150-52; and aging, 27; and dementia, 31-45; and environment, 61-62, 64-72; and fluctuations, 30; and strengths, 27-30. *See also* cognition; dementia; language; mood and emotions; physical abilities; stages of dementia

accessibility. *See* dementia friendly; disability; environment; pre-program spaces; stigma

activities, 123-24; in combination, 124, 131; and content, 98; and engagement, 171; and environment, 65-70; and frustration, 149; and relationships, 149; and self expression, 137. *See also* conversations; hands-on activities; interactivity; just right challenge; process over product; shared experience

adaptation in the moment, 134, 136; *vs.* invention, 149-50; when and how much, 43-44, 129-30. *See also* activity; approach; environment; Environment Assessment Template

adapting activities, 123; conversations, 144-46; hands-on activities, 150-58

adapting environment, 58-59; exhibition spaces, 64-70; hands-on spaces, 70-72; pre-program spaces, 62-63

aesthetic experiences, 14

Alzheimer disease. *See* dementia

Alzheimer's Disease International, 10

Alzheimer Society, 10-12

approach, 83-119; and engagement, 171; and person/participant-centred, 83, 85, 118. *See also* communication; *Model for Successful Engagement*; questions

art appreciation, 136. *See also* conversations

Artful Moments, 5-6; and philosophy, 17, 27, 146; strengths, 8-9. *See also* evaluation; *Model for Successful Engagement*

assessment, 58-59, 65; *vs.* diagnosing, 99. *See also* reading the room; Scope of Practice; therapy/art therapy

attention, 32. *See also* cognition

behavior, changes, 169; and disengagement, 169-71. *See also* dementia; challenging situations; cognition

brain changes. *See* dementia

Canadian Institute of Wellbeing, 13, 175

Canadian Museums & Dementia Survey, 4

caregiver/care partner. *See* family and friends

challenging situations, 97; with family and friends, 107-12

cognition, 31-36; anecdote, Lucy (judgment and self regulation), 35; and attention, 32; and initiation, 35, 144, 155-56; and insight, 36; and judgment, 36; and memory, 32-33; and in the moment, 33; and new learning, 33; and organization, 35; and planning, 34; and problem solving, 35-36; and processing speed, 35; and self regulation, 36; and sequencing, 35

communicating; with family and friends, 107-9; by phone, 115-16

communication, 37, 83; and changes, 169; and clear language and speed, 94-95; and feedback, 104-5; and multi-modal, 117; and non-verbal, 93, 95-97; and role of facilitator, 90-93; and second languages, 95; and sharing expectations, 90; and speed and pauses, 93, 133; and strategies, 93-97; and supporting memory, 94; and virtual, 116; and written, 115. *See also* approach; expression; language; understanding

community partners, 8, 44, 77, 158-59. *See also* staffing

content *vs.* activity, 124

conversations, 136-37; and approach, 144-45; and dementia, 137; and physical and sensory interventions, 137, 140, 147-48; and planning and logistics, 142-48; and role of facilitator, 145; and selecting objects, 138-42; and sensitivity and triggers, 139; and storytelling, 146-48; and strategies, 145-49; and subject

About the Authors

A core value in our work is the sharing of knowledge. As a team, this has been with us since the beginning. Together we have combined our skills, passions, and areas of expertise to develop a program that embraces the social and well-being potential of museums along with the rigor expected from museum programs. Our work is guided by extensive knowledge and best practices in dementia care. We continue to learn from each other and collaborate on a program that we love. We are so pleased to share our experiences with you.

LAURIE KILGOUR-WALSH

Laurie Kilgour-Walsh has been the Lead of Wellness and is now Head of Programs and Learning at the Art Gallery of Hamilton since 2006. During that tenure, Laurie has led educational and interpretive programs for audiences of all ages and abilities, creating programs that are responsive to the individual strengths and interests of participants. She is now developing a larger mandate for arts and well-being within the AGH's public program to support diverse audiences with a range of abilities and interests.

Laurie led the inception of *Artful Moments* in 2009 and continues to lead it through numerous diverse initiatives in support of best practices in museum-based programs. Following many conversations with peers about *Artful* Moments, and how others can create similar experiences for their audiences, Laurie is excited to share the collected learning and experiences of the past decade through this project.

With a background in fine art and art history, many years spent working in museums, and an eclectic collection of education and professional development experiences, Laurie brings a passion for art and museums, focusing on the socially connective and empowering potential of creative experiences. Laurie is also a practicing artist and an avid museum visitor.

JANIS HUMPHREY

Janis Humphrey is a retired nurse who worked in the field of dementia care for over twenty years. Janis holds a bachelor's degree in nursing from McMaster University and a master's degree in Health Administration from D'Youville University in Buffalo, New York.

Janis has worked to raise the awareness of dementia, and its impact on the person and family, as well as examining the role communities can play to enhance the lives of those living with this disease. Janis was the clinical lead for the inception of *Artful Moments* in a hospital setting, and her knowledge and vision continue to guide this work. In partnership with the AGH, Janis has been researching the connection between art and dementia. Through the publication of their work, the focus has been to translate the findings and continue developing relationships between museums and people living with dementia.

Museums are a trusted source of information and a valuable repository of knowledge. Janis believes that *Artful Moments* provides the framework to engage individuals in the world of museums. Through engagement, one can explore, share experiences, and create their own masterpiece. The *Artful Moments* model provides an opportunity to enhance an individual's sense of well-being.

Janis believes in the importance of living in the moment; the emphasis is on the process, and the connections made along the way, which is where the joy lies.

MAUREEN MONTEMURO

Maureen Montemuro graduated with a BScN from the University of Toronto followed by a MHSc degree from McMaster University. She retired in 2014 after working in the nursing field for forty-five years. For the past twenty-two years of her career, she focused on clinical practice, education, and research with older adults and completed her career working as a clinical nurse specialist (CNS) in dementia care.

As a CNS, Maureen worked with her institution and long-term care homes to develop, implement, and evaluate an educational program called *Gentle Persuasive Approaches (GPA) in Dementia Care*, to train healthcare staff across Canada. Later she became involved with the AGH in the development of *Artful Moments*.

Since retiring, Maureen has volunteered at the AGH, playing a key role in designing, implementing, and evaluating *Artful Moments*, now presented for people living with dementia and their loved ones in the community. Maureen has found this volunteer work to be a mutually beneficial endeavor as she can contribute to the program because of her background while also developing knowledge and skill for herself in art appreciation and art-making at the AGH in her retirement years—a win-win!

KATHY MOROS

Kathy Moros retired from her thirty-eight-year career as an occupational therapist in 2021. She dedicated most of her career to assessing and treating people living with dementia in a specialized inpatient hospital program, educating families and staff about dementia, presenting at conferences, and participating in dementia-related research. Kathy has also contributed to student learning by being a tutor and clinical preceptor for the Occupational Therapy program at McMaster University (Hamilton).

Kathy has been part of *Artful Moments* since its inception, assisting with the initial development of the educational curriculum, participating in the associated research project, and publishing the research results.

Although now retired, Kathy's passion for the *Artful Moments* program continues as she volunteers her time to further develop the educational curriculum with the goal of expanding access to *Artful Moments* for people living with dementia in her local community and beyond.

SHANNON STANNERS

Shannon Stanners is a speech-language pathologist with Hamilton Health Sciences. A highlight of her career was her eleven years' working with individuals with dementia in the Behavioural Health Unit at St. Peter's Hospital.

Enhancing communication with individuals with dementia had always been a key focus and passion of her role on the team, working alongside Maureen and Kathy, under the inspirational leadership of Janis Humphrey. In *Artful Moments*, through their collaborative project with the AGH, she witnessed firsthand the happiness and engagement that the participants had during the program.

She eagerly rejoined this incredible team, now extending the work to other museums. With clinical experience, as well as personal experience caring for loved ones with dementia, she has experienced *Artful Moments* both as a team member and as a care partner alongside a participant in the *Artful Moments* program. She values the program deeply and has observed the positive impact on her loved one's engagement, social connectedness, confidence, and well-being.

ABOUT THE AGH

Founded in 1914, the Art Gallery of Hamilton is the oldest and largest art museum in Southern Ontario, with a permanent collection of over 11,000 objects that is recognized as one of the finest in Canada. The collection comprises historical Canadian and International art and contemporary Art and in recent years has focused on collecting work by Black, Indigenous, artists of color, and women artists. The exhibition program balances traveling exhibitions and work from the collection, often placing works from different times and places together to inspire a critical conversation.

In the past decade, the AGH has delivered a public program focused on the power of visual art and exhibitions to enrich social connection, particularly when paired with experiential and creative learning. We have had particular success developing programs to address specific wellness needs and communities using the arts to support people's social, emotional, and physical well-being in meaningful ways, regardless of abilities, circumstances, or prior experiences with art.